William Ansell Day

The Russian Government in Poland

William Ansell Day

The Russian Government in Poland

ISBN/EAN: 9783337294670

Printed in Europe, USA, Canada, Australia, Japan

Cover: Foto ©ninafisch / pixelio.de

More available books at **www.hansebooks.com**

POLAND.

WITH A

NARRATIVE OF THE POLISH INSURRECTION OF 1863.

BY W. A. DAY.

LONDON:
LONGMANS, GREEN, READER, & DYER,
PATERNOSTER ROW.
1867.

WYMAN AND SONS,
CLASSICAL AND GENERAL PRINTERS, GREAT QUEEN STREET,
LINCOLN'S INN FIELDS, W.C.

PREFACE.

THE materials for the following narrative were collected by me during three visits to Russia and Poland in the years 1863, 1864, and 1865. My sources of information were various.

From Lord Napier, then the English Ambassador at St. Petersburg, from Mr. Lumley, the Secretary, and from Mr. Michell, the first Attaché of the Embassy, I received from time to time very valuable information. They necessarily heard statements from persons who represented all the parties interested in the Polish question, as well as the views put forward by the representatives of other European powers in St. Petersburg, and I am greatly indebted to them for the assistance they afforded to me. Mr. Michell especially, from his long residence in Russia and his intimate knowledge of the institutions and state of public feeling in the empire, gave me an amount of assistance that I could not have procured elsewhere. At Warsaw the Consul-General, Colonel Stanton, and the Vice-Consul, Mr. White, were equally ready to aid me; and Mr. White's long connection with Poland, and his unequalled experience of the men and parties with whom in the course of my narrative I have to deal, gave the greatest weight to his views and criticisms.

In the official, commercial, and general society of St. Petersburg, especially among the English and German residents, there were great differences of opinion upon political questions, and I had the advantage of hearing the views of all parties and the statements of facts with which they were supported.

It is difficult for me to set out with precision my sources of information among the Poles. Reasons obviously exist why in this case names should not be given, but I trust the perusal of my work will show that I was well informed as to their views, and have done full justice to them. I may, however, mention that I received much information from Count Joseph Zamoyski, and that it was valuable alike from its unquestionable authenticity, and from the moderation of his own views.

Among the Russian officers from whom I received information, I may mention Count Berg, Viceroy of Poland; General Mouravieff, Governor-General of the North-western provinces; Count Osten Sacken, head of the diplomatic Chancery at Warsaw; Prince Tcherkaski and M. Milutine, two of the three members of the Commission for settling the peasant land question in the kingdom of Poland, the former of whom is now Director of Posts and the latter is Secretary of State for Poland; Prince Emile Wittgenstein, commandant of one of the Russian corps operating in the kingdom; Prince Pierre Ouroussoff, Chamberlain of the Emperor, and a member of the court-martial at Wilna; General Lebedeff, who had charge of the political prisoners at Wilna; Colonel Annenkoff, son of the governor of the South-western provinces; M. Westman, head of the private chancery of Prince Gortschakoff; M. Zablotski, Secretary of State; M. Pierre Semenoff, who represented Russia some four years since at the Statistical Congress; Colonel, now General Romanoffski, at that time editor of the *Invalide Russe*; Captain Koutzinski, commandant of the Château of the Viceroy in Warsaw; and M. Rumine, one of the judges recently appointed to preside over the peasants' courts. These gentlemen advocate many different forms of opinion in Russia, varying from the strict conservative principles of the Emperor Nicholas to the somewhat indefinite creed of modern liberalism; on the whole, I am persuaded that they fairly represent the opinion of the educated classes in Russia of the present day.*

I have striven in the following pages to represent fairly and impartially the conduct and the aims of all parties. It is, perhaps, impossible to regard the actions which pass before our eyes, and the men whom we have seen and with whom we have had personal intercourse, entirely from a historical point of view; and I cannot hope that my narrative will be free from error. All that I can urge is that to the best of my ability I have studied the question, have endeavoured to regard it dispassionately, and have recorded my exact impressions of the men and the events I have endeavoured to portray.

St. Swithin's Lane, London,
   30th October, 1866.

---

* I give these names without hesitation, as in every instance where information was given me it was fully understood that I intended subsequently to avail myself of it for the purposes of the narrative I was preparing.

CONTENTS.

CHAPTER I.

Policy of the Emperor Nicholas.—Suppression of Polish Universities.—Education of Polish Youth.—Its Revolutionary tendency.—Disaffection among them in after-life.—Effect of this System.—Polish Catechism.—Death of Nicholas.—Russian Liberals.—Views of the Emperor Alexander.—Emancipation.—Sympathy with the Poles .... *Page* 1

CHAPTER II.

Close of Crimean War.—State of Poland.—Visit of the Emperor to Warsaw.—Reforms introduced.—Formation of the Agricultural Society.—Improved Condition of the Country.—Disaffected Parties.—Religion and Races in Western Provinces.—"The Emigration."—The Democratic Party.—The Roman Catholic Church.—Patriotism of Polish Women 18

CHAPTER III.

Relations of Landlord and Peasant in the Kingdom of Poland.—Ancient Freedom of Peasants.—Their Reduction to Servitude.—Tyranny of their Masters.—Servitude in Lithuania.—Personal Enfranchisement in the Kingdom, and its Evil Effects.—Legislation of Polish Diet.—Subsequent Reforms by Russian Government.—Inventories.—Views of Poles on Land Question.—Legislation of Austria and Prussia upon it.—Necessity for effecting a Settlement favourable to the Peasants 33

CHAPTER IV.

Commencement of "Unarmed Agitation" in Warsaw.—Meeting in the Old Square.—"The Warsaw Massacre."—Address to the Emperor.—Indecision of Prince Gortschakoff.—The Delegation.—The Funeral.—Conduct of the Delegation and its Dissolution............ 50

CHAPTER V.

Embarrassment of Government.—Suppression of the Agricultural Society.—Liberal Institutions granted.—Polish Demonstrations.—Suppression of Disturbances.—State of Warsaw.—Death of Prince Gortschakoff .... *Page* 64

CHAPTER VI.

Count Lambert.—Declaration of State of Siege.—Demonstration of 15th October.—The Blockade of the Churches.—Mourning.—Attempted Murder of General Luders.—Appointment of Grand Duke Constantine as Viceroy.—The Marquis Wielopolski; his Character and Policy.—Attempts to assassinate the Grand Duke and the Marquis.—Distinction between the Kingdom of Poland and the Western Provinces.—Address of Polish Proprietors.—Count Andrew Zamoyski; his Exile 78

CHAPTER VII.

Revolutionary Press.—Plan of an Insurrection.—Increase of Agitation in Western Provinces.—Demonstration at Wilna.—Repressive Action of Government.—Celebrations at Kovno, and throughout Lithuania.—General Disaffection.—Wavering Policy of General Nazimoff.—Its Effects 94

CHAPTER VIII.

Conflicting Views of the various parties among the Poles.—The Conscription. — Outbreak of Insurrection. — Massacres.— Despatches from the Consul-General at Warsaw.—Proclamation of the Central Committee.—Conduct of the Proprietors.—Revolutionary "Order of the Day."—Attempt to poison the Marquis Wielopolski 109

CHAPTER IX.

Excesses of the Insurgents.—Their Position, and Character of their Bands.—Battle of Wengrow.—Progress of Revolt.—Concentration of Russian Troops 126

CHAPTER X.

Policy of Prussia.—Her Government of Posen.—Convention with Russia for Rendition of Criminals.—Debate in Prussian Chambers. —English Despatches.—Policy of Austria.—Loyalty of Peasants and Clergy in Galicia.—Anti-Russian Feeling of Austrian, French, and English Press .... *Page* 134

CHAPTER XI.

The Emperor Napoleon.—His presumed Designs on Prussia.—Exasperation of the French People.—Temporizing Policy of the Emperor.— Sympathy in England with the Insurgents.—Debate in the Lords. —Despatch of Lord Russell.—Reply of Prince Gortschakoff 144

CHAPTER XII.

Langiewicz's Campaign; his Defeat.—Resumption of Power by the National Government 155

CHAPTER XIII.

The National Government.—The Peasants and the Government.— Public Feeling in Russia.—Addresses to the Emperor.—The Amnesty.—Its Reception by Insurgents.—English Cabinet 168

CHAPTER XIV.

Moral Force.—Fabricated Intelligence.—Mouravieff.—Mourning Proclamation.—Debate in the House of Lords.—Property-tax.— Sequestrations 190

CHAPTER XV.

Serinkoffski, his Capture and Execution.—Attempted Murder of the Marshal of Nobility at Wilna.—Death of Nullo.—Rising in Kieff.—Wysocki's Invasion.—Letter of a Patriot Pole............... 206

CHAPTER XVI.

The Six Points.—Public Opinion in Russia.—Diplomatic Correspondence.—Analysis of the Six Points.—Proclamation of the National Government.—Cessation of Foreign Interference 229

CHAPTER XVII.

Dispute between the White and Red Parties.—Public Opinion in Russia.—Resignation of Wielopolski.—Embarrassing Position of the Grand Duke.—Excesses of the National Government.—Robbery of the Treasury.—Compulsory Loan.—Death of Lelewel.—Hopeless Character of the Revolt. — Resignation of the Grand Duke.—Appointment and Character of Count Berg.—His Policy.—Attempt upon his Life.—The Sacking of the Zamoyski Houses.—Suppression of Mourning.—Close of the Insurrection .... *Page* 241

CHAPTER XVIII.

Résumé of the Narrative 263

Appendix A. 277
Appendix B. 279
Appendix C. 285
Appendix D. 287
Appendix E. 288
Index 327

THE RUSSIAN GOVERNMENT IN POLAND.

CHAPTER I.

Policy of the Emperor Nicholas.—Suppression of Polish Universities.—Education of Polish Youth.—Its Revolutionary tendency.—Disaffection among them in after-life.—Effect of this system.—Polish Catechism.—Death of Nicholas.—Russian Liberals.—Views of the Emperor Alexander.—Emancipation.—Sympathy with the Poles.

IN the following pages I shall endeavour faithfully to trace the rise and progress of the rebellion in Poland; to point out what were the causes which nominally provoked it, as well as the more remote and powerful agencies from which it really sprung. It will be my province to show how the ancient animosities of religion and race prevailed over the humanizing influence of common interests, hopes, and aspirations, and how noble plans for the advancement of civilization and freedom withered beneath the hand of the conspirator and the angry breath of war.

In the course of my narrative I shall glance at the long train of injuries which were heaped upon a subject race, and show how consistent and how vain were the efforts of power to trample out the memory of past history, and eradicate the hopes of future national independence.

An aristocracy proud of its hereditary fame, and writhing beneath the wounds which a remorseless conqueror inflicted, will be seen in sullen dignity to reject the hand of reconciliation and friendship which the son of their oppressor extended to them; they will be seen disdainfully to ignore the liberal institutions he conferred, and which would have opened the way to self-government and constitutional freedom; and, abandoning the high position which a landed aristocracy should never abdicate, do nothing to prevent the rising liberties of their country from being risked on the desperate hazard of intestine war.

Again, now lowering in the distance, and now frowning in the foreground, will be seen the shadowy outline of a revolutionary *Vehme*. Without property, without honour, without aught to recommend them, save the headlong valour which but half redeems them from the condemnation they deserve, the leaders of the socialist propaganda will force themselves into the strife. Before their bolder and more resolute counsels, the feebler will of the aristocracy will bend; terrorism will be the means resorted to for carrying on the struggle, and murder be avowed as a legitimate instrument of war.

In Western Europe we shall see two mighty nations greatly moved by Poland's efforts to be free. Goaded into excitement by exaggerated rumours of cruelty on the one side and prowess on the other; deceived by documents audaciously forged and possessing about them all outward signs of authenticity; misled by circumstantial falsehoods gravely propagated by men who should have known the truth, and the worst and vilest of them endorsed by a powerful nobleman in the House of Lords; we shall find there have been moments when war and peace hung on the chance decision of an hour, the intrigues of a cabinet, or the response of an ally.

Sometimes, also, the indecision and the folly of the Russian authorities will be strikingly apparent, and the signs of their weakness will be traced in the spread of anarchy, the terror of the loyal, and the augmented power of the party of revolt; sometimes, also, we shall have to condemn their acts of arbitrary power, their injustice and disregard to the rights of property, when that property was the possession of their foe.

Through the varied intrigues of courts and councils, through the secret consultations of rebel leaders, and the daring exploits of the men who obeyed them, it is impossible in all cases to pilot the way to truth. The events I chronicle are scarcely those of yesterday, the flush of triumph yet lingers on the brow of the conqueror, the tear yet glitters in the mourner's eye, and only a few months since the strife yet lingered on amid woods and morasses, and ever and anon was embittered by some dark assassination or some high-handed act of power. The materials for history are here, but the men who collect and offer them for acceptance can scarcely be impartial; and if the author is sometimes misled by the spell of their patriotism or the contagion of their zeal, such errors may well be forgiven him if he endeavours impartially to perform his allotted task.

After the suppression of the Polish revolt of 1830, the Emperor Nicholas appeared resolved to obliterate the very memory of Poland. Himself a man of stern and unbending determination, he over-estimated his power, and strove to accomplish that which was unattainable. The master of a million of soldiers, he could wage war at his pleasure, and make peace at his will; but the power that he wielded, though it sufficed to embroil the world, was impotent to crush out one national tradition or to obliterate one historical memory. This truth he from time to time recognized, as he admitted at moments the impotence of his policy; but his proud nature forbade any public acknowledgment of his errors, and he persevered in a fatal consistency of action, though he knew it would bring him nothing but disappointment. This, indeed, was one of the errors of a mind which had within it many of the attributes of greatness; within the limited range of his prejudiced vision, he was wise and just, and almost magnanimous; but he possessed not that magnanimity which impels a great man to admit that he has erred, and in the face of the world to alter his avowed policy.

When the revolt was crushed out, and its leaders punished, it would have been the part of a wise and far-seeing prince to have bound up its bleeding wounds, and whispered hope to a discomfited and prostrate race. He would have found in their gratitude a securer tie than their fears ever afforded him, and would have converted men who detested him into loyal and loving subjects.

But from his point of view rebellion was a crime so loathsome and horrible that nothing could justify and nothing extenuate it; in this instance, too, the crime was yet blacker than in ordinary cases, for it was combined with a hatred to that great and sacred empire of which he was the divinely-appointed ruler.

Instead, therefore, of attempting to conciliate the Poles,—instead of seeking to attach them to his country and his crown by the creation of liberal institutions in which they might fill places of trust and dignity, he resorted to an unwise and arbitrary series of measures, by which he tried to merge Poland and the Poles in Russia, and tried in vain.

Warsaw and Wilna were the seats of two universities, where men of the Polish race had long been educated; they possessed libraries and collections, the relics of old times, the memorials of an age when Copernicus taught and Sobieski ruled. These institutions were regarded by the stern Emperor as memorials of that past which it was his mission to crush out; if he suppressed them, he thought he should destroy two of the rallying-points of disaffection and revolt; so his mandate went forth, and the universities were closed.

The libraries and collections they had contained were transferred to St. Petersburg and Kieff, and Poland and the Western Provinces were deprived of their accustomed means of education.

No longer possessing them in their own neighbourhood, the nobles of the kingdom and the Western Provinces were compelled to send their sons to the distant universities of Kieff, Moscow, and St. Petersburg.

Some of the poor students, who were unable to afford the cost of an education, were supported at these universities by the Government, on condition, after leaving it, that they should pass several years in the public service.

Thus, far away from their own land, the Emperor anticipated that they would forget the misfortunes of their country, that they would cease to look back on its past history with vain repining, and that they would devote all their energies to the service of the Empire.

The result did not answer his expectations; in many instances it prevented the poorer proprietors from affording a liberal education to their sons, and frequently the wealthier classes refused to part with their children, as they objected to the long and remote separation rendered necessary by their distance from the Russian universities. The corruption which was so rife in the public service rendered the wealthier proprietors unwilling that their sons should enter its ranks, and they therefore sent them very frequently to some German university to receive their education, and left them to gather it as best they could in the course of foreign travel.

A large portion of the Polish youth was thus brought up in idleness, among scenes where every tradition was associated with the history of their race, and where the only recognized standard deemed worthy of emulation were the patriots who had tried to free their country from the foreign yoke.

Education was thus in a measure checked by this act of power; but, nevertheless, large numbers of Polish students went to the principal Russian universities, where, instead of losing their nationality, it became more than ever confirmed.

Sometimes in periods of political excitement they banded themselves together as a distinct and separate body, neither sharing in the sports nor sympathizing in the pursuits of the other students. Thus, in the university of St. Petersburg they formed one-third of the whole students, and in that of Kieff they were comparatively even more numerous; in the former they partially, and in the latter they altogether, refused to associate themselves with the Russians. Oftener, however, they took the lead in daring political speculations, supported the most advanced liberal theories, and endeavoured there, as it will be afterwards seen they did subsequently upon a wider arena, to prejudice their Russian fellow-students against all the forms of a despotic government.

His university course ended, the Pole generally entered the public service, where his talents and industry were certain of meeting recognition and reward; for in every Pole who entered his service the Emperor saw a deserter from the camp of the enemy, one who had abandoned the idle hope of reviving an extinct nationality, and had identified himself with the greatness and the fortunes of Russia. Yet the allegiance of such a man too often sat lightly upon him, and we shall see that the result of the system of the Emperor Nicholas was but a Pyrrhic triumph.

The injuries to which youth is subjected by oppression root deeply in the mind, and it is little to be wondered at if these Polish students, the sons for the most part of the insurgents of 1830, were dissatisfied with the Government they obeyed, and the country which had trampled on their native land.

As they grew in years, such feelings strengthened, and however much the history of their country was unfavourably coloured by Russian scribes, *they* pictured her in the warm tints of a glowing patriotism; they thought of her as the Poland which had saved Vienna and menaced Moscow, and they imaged her as the land of chivalry, of freedom, and of song; they regarded the stormy gatherings of feudal chieftains as the legitimate expression of the national will; and in the repeated partitions of Poland they allowed for none of those circumstances which almost rendered them inevitable, and saw in them nothing save their guilt.

It is natural that minds thus impressed with a sense of wrong should regard with deep detestation the forms of government by which they were surrounded; and that they should behold in them the machinery by which arbitrary power kept down the expression of opinion and the progress of free thought.

The Polish student, dissatisfied with what was, solaced himself with chimerical visions of a future which will never be. Crude and impracticable theories of socialist scribblers, wild notions of ultra-theoretic liberalism, dreams of impossible changes, and of a perfection in institutions of which no institutions are capable, filled his mind and animated his exertions.

Had the free interchange of thought been allowed in Russia, and these opinions been fairly tested in the broad sunshine of public discussion, a general diffusion of liberal ideas might have resulted from it, but it certainly would have stopped the rank and poisonous vegetation which was silently germinating in that intellectual dungeon.

Impressed with the wildest and most extravagant ideas, the Pole, when he entered the public service, used his influence to procure converts to them. He associated with men of liberal opinions among the Russians, and endeavoured to win them over to his own anarchical theories.

While holding office under the Government, too often he was

encouraging others to attempt its overthrow; too often he betrayed the secrets his official position alone enabled him to acquire, and thought all deception honourable and just which served, however remotely, the interests of his country.

Employed in the interior of Russia, he was frequently remarkable for his grasping and avaricious tendencies, and was not too scrupulous as to the means he employed to gratify them. He desired to amass a fortune, that he might spend it thereafter in the service of Poland; and if, in collecting it, he gave dissatisfaction to the people, that dissatisfaction would only recoil on the institutions he longed to destroy.

For the furtherance of the same political ends he endeavoured unduly to advance his countrymen in public life. In every province where a Pole was in high employment, it was certain that the lesser appointments would be thronged with his compatriots, and thus throughout the Empire all branches of the administration were crowded with men who were the secret enemies of Russia.

Of course, in the public service there were many men who would not stoop to such courses; men of high honour and independent will, who would not sully their reputation by any such combination of perfidy and self-interest.

The policy of the Emperor Nicholas on the subject of education was consistent with the measures he adopted in other branches of the administration.

The study of the ancient history of Poland was forbidden, or permitted only in the feeble and garbled treatises of Russian scribes; as though every battle-field had not its memory, as though every tomb in the churches, every banner that mouldered on their sacred walls, did not teach some passage of her history to Poland's persecuted sons. The works of foreign authors were rigorously forbidden, and secret commissions punished their study with imprisonment and exile; the visits of foreigners were as much as possible discouraged, and they were subjected to numberless vexatious restrictions, having their speedy departure for their object; while the trade and manufactures of the country languished under the blighting influence of prohibitive tariffs, and the multitude of unwise regulations official pedantry imposed.

The custom-house frontier between Russia and Poland was abolished, and the prohibitive system of the Empire was introduced in all its severity; a commission of the secret police settling in Warsaw filled the prisons with the most enlightened citizens, while the Polish youth were drafted into the military service in such numbers that for a whole generation the population of the country decreased, and the last vestige of independence—the national army—was merged in the imperial forces.

Such was the system on which the Emperor Nicholas governed Poland, and he never swerved from it. The revolution of 1830 was terribly avenged in a civil administration denationalized, a blighted commerce, an army that had ceased to exist, and a land lying prostrate at the feet of implacable power. A generation was born and grew up under this relentless sway, and one of the last acts of his reign was to destroy a whole quarter of Warsaw, that he might add a glacis and an outwork to the citadel with which he overawed the town.

Yet the measures he took to blot out the nationality he detested were singularly unfortunate; the annihilation of the frontier on which he relied as a means of introducing the Russian element into Poland served, on the contrary, to bring together the scattered members of the Polish race. Warsaw once more became the capital to which the wealthy nobles of the Western Provinces, as well as of the kingdom, resorted; and in spite of their long alienation from each other, it was soon apparent that their feelings and interests were the same. Indeed the very fact of nobles of the provinces dwelling for the most part among Russians made them more decided in their Polish sympathies and policy than even their kindred in the Congress kingdom.

The Polish proprietors perseveringly endeavoured to implant a national feeling antagonistic to Russia, in the minds of the common people. In the Western Provinces the Polish race, as will hereafter be seen, numbered only some ten per cent. of the entire population. The remainder were of Russian, Lettic, or Jewish origin. Amongst them the Poles incessantly toiled. They often professed not to understand Russian, and peasants who used that language were handed over to the agent, while those who spoke Polish were thrown into direct communication with their proprietors. Self-interest thus prompted them to understand and speak the language of their masters. The language once learned, it was easy to persuade them that they were Poles, to teach them vague lessons of their country's former history, to shake their political allegiance, and to undermine their religious faith.

Among the Lettic race, the Roman Catholic clergy were equally active. The community of faith was a link between them and their pastors which was wanting in the relations of the latter with the Russian serf, and the clergy ably propagated political views which might tend thereafter to win back the Western Provinces to the profession of the true faith. The result was that when the Emperor Nicholas died, the Western Provinces were far more Polish than they had been previously to the revolt of 1830.

The principles which I have attributed to many of the Poles find expression in a curious document which was circulated extensively among them, a translation of which I subjoin. It is known as the Polish catechism; its authenticity has indeed been questioned by those who were interested in repudiating it, but there is not the least reason for attaching any credit to the denial. It reads thus:—

"In the great hour of the re-establishment of our beloved country, everyone having a right to call himself a son of Poland must sacrifice on the altar of liberty, and must not suffer the spark that animated Poland in all her misery to be extinguished. This spark will soon become a fire spreading over the whole world, and the Polish nation, like another phœnix, will arise from her ashes and appear as the protector of oppressed nations and champion of the mission of civilized Europe. Let us remember, brethren, that Phœnicia and Venice ruled the world not with arms but with intellect, riches, and knowledge. Let us imitate their example, and act in accordance with the following measures proposed by a man completely devoted to his country.

"Poland is a land fitted for commerce and civilization; there was a time when she ruled with her glorious and unconquerable arms; but the views of Providence are unfathomable, and she is now called to rule by the power of her intellect, commerce, and civilization. Look at England, a truly commercial nation, but the most powerful in the world. She rules it on the sea, Poland on the land. The colonies are the prop of England's wealth, but they are at a distance. Poland has likewise an India,—Lithuania and the Ukraine. These colonies form one with Poland, and if this agitation is ably conducted, they can never be separated from her.

"I offer to our brethren in blood and in religion, the following counsels to enable us to act with union, that we may reach the goal.

"1. In the annexed provinces the landowners must endeavour not to part with their property; if they are obliged to do so, let a Pole be the buyer, in order to prevent the Russian element from spreading. The suffering brethren landowners must be helped, the Russian landowners must be subjected to all kinds of annoyances; nothing must be sold to them or bought from them; lawsuits must be instituted against them; they are sure to lose, as the judicial offices in the country are occupied by Poles likewise. Thus they will be forced to sell their unrighteously acquired property and to return to their Muscovy. The land sold by Russians must be bought, even if it were necessary to form a company for the purpose. Thus in time all the power and profit will be in our own hands. Let us help our country and be useful to her.

"Let greedy Russia think the Ukraine and Lithuania her property; but she won't understand who will have the material profits of those provinces.

"Besides this, these measures will hinder the union of these provinces with hated Russia, and if we profit by the stupidity and want of enlightenment of the local popes (priests), and work upon their avarice with money, we can lull these men, whose antagonistic creed renders them our most inveterate foes.

"If we act well, we may make the people adjure their false faith, or at least inspire them with less confidence in their popes; and this will be sufficient to arm the people against them.

"2. As the Russians are in general uneducated, lazy, and

self-confident, the Poles must try to be particularly well educated, to be able to get the best and most useful places, and thus to be the moral arbiters of that dull nation.

"3. Persons specially educated must try to serve in Russia without paying attention to the idle talk of those who know nothing of political secrets, who say that it is dishonourable for a Pole to serve Russia; for, being in the Russian service for his country's sake, every Pole makes a great sacrifice for Poland.

"4. Only profitable places must be accepted; as soon as a fortune is made, leave Russia, and return to your country; thus the money got in Russia will belong to our brethren; thus not only your sacrifice is repaid, but you impoverish the enemy; all means thereto are not only allowed, but necessary; the claws of the foe are thereby cut. Strive by all means to make a fortune at the expense of the Russian treasury; it is no sin and no crime, because, robbing Russia, you disable the enemy and enrich your country. The Holy Church will pardon you, as thereby you do good to your brethren. Jesus Christ himself, who has ordered us not to kill each other, has, nevertheless, permitted arms to be raised against the foes of Israel; this expedient, moreover, is not murderous, and depriving the robber of wealth, you will give it to your poorest brethren. When your country will be free, it will be strong.

"5. Strive to obtain an important post, and when you have the power, protect your brethren and give them good places too. All means are legitimate for this purpose, even if they appear base to others; remember that all this is done for your country's sake, and thus your baseness will be looked upon as a great sacrifice by your countrymen. As to what others say, pay no attention to it, and continue your work. The Russian particularly likes flattery, and, blinded by it, will rather give a place to you than to his own countryman (though worthier of of it than you), whose rude nature does not enable him to assume polite manners; and thus flattery being the surest arm against the enemy, must be used in all cases where it can be of use. When we shall thus occupy all the important posts in Russia, she will herself become our tributary.

"6. Do not serve long in the Russian army, because when

you obtain a high rank you necessarily become the instrument of the nation hateful to you, and must carry out its plans. In general, remain in service as long as you have means to enrich yourself; as soon as you have made your fortune, leave the service and settle amongst your own countrymen, or else your treasures might again pass to the foe.

" 7. As to the civil service, remain in it as long as you can, and mount on the highest steps; do not accept the post of the highest statesmen, but try to be their help, to be near them, in fact. In the first case the Government will have no confidence in you, and will not make you acquainted with its plans. In the second, if you know how to manage your superior, and to gain his confidence, all the secrets of the Government will become known to you, and through you to your countrymen. If the Government is betrayed, your superior will have to answer for it, while you will remain in the shade and reserve yourself for the further service of your country.

"8. Be in every case your superior's right hand, and to gain his confidence, neglect nothing; even abuse your countrymen in his presence, and condemn their actions: there is nothing easier than thus to persuade a Russian of your attachment to Russia and the Government. Having thus stolen into your superior's confidence, you may secretly protect your countrymen.

"9. If you remark a member of the Russian society hostile to your countrymen, strive to gain his friendship, and make your countrymen acquainted with him; thus, if you cannot destroy the foe, at least, knowing his plans, you will be able to avert the evil by fighting him with equal arms. When Russia is filled up with our agents, and covered with a network of our brethren united in action, it will be ours, and with time, acting systematically and assailing the weaker points of Russian society, we shall make it acquiesce with us in the necessity of Poland's separation.

"This can be done without any armed power or loss of blood; and we shall thereby be stronger and more powerful in the future.

" 10. Remember that Russia is your greatest foe, and that a member of the Greek religion is a heretic, and thus freely affirm that you are brothers, that you have nothing against the Russians, only against the Government; but in secret try to revenge yourself on every Russian; he can never be your friend, as he hates the Catholic religion and Poland, and will always be ready to help his Government in its hostile measures against them.

"11. Always tell the Russians that Germans are the greatest enemies of Russia and Poland; that they destroy the union between the two nations, as their policy requires it.

"Russians hate the Germans, and will always credit your words; this is the best argument you can use, and thus lull the foe to sleep by appearances of friendship. When any of your plans are discovered, make the blame fall on the Germans; you will thus avert the blow from yourself and incite one enemy to destroy the other, while you escape suspicion. When you speak with a Russian, try to make him lose his patience; his stupid and frank nature makes him disclose everything in a quarrel; this only is necessary to you,—knowing the plan of the foe, you can act against him.

"12. In the society of Russians, try to be silent, and do not disclose your views, as it is not profitable. Attack the Russian in your own society; first attack the hateful Government that he serves like a slave, then reproach it with domination over other nations; reproach him with want of heart and sensibility for his oppressed brother Poles. Try to wound his self-love, and then, at the end of the conversation, you will make of him a devoted servant in all your enterprises. The Russian with his rude and frank nature is always full of self-esteem, and the title of 'barbarian' enrages him. To be freed from this odious epithet, he is ready to plunge a knife in the breast of his own countrymen. When necessary, wound his self-love, and profit by it.

"13. If your foe is strong and cunning and understand you, try to destroy him, and use the surest arm thereto,—an influential German. The German hating the Russian element, will help you in this; your foe will perish, thinking he owes his fall to German influence. Thereby you will still more prove that the real enemy of the Russian is the German, and you, exciting no suspicion, will make a friend out of an enemy, who will help you in your plans. Amen."

The death of the Emperor Nicholas and the termination of the Crimean war, gave a great impulse to the Liberal party. The tyranny which for thirty years had weighed down their energies was at length removed. That imperious and commanding figure, which had filled so important a part on the stage of their history, was gone ; his resolute will no longer directed the destinies of Russia ; his settled policy, which for so prolonged a period had been unquestioned, was now open to discussion and hostile comment, and the nation, aroused from its long trance, demanded upon what principles its future government was to be based.

There were men in Russia of eager and daring minds, who had travelled in foreign lands and attentively studied the institutions they found existing there. Keenly alive to the defects of their own system, they anxiously anticipated the period when their native land also should enjoy constitutional freedom. In the disastrous peace of 1856 they read the downfall of despotic power. What, they asked, had their patriarchal government secured them ?

It had built up, at a vast expense of treasure and of suffering, a huge army ; to feed that army Russia had been yearly drained of multitudes of men, whose labour was required in her untilled fields or her failing manufactories ; it had been the idol and the boast of the late Emperor, and had given him for a long period great influence in Europe ; the hour of trial came, the idol was shattered, and the priest lay dead before the violated shrine ; the sole result of years of repression and military rule was to show that the army which could govern reluctant citizens broke down when it was arrayed against a foreign foe.

Corruption also was eating away the vital powers of the State. Employés, who had no private means, and whose insignificant salaries were unequal to afford them a competence, were the masters of stately mansions, splendid equipages, and pompous retinues of slaves ; justice was for sale ; public honours were showered on worthless men ; officials fattened and the people starved.

Such were some of the charges brought against the Government by the able and earnest men who desired an immediate change, and they made these and many similar allegations the basis of their attacks on the existing order of things. Must there not, they asked, be something rotten in the system which had so hopelessly broken down in the first moment of severe trial? and was it not certain that nothing but disaster could thereafter be anticipated from a bureaucracy so constituted that its employés could only live by robbing their country?

Perhaps, in their pursuit of theoretic improvement, these men under-estimated the difficulties of their intended task; no jurist, for example, who knows the operation of our system of trial by jury, will feel very sanguine as to its working well in Russia, nor will any statesman feel confident that the parliament they are anxious to constitute would use with wisdom and moderation the powers they should thus obtain.

Public opinion is not moved in Russia as easily as in England; but at this juncture there was a strong and increasing tendency towards constitutional government, and it would have been scarcely possible to have adhered to the system of the Emperor Nicholas.

Nor was such an adherence intended. We are told that in the sad and darkened chamber where the late monarch died, a solemn scene had taken place;—that, calling his successor to his side, the dying man had besought him, for the sake of the Russia that son had always loved, for the sake of the diadem so soon to descend upon his brow, for the sake of the people so soon to be committed to his charge, to govern Russia as *he* had never done; the approach of death was manifesting to him truths to which during life he had been blind, and he urged upon him the emancipation of the serfs, and expressed his sorrow at not having himself accomplished that salutary work.

These warnings were scarcely needed; the Emperor Alexander had studied the history of his country; as a philanthropist he desired, as a statesman he saw the necessity of emancipation; he saw also that wide-spread reforms were needed, and he resolutely devoted himself to their accomplishment.

The state of public affairs was such as demanded the exercise of most unwavering courage and constancy directed by consummate prudence. On one side were the great nobles, men whose estates yielded enormous revenues, which they spent about the court at St. Petersburg; their social importance had hitherto been accompanied by vast political influence, and they formed, as it were, a Pretorian guard about their sovereign, from whose influence he could with difficulty escape. On the other side were the people, numerous, uneducated, without organization or leaders, but possessing in themselves an immense power, capable of crushing whatever opposed it, if it were once given a direction and a policy.

These uneducated masses were conscious they had been wronged; they knew enough of their past history, they felt enough their present degradation, to convince them that they were entitled to freedom, and to induce them to regard their masters as aggressive and unjust oppressors. The Emperor observed the threatened storm, he saw the only hope of salvation for the State consisted in avoiding the wild excesses of democracy on the one hand, and the confirmed supremacy of an exclusive oligarchy on the other. He knew that the counsels of wisdom and moderation on which he was prepared to act would be supported by a great mass of enlightened public opinion, and he was resolved that no considerations of personal danger, and no desire for personal repose, should deter him from performing the great task which, to be done with security to Russia, must be done at once.

But the Emperor was too observant, and knew too well the character of the people over which he ruled to imagine that emancipation could stand alone; he knew it would alter the relation in which every class of society stood to himself and to every other class; and he felt that, to consolidate the freedom he was about to grant, it was necessary he should confer institutions which should be at once its embodiment and safeguard.

While such were the views he entertained with regard to Russia and the provinces of ancient Poland incorporated with her, his views with regard to the Congress kingdom of Poland were not less liberal and enlightened. I shall have hereafter to show, that although personal servitude did not nominally exist there, the peasants of the kingdom were as degraded as the serfs of the empire, and that their condition as greatly required the interposition of an enlightened and progressive government.

In addition, however, to any claims which the peasants of Poland had on the consideration of the Government, the condition of the country and its inhabitants excited deep commiseration in Russia. Despite the antagonism which had for centuries divided these two great members of the Sclavonic family, despite the long account of mutual injuries and the bitter recollections of ancient feuds, it was impossible for Russia to view Poland, in this the hour of her downfall and humiliation, without entertaining for her a generous sympathy, and without desiring to raise her from her low estate. Moreover, the Liberals of Russia deprecated the policy which the Emperor Nicholas had pursued;—How could they strive for freedom in Russia, and yet countenance the policy which had enslaved Poland? How, when they desired the spread of public education and enlightenment, could they approve the act which had closed the universities of Warsaw and of Wilna, ransacked their treasures, travestied the history, and would fain have blotted out the very memory of Poland? How could they, who were anxious to struggle for self-government in Russia, countenance the harsh and grinding system which denied all power to the Pole?

There was in Russia a feeling that the inhabitants of the kingdom had been harshly and cruelly treated, and the kindly sentiments the monarch entertained towards Poland found a cordial echo in the feelings of the Liberal party in Russia.

CHAPTER II.

Close of Crimean War.—State of Poland.—Visit of the Emperor to Warsaw.—Reforms introduced.—Formation of the Agricultural Society.—Improved condition of the Country.—Disaffected Parties.—Religion and Races in Western Provinces.—" The Emigration."—The Democratic Party.—The Roman Catholic Church.—Patriotism of Polish Women.

THE Crimean war was closed by the peace of Paris, signed 31st March, 1856. During that arduous struggle Poland had given no sign of life; and not the faintest whisper arose from her cities, or her silent plains, which told the world she was resolved to re-assert her ancient freedom. Perhaps in secret she cherished dreams of winning back again her fallen independence; but if she did, those visions found no expression, and there was nothing to indicate to the world that her ancient spirit yet survived. A few regiments of militia, a few reserved battalions of inferior soldiery had kept in check the land which, twenty-five years before, had haughtily challenged Russian supremacy on the battle-field of Grockovo. It seemed as though a quarter of a century of servitude had trampled out all hope and expectation for the future, and as though Russia had at length succeeded in incorporating Poland virtually, as well as in name, in her vast empire. Neither had Poland shown any indication of political life when in 1848 almost every European nation was in arms; then when the wildest visions of political enthusiasts found a momentary realization, when dormant nationalities were everywhere rousing themselves, the champions of freedom listened for the battle-cry of Poland; but Poland gave no sign. At her very gates the war was raging, and she made no effort when the struggling liberties of Hungary were being trampled out to save a people whose cause, she might well have thought, was intimately connected with her own. The Polish soldier was seen marching in the Russian army when

Kossuth fled and Georgey capitulated; and, while he apparently thought nothing of the liberties of his own land, he became an obedient instrument to trample out those of another.

In the Crimea the valour of the Polish soldiers had been very remarkable, and no whisper of disaffection had escaped them, nor was there any reason to believe that they hoped for a revival of national independence.

Such was the state of Poland, and such the apparent disposition of her inhabitants, when, shortly after the peace of Paris, the new Emperor visited Warsaw.

He came there anxiously desiring to benefit his Polish subjects; he trusted in their loyalty, he was grateful to them for their valour, and he thought he could attach them to his crown and his dynasty by the silken cord of kindness and conciliation.

His first act demonstrated in how different a spirit he proposed to govern to that which his father had evinced.

Since the rebellion of 1830, the Poles, a deeply bigoted race, had remarked that their monarch had never graced the Catholic cathedral with his presence. The short and sullen visits he had paid to Warsaw had been marked by no act of condescension, cheered by no evidence of abating wrath; he came to require an account of his stewardship from his viceroy, Paskievitch, but he made no effort to win the love of a people he governed with the sword. One of the first acts, however, of the new sovereign was to attend a solemn Te Deum, which was chanted in the Catholic cathedral in honour of his visit; and at this service all the civil functionaries of the kingdom were present.

Immediately after this ceremonial he received the marshals of the Polish nobility, assured them of his beneficent intentions, and expressed a hope that they would assist in giving them effect. He lauded the valour the Polish soldiers had displayed before the walls of Sebastopol, and, coupling together the names of the kingdom of Poland and the grand duchy of Finland, he stated that both were as dear to him as any of the provinces of Old Russia, and both should as greatly experience his protecting care; but at the same time, he added, "for the good of Poland and for the good of the

Poles themselves, it is necessary that your country should remain ever united to that of the great family of the Emperor of Russia."

In this address the Emperor made use of an expression which offended the jealous pride of the Polish magnates. Desirous of really benefitting the country, he feared the impractical character of the Poles would induce them to depreciate real improvements in their wild pursuit of impossible theories. Once, or more than once, therefore, he used the expression in addressing them, "Let us have no reveries, gentlemen" ("Messieurs, pas de rêveries"); and this phrase was chronicled against him as a grave offence. Notwithstanding these murmurs, however, the relations established between the sovereign and his subjects on the occasion of his first visit were cordial. An amnesty was granted, by which, with a few inconsiderable exceptions, all emigrants were allowed to return to Poland; were restored to their civil rights, and were secured against all legal prosecutions or inquiries. Shortly afterwards a similar amnesty was granted to the emigrant Poles of the Western Provinces.

The recruitment, which had pressed so heavily on the people of the Congress kingdom, was suspended. Some remissions of taxation were effected, and many pardons were granted to offenders who had been condemned for political crimes.

Steps were also taken to secure the filling up of various episcopal sees belonging to the Roman Catholic Church. These sees had been for some time vacant, and the affairs of the various dioceses had been intrusted to mere administrators. To effect this end a Papal bull was required, and the necessary application was made for procuring it. Some alterations were also made in the laws regulating marriage, by which all questions connected with it were committed to the jurisdiction of the Church.

At the same time preliminary measures were taken for the re-establishment of the university at Warsaw, and a Faculty of Medicine was at once constituted there.

Many other minor reforms and improvements were introduced; but the step which was destined to be eventually attended with the most marked results was the permission which the Government accorded to certain proprietors to form an agricultural society for the kingdom of Poland. This society, as originally contemplated, would have consisted of three or four hundred members, and have been exclusively confined to the landed proprietors of the Congress kingdom. Soon, however, its numbers enlarged, and it became a centre round which the Poles of Galicia, Posen, and the Western Provinces rallied. Its numbers, at the time of its dissolution, had swelled to about 4,000 members. It had committees sitting in permanence throughout the whole year, and had become more like a parliament than a mere agricultural society.

In the same year a commission was appointed by the Government for inquiring into the best mode of dealing with the land question, so far as the peasants were affected by it; the object being to secure to them the land they fairly claimed, while the proprietors were protected from undue sacrifice.

In the month of July two decrees were issued, which further evidenced the desire of the Emperor to study the legitimate wishes of the Poles. By the first of these the general military governors in the different governments of the kingdom, with the exception of Warsaw, were replaced by simple *commandants de place;* and by the second, the administration of posts and custom-houses in the kingdom was detached from the central administration at St. Petersburg.

The altered policy of the Government soon produced beneficial results; the iron rule beneath which the country so long had crouched was relaxed; trade was opened up in various directions; oppressive tariff regulations were abolished; the old passport system, under which the country was one vast prison, was done away; and the same immunities were extended to the kingdom as the most loyal provinces in the empire possessed.

The laws relating to the press were no longer strictly observed; state prosecutions were abandoned; political prisoners were released; the fortresses were empty, and the exiles were returning to their former homes.

The ecclesiastical jurisdiction of the Roman Catholic Church was restored; and in the commission sitting at St. Petersburg for the reform of the tariff Poland had her representatives.

It was then that sanguine men believed that a great future was in store for their country; in her geographical position they saw the surest guarantee for her commercial importance; lines of railway from St. Petersburg, Berlin, and Vienna were all converging to her ancient capital. A large carrying trade sprang up between Hamburg and Warsaw, and the latter city was full of foreign goods. Poland was evidently becoming the highway to Europe, and had only to be patient to acquire more than she had ever lost.

The changes that were occurring about them stimulated many of the proprietors to exertion and enterprise; they could not see movement on all sides, and themselves be still; so they joined in various commercial undertakings, and assumed their direction.

Wherever a Polish proprietor, either in the kingdom or the Western Provinces, was possessed of capital, new sugar-factories or distilleries sprung up on a great scale; agricultural machines were largely imported and extensively used; the mineral productions of the country were attracting attention; magnificent hotels were being constructed; municipal improvements were everywhere being effected, and in Warsaw gas was introduced. Simultaneously with these evidences of returning prosperity, the price of land increased, building speculations were undertaken, and Polish companies were formed for the construction of two new lines of railway. Thus the liberal policy of the Government gave hope and prosperity to Poland. War, conscription, pestilence, and want had thinned the mourning land; but now peace was restored, the conscription was abandoned, and employment was driving away pestilence and want.

Yet there was a party in Poland who regarded all these signs of advancement with suspicion; they cared not for peaceful triumphs, the spread of commerce, or the introduction of liberal institutions; they knew their country had been wronged, and they burned to avenge her injuries. National independence had been their object thirty years before—it was their lode-star still. They thought of that scroll whereon the Constitution the first Alexander gave was blazoned, and remembered with bitterness that it was paraded as a trophy before every stranger who spent an hour among the collections and curiosities of Moscow. They thought of the monuments of Russian victories, victories won over those they designated as their subjects, which were to be seen on every side. They recalled the iron rule of Nicholas, and asked if a few fair words from his successor availed to sweep its memory away. They thought of the patriots who had suffered death, or who in Siberia had found a living tomb, and, folding around them a mantle of implacable resentment, they rejected the well-meant overtures of the Government.

And here the very clemency of the Emperor swelled the tide of disaffection. He had generously recalled all those who for political offences had been banished in his father's time; and they came back, the men who had fought, intrigued, and suffered in the cause of Poland, their hearts full of bitterness, to fight, intrigue, and suffer once again. They came back as exiles always do, untaught by adversity, unlearned in the signs of the times; they came back, ignorant of the power of Russia and of the feelings, hopes, and prejudices which had grown up amongst their own people; they came back, having learnt nothing and forgotten nothing, to parade the history of their woes, and to preach rebellion as a sacred duty.

It is necessary to understand the constitution of society in Poland, and the different parties into which the Poles were divided, in order to comprehend how far the agitation which I shall have to record, and the subsequent revolt, were really entitled to be regarded as a national movement.

In the Congress kingdom, out of a population of nearly 5,000,000 souls, about 263,000 are called noble. They represent those who in old time, by virtue of property, descent, or the favour of the reigning king, were ennobled; and the position thus conferred on them is somewhat analogous to that of freemen in our ancient boroughs. Some of these nobles are men of large estate and great influence; such, for example, as Count Andrew Zamoyski and the Marquis Wielopolski. By far the greater number of them, however, are men of neither property nor position, and their only inheritance is the title of noble, and the trifling immunities it confers. Nobles of this class are generally known as Schliacta; and the driver of a hired carriage and the waiter at an hotel not unfrequently belong to it.

The shopkeepers, artisans, and mechanics of the larger towns hold much the same relative position to the proprietors as they do in England; like them they are to a considerable degree dependent upon their customers and employers, and the views held by the latter are likely to some extent to influence them.

The peasants are divided into two classes,—those who hold land, and those who, having none, are mere farm labourers or servants. The former have no sympathy whatever with the political views of the proprietors. I shall hereafter show how it happens that the utmost distrust and hostility exists between them, and how utterly the "national" aspirations of the nobles are repudiated by the occupying peasants.

The peasants who hold no land (proletarians) are in a peculiarly unfortunate position. A large proportion of the rent due to the proprietors has hitherto been paid in labour, and this labour has been valued at a very low rate. The proprietor, therefore, having already the command of a considerable number of hands, requires but little additional assistance, and either refuses to hire more labour or, if he does hire, procures it on very inadequate terms. There is not, as in England, a regular demand for labour, and a regular rate of wage; and the landless peasant knows, if he quits his present employer, that he may starve before he finds another. It is very common to find two families of this class living in one hut containing two rooms; for this hut, together with the keep of a cow and a pig, they work four days a week, and are paid only 5*d.* a day for their labour. Men of this stamp are much in the power of their employers, and during the revolt it frequently happened that work was given to them on condition that they, or some member of their family, would join a band of the insurgents.

Such being the division of ranks in the Congress kingdom, it remains to point out the social difference which exists between those in the Western Provinces. It will hereafter be seen that the serf in the latter is better off than the peasant in the former district; that the freedom conferred on the inhabitant of the grand duchy of Warsaw, in 1807, by depriving him of his title to his land, and placing him completely at the mercy of the proprietor, reduced him to a state of misery and dependence, to which the serf of the Western Provinces has never been brought down. In the Western Provinces the proletarian class does not exist, and therefore the nobles, when the rebellion broke out, had no retainers whose active assistance they could command.

In the Western Provinces there is a difference of race between the nobles and the majority of the peasants. Instead of being for the most part Poles, the numbers of that race average only 10·4 per cent. of the entire population, while the Russian or Ruthenian races amount to nearly six times that number. The following is an analysis of the population:—

Russians and Little Russians	5,952,513
Letts and Lithuanians	1,614,660
Poles	1,046,947
Jews	1,139,633
Other nations	114,618
	9,868,371*

A yet more important distinction than that of race is to be found in the difference of religion. The number of inhabitants professing the Greek faith is 6,707,570, while the number belonging to the Roman Catholic and Armenian churches is only 2,597,627. The Catholic peasant has generally been led by his interests to side with the Government in the insurrection, and has done his utmost to put it down; but occasionally the promptings of the Catholic priesthood have induced him to render aid to the insurgents, and to discard mere considerations of selfish policy at the call, as he has been taught to believe, of his country and his Church. The Greek peasant has been exposed to no such advocacy; the clergy of his Church have been faithful to the Government and preached the duty of loyally obeying it; his own interests

---

* See Appendix A. The discrepancies in some of the statistics in Herr von Buschen's work are explained at length in the preface to it.

have pointed in the same direction; and thus, in all cases, the peasants belonging to this creed have been opposed to the revolt.

Although the Poles are thus outnumbered in the Western Provinces, they represent their intelligence, wealth, and education, and they therefore claim to be considered as the nation. Stupid, uneducated, and incapable of thought, the masses, the Poles contend, are unworthy of consideration. The only men whose wishes and interests should be consulted are those who have for centuries absorbed all political power and all civil rights.

It is hard to recognize the truth of this doctrine, and it is strange to hear it enunciated by those who claim the support of liberal politicians, and the active assistance of revolutionary propagandists. The present degradation of these suffering masses is owing in no slight degree to the long-continued tyranny of their Polish masters, and now those very masters would take advantage of their own wrong, and claim to be the representative men of the people who so long have groaned beneath their oppression.

If an additional reason were required to show that the nobles and proprietors should not be recognized as the nation, it would be found in the influence the settlement of the land question and the spread of education is sure to exercise in future. Some millions of men are about to be endowed with land, are about to receive education from the State, and to be freed from a thraldom which has prevented their physical and moral progress. Very likely it may be generations before they will produce individuals capable of taking a prominent part in the government of their country; but we may be sure that that time will come, that great organic changes are now in progress, and that the non-Polish races will hereafter be as overwhelming in property and influence as they at present are in numbers.

There are several distinct sections among the Poles who take part in politics.

"The Emigration," consisting of political refugees and their families, are principally situated at Paris, and may be divided into two classes.

The aristocratic party, which acknowledges Prince Czartoriski as their leader, seek to re-establish a kingdom of Poland, to be ruled by an hereditary monarch. In such a kingdom the great territorial families would, doubtless, exercise immense power, and if the old were to be any guide to the framers of a new constitution for Poland, their efforts would result in the establishment of oligarchical rather than popular forms. The success of this party would assuredly afford no security for constitutional freedom; never yet have the Polish magnates evidenced a real desire to promote the welfare of the people; for the liberal constitution of 1791 was an attempt to meet the exigencies of a moment full of difficulty, and cannot justly be deemed a proof of sympathy with the masses; and at all other periods there has been wanting the slightest tendency to liberality or constitutional freedom. When we think of the Polish history of that day, we recall Lamartine's words:—" Dumouriez found the Polish aristocrats corrupted by luxury, enervated by pleasures, employing in intrigues and fervent language the warmth of their patriotism. Sapieha, the principal leader, was massacred by his nobles. Pulaski and Micksenski were delivered up wounded to the Russians. Zaremba betrayed his country. He (Dumouriez) broke his sword, despairing for ever of this aristocracy without a people; calling it, as he quitted it, the Asiatic nation of Europe."

Has the character of the Polish noble greatly changed since then? Are the men who have squandered life and its opportunities in the dissipations of foreign capitals likely there to learn great lessons of wisdom and of patriotism? Is not exile always an excuse for neglected duties, and abilities allowed to run to waste? But, supposing among the habitués of Paris and of London there are some men of higher purpose and of sterner mould; supposing there are some whose only aim is the renovation of their country, and the vindication of her injured fame; even then the question will arise, to be answered with doubt and hesitation,—Is it possible for those who long have been exiled from their native land, those whose intercourse is necessarily, to a great extent, with the intriguing agents of a vanquished party, to form so calm a judgment of all that occurs during their absence as to qualify them for power on their return?

All history seems to deny it. Exiles who return are biassed by former recollections and old party ties; for them their country has stood still since their departure, and they expect to find it unaltered when they are restored to it. If, therefore, the insurrection had terminated in the triumph of this section of the "Emigration," the liberal party would have gained nothing by their change of masters.

Alive to this fact, there has long been in existence a democratic party among the Emigration, who up to the outbreak of the insurrection were violently opposed to the aristocrats. This democratic party recognized Louis Mieroslawski as its head, and professed the ordinary dogmas of the Mazzini school. The supporters of this party in Poland were principally young men, and those who, having neither property nor employment, had no dread of revolution.

There was in Poland a third party, consisting in the main of those who had property to lose, and experience which taught them to put little faith in revolution. These men desired to develop the resources of their country, to educate her people, to promote the construction of roads, canals, and railways, to encourage her manufactures, and to improve her agriculture. They believed by such means Poland would grow so greatly in power, that arrangements with Russia might be won from her in a few years which would be far more beneficial in their character than any concessions she could hope to wring by force.

With the exception of the immediate followers of Mieroslawski, one ancient institution was the centre round which these different parties rallied, and it was her interest to unite them all in opposition to the power of Russia. The Roman Catholic Church has great sway over the Poles, and we cannot wonder at her power. Brave, eloquent, impassioned, they have produced poets and soldiers, but not, with rare exceptions, philosophers and statesmen. Patriotism is with them a sentiment rather than a principle; a sentiment illustrated by song and hallowed by their Church. Their national anthem is no half-boastful chant, which almost as a right demands the assistance of the Most High;* it reads like the wail of a supplicating people, who follow their clergy to the altar of mercy and of help.

And that Church had made great sacrifices for Poland: many were her ruined altars, and far-stretching her forfeited estates; she knew the perils of conspiracy, and the penalties of detected guilt, yet there she stood unhesitating in the van of the national movement, prepared again to struggle, and if need be to suffer in her children's cause.

* Mr. Edwards, in his work "The Polish Captivity," thus translates it:—

I.

"O Lord, who for so many centuries didst surround Poland with the magnificence of power and glory; who didst cover her with the shield of Thy protection when our armies overcame the enemy; at Thy altar we raise our prayer: deign to restore us, O Lord, our free country!

II.

"O Lord, who hast been touched by the woes of our injured land, and hast guided the martyrs of our sacred cause; who hast granted to us, among many other nations, the standard of courage, of unblemished honour; at Thy altar we raise our prayer: deign to restore us, O Lord, our free country!

III.

"Thou whose eternally just hand crushes the empty pride of the powerful of the earth; in spite of the enemy vilely murdering and oppressing, breathe hope into every Polish breast! At Thy altar we raise our prayer: deign to restore us, O Lord, our free country!

IV.

"May the Cross which has been insulted in the hands of Thy ministers give us constant strength under our sufferings! May it inspire us in the day of battle with faith that above us soars the Spirit of the Redeemer! At Thy altar we raise our prayer: deign to restore us, O Lord, our free country!

V.

"In the name of His commandments, we all unite as brothers. Hasten, O Lord, the moment of resurrection! Bless with liberty those who now mourn in slavery! At Thy altar we raise our prayer: deign to restore us, O Lord, our free country!

VI.

"Give back to our Poland her ancient splendour! Look upon our fields soaked with blood! When shall peace and happiness blossom among us? God of wrath, cease to punish us! At Thy altar we raise our prayer: deign to restore us, O Lord, our free country!"

The enemies of the Catholic Church contend that she is animated not by the love of liberty but by the desire for sway. They point to Galicia, and remind us that she has never in the cause of freedom protested against Austrian rule; yet the yoke of Austria has pressed as heavily on the Polish neck as ever did that of Russia. When Galician peasants were murdering their masters, the Catholic Church shuddered not at the political St. Bartholomew, the pulpits resounded to no eloquent denunciations, and the Vatican was also dumb; how does it happen, they inquire, that under one dominion this Church is the champion of liberty, while under the other she is the willing slave of power? The reason, they reply, is very apparent. Austria is the faithful disciple of the Papacy; Russia obeys a rival and schismatic church. The one endows her Catholic clergy with broad lands and ample immunities; the other visits them with the penalties of treason when they struggle against her rule. Rome is ever the same; her own aggrandisement, her own spiritual power, are the only objects of her care; she was never yet the disinterested friend of freedom, though often for a period she has advocated its cause; often she has given utterance to liberal sentiments and clothed them in glowing language; often has she whispered courage into the fainting heart, and nerved the patriot arm. It is easy to reverse the medal, to record a thousand scenes where she has leagued herself with the tyrant and the persecutor; where she has shown that she loves not freedom, and cares nothing for progress or enlightenment;—but it is idle to search for examples when so striking an instance is before us.

In those portions of ancient Poland which are now governed by Russia, Rome cordially allied herself with the national cause. She did so, because in an independent Poland she knew her creed would be established; she anticipated that the success of a Catholic aristocracy would enable her to convert the Greek population; and she foresaw an illimitable vista of struggles and of triumphs which would carry her influence and her spiritual ascendancy to the frontiers of Old Russia.

When the Papacy, they contended, is once committed

to a policy, she has no difficulty in finding enthusiastic
and able men to carry it into effect. Her priests, deprived
by the law of celibacy of the opportunity of indulging
those domestic tastes which make men amiable and un-
aspiring, are ever ready to obey her call; and thus in
every parish of Poland she had an agent; in every monastery she had a brotherhood, whose only aims were the
aggrandisement of their Church and the freedom of their
country. These men were not hampered by the ties of wife
and child; if they read a rebel proclamation, or administered
an unlawful oath, they incurred some personal danger, but
involved not the helpless in their doom; if they were sent
into exile, far from their old associates, their lot might
certainly be hard, but it would be cheered by the reflection
that they suffered for the performance of their duty; while
if a sadder fate awaited them, they would die with the
ennobling conviction that they had fought the good fight, and
perished in the cause of their country and their God. When
it is remembered that these men were Poles, that they had
suffered much under the rigorous administration which for
thirty years had manacled their country,—that from earliest
boyhood they had regarded the Russian supremacy as a hateful
and foreign yoke, it will be evident that they would strain
every effort to assist the insurgent cause. Their love for their
country, their desire for distinction, their reverence for their
Church, combined to impel them in the same direction,—
hostility to Russia, and resistance to her policy.

In the women of Poland the clergy had most efficient
auxiliaries. Beautiful, enthusiastic, full of life and energy,
they threw their enormous influence into the scale of revolution. To them the strife seemed a holy and a national one.
They thought it might be attended with difficulty, with
danger, and with loss; they did not conceive the possibility
of eventual failure. Thus as day by day they met together,
their conversation and their thoughts were wholly fixed on the
coming struggle; everything else was forgotten, every other
duty was laid aside to prepare for it; even amusements were
neglected in the fierce excitement of the period. The theatres
were empty; there was no sound of music or of dance; and

the only song which was heard on all sides was that suppliant hymn which prays for freedom, to be extorted by the sword. And then, as they sat and talked of the liberty they hoped to win, their busy fingers plied the needle and blazoned banners for the future war. From one of them the features of the Virgin meekly smile; a second bears the Polish cross upon a ground of white, while on the reverse side is to be seen a sable crown of thorns; some, again, are rich with emblematic symbols, and all the pageant pride of Northern heraldry. Those banners have never glanced in the van of a successful war; they have floated in the woods and plains of Poland; they have been followed by the wild bands of guerilla leaders; they have been captured in ignoble skirmishes, and are now exhibited among other trophies in the armoury of Tsarskoe,— trophies that painfully remind the visitor of the vain struggles of a noble race, and make him wonder at the misplaced pride which leads a gallant nation thus to exult over their vanquished fellow-subjects.

CHAPTER III.

Relations of Landlord and Peasant in the Kingdom of Poland.—Ancient Freedom of Peasants—Their reduction to Servitude.—Tyranny of their Masters.—Servitude in Lithuania.—Personal Enfranchisement in the Kingdom, and its Evil Effects.—Legislation of Polish Diet.—Subsequent Reforms by Russian Government.—Inventories.—Views of Poles on Land Question.—Legislation of Austria and Prussia upon it.—Necessity for effecting a Settlement favourable to the Peasants.

THE condition of the peasants in Poland and the Western provinces deserves more than a passing notice. The success or failure of the insurrectionary movement depended on the course they took. Armed battalions, no matter with what sagacity they may be governed, cannot hold in slavery a numerous and hostile race. Poland, with its twenty-two million of inhabitants, would never have been subjected save for her internal feuds, and she could never be held in bondage if her unanimous people determined to be free.

There are, however, deep-seated causes for the alienation of her classes, and the bitterness of her internal feuds. A wide gulf spread itself between the noble and the peasant, which a few words of interested kindness are insufficient to span. The bitter wrongs of five centuries, their grinding oppression, their cruel tyranny, have left behind them traditions which forbid reconciliation or confidence.

A review of the history of the mutual rights and duties of noble and serf will show how little gratitude or deference the former was entitled to receive; and will explain how vain was the reliance he placed in the disposition of the liberated serf to follow his guidance.

The peasants in ancient Poland enjoyed considerable liberties till the year 1374, and their condition appears to have been as favourable as that of the same class in the nations of

Western Europe. The two succeeding centuries are held to be the proudest and most triumphant that Poland ever enjoyed. Let us see amid the glitter of this prosperity if the condition of the peasant improved.

In 1374, King Louis d'Anjou conferred on the nobility charters and privileges by which the peasants were reduced to servitude. From that date to the end of the reign of Sigismund Augustus (1572) a gradual system of spoliation went on, by which the serfs were deprived of every political and civil right.

All the land, as well as the serfs who lived upon it, became the absolute property of the lord of the soil; he had the power of life and death over his slave, and uncontrolled jurisdiction over the whole extent of his estates. If a nobleman murdered a serf, the only penalty was a trifling fine, which he paid to the master of his victim,—a fine not for the crime he had committed, but for the pecuniary loss his fellow noble had sustained.

The accounts of this state of wretched debasement are not derived from Russian scribes; we learn them from no travestied history composed by the minions of a Frederick or a Catherine; they are to be found in the records of impartial historians, and sadden the pages of patriot authors.

Lelewel, the well-known Polish historian, whose sympathies were all in favour of the country where he was born, and for which he so greatly suffered, has left passages on record which surpass, in gloomy interest, the darkest records of antiquity.

"You talk of liberty," says André Fritz Madrzewski, in his work on the reforms needed for redressing the wrongs of the republic, "when you have nothing but barbarous slavery which leaves the life of a man at the mercy of his master. The nobility regard the cultivator and the plebeian as dogs; that is the expression used by these abominable men, who, if they kill a peasant, whom they call the rubbish of the earth (chlop), say they have killed a dog." *

King Stanislaus Leszinski in exile said, speaking of the

---

* History of Poland, by J. Lelewel, vol. ii. pp. 159, 160 (Paris. 1844).

peasants, "Men so necessary ought certainly to be considered, but we hardly distinguish them from the cattle we keep to cultivate our ground. We often spare their strength less than that of the cattle, and often, by a scandalous traffic, we sell them to masters as cruel, who force them by excessive labour to pay the price of their new servitude. I cannot think without horror of the law which imposes a penalty of fifteen livres only on any noble who kills a peasant. We regard these men as creatures of a different kind, and we almost refuse to allow them to breathe the same air with ourselves."*

At the commencement of the seventeenth century, in the reign of Sigismund III., the condition of the peasants was thus described by the priest Skarga :—

"And the sweat, and the blood of our peasants, which flow incessantly, and moisten and redden the whole earth,—what a terrible future they are preparing for this kingdom! I know of no country in Christendom where the peasants are so treated. And you cry out against absolute power, which no one wishes or is able to impose upon you. Hypocrites and declaimers! 'You have destroyed my vine,' saith the Lord; 'Why crush ye thus my people, crushing it as the millstone crusheth the corn?' By what right do you obstinately refuse to change this infamous law? These peasants are your neighbours. They are Poles like you. They speak the same language, and are children of the same country. Formerly the Christians gave liberty to their slaves when they baptized them, and became their brothers in Jesus Christ; but you, you dare to keep Christians, who are your fellow-countrymen, in bondage. I know that you do not all act in this manner; but those who commit such crimes, how do they not blush in the face of Christendom, which beholds them, and of which they call themselves members." †

The oppression increased till the end of the reign of the last king. "One has no more regard for this vile, wretched, detestable, cursed race. It is not enough to qualify it, '*chlop*,' its impure blood having drawn down on itself the curse of its origin as soon as it left Noah's ark; it is the impious race of

* Lelewel, vol. ii. p. 294.   † Edwards's Polish Captivity.

Ham." The peasants were thus insulted by injurious epithets; the injurious language was only a preliminary to every species of injustice.*

When the duchy of Lithuania was first united to Poland, under the Lithuanian prince Jagellon, its peasants were entirely free. This freedom was an insuperable bar to the Polonization of Lithuania, and the Government did all in its power to destroy it. With this view, titles and coats of arms, charters and privileges, were conferred on the Lithuanian nobility, which placed it on an equality with that of Poland. Consequent on these innovations, dissension ensued between the different classes in Lithuania; the democratic equality of former times gave place to the aristocratic spirit of Polish civilization; and when, in 1569, Lithuania was finally united to Poland, the peasant population of the duchy had lost almost all its liberties.

Two centuries afterwards, when Russia finally annexed Lithuania, serfdom had become so thoroughly established there, that not only had the nobles a right to possess slaves, but towns and simple citizens had the same privilege. This has never been the case in Russia.

After the various partitions of Poland, Russia confirmed the rights of the nobles over their serfs in the Western provinces; Austria and Prussia also made but little change in the relations between the serfs and their masters; and although Austria had nominally abolished serfdom, the peace of Tilsit and the constitution of the duchy of Warsaw found the proprietors and peasants in much the same condition as they had been left in by Stanislaus Augustus.

The fourth article of the statute constituting the duchy of Warsaw, dated 22nd July, 1807, was couched in the following terms:—

"Slavery is abolished. All citizens are equal before the law; security of the person is placed under the care of the tribunals."

These brave words brought with them no relief. The personal freedom conferred upon the peasant vested the land he

---

* Lelewel, vol. ii. p. 289.

had occupied exclusively in the proprietor; the latter allowed the peasant to continue to hold it, but subjected him to rents, task-work, and other obligations without number and of all kinds.

In December of the same year another law was enacted, giving the peasants the right of removal, which, as serfs, they did not possess; but this law was in its operation entirely illusive; for in addition to the love of the Sclavonic peasant for the hut in which he was born, and the fields which the labour of his ancestor reclaimed, he was firmly persuaded that no other proprietor would let land to him if he once quitted that of his old master.

The laws of 1807 in effect proved injurious to the peasants. So long as the peasants were slaves, their masters allowed them to remain in undisturbed possession of the quantity of land required for their subsistence; but after they were freed, the proprietors endeavoured, under various pretexts, to resume the land they held, and to add it to their own estates. Sometimes, also, they let it to German colonists, richer, more industrious, and more skilful than the Polish peasants, and who could establish no possessory or customary interest in the property which might hereafter interfere with the absolute rights of the owners of the soil.

Thus, one by one the peasant holders were rooted out, and the number of landless men (proletaries) increased, until it amounted, in 1856, to the enormous proportion of 1,165,857, out of an agricultural population of 2,782,133. Thus, nearly one-half of the peasants had lost their land, and were reduced to the condition of farm labourers.

The fifth article of the law of 21st December, 1807, obliged the peasants to surrender the houses they had themselves built, the cattle they had reared, the crops they had sown, the very agricultural implements they used; for, although by that law the liberty of the peasants was decreed, it yet enacted that every one who quitted his field and his master was to abandon to the latter all the objects named,—objects which had been the painful reward of the industry of many generations.

The Congress of 1815 secured a constitutional government

for Poland, and as our Foreign Minister wished to see it revived, it will, perhaps, be instructive to place on record the tendencies of its former legislation.

The laws which it enacted, and which finally regulated the organization of the rural parishes (*gmina*), and the rights and duties of the mayors (*gmniani woït*), seem more fitted for the times of Skarga than the period when, in the nineteenth century, constitutional government reigned at Warsaw.

Any property composed of ten peasants' huts could, under a law of 3rd of February, 1816, be formed into a distinct rural parish, or several properties could be united into one parish. The formation of these parishes was in no way dependent upon the authorities, or made subordinate to the administrative wants of the district, but was entirely subject to the uncontrolled will of the proprietors.

By a law of 30th May, 1818, every owner of a village is *ipso facto* mayor of the parish, by virtue of his property, and unites in himself the rights of the proprietor and the administrative and legal power. He apportions and collects the taxes, sues those who do not pay them, superintends the police, arrests suspected persons, publishes the orders of the superior administration, maintains the roads, bridges, and ferries through obligatory labour, draws up the lists for the conscription, judges offences in the first instance, gives and refuses passports, has general superintendence of the conduct of the peasants, and, in short, has all the administrative power of the district vested in him. He has the right to condemn the inhabitants of his parish to seven days' imprisonment, 10 roubles fine, or 20 strokes of the rod.

Sometimes the mayor is himself a party interested in the causes he tries, and then he makes every endeavour to disguise the truth, and by describing himself in different ways, to prevent the superior authorities from detecting it.

The mayor has the right to delegate his functions to a substitute of his own choosing. Out of 3,069 parishes in Poland, it appears that at least 1,634 are administered by such substitutes. The greater part of these men are chosen from the lowest class of intendant, men whom Lelewel describes as being in the eighteenth century " an impious race, base flatterers of their masters, stealing to enrich themselves, tyrants of the peasants, whom they despised and hated, without pity and without remorse, who firmly grasped the whip in inflicting punishment according to their pleasure."* The salary of these men rarely exceeds 300 or 400 francs a year, and often is not half as much.

The perpetual grievances to which the peasants are subjected by this union in the same person of the various characters of proprietor, plaintiff, judge, and jury, may readily be imagined; and the temptation to the proprietors to abuse their power is strengthened by the knowledge that the law imposes no serious responsibility upon them, and that their misdeeds will be shielded by the guilty connivance of an administration solely guided by the Polish nobility.

As an example of the tyrannical conduct of the proprietors, the instance may be cited of the persecutions suffered by the peasants on the estate of Garnek, belonging to M. Grodzicki, and situated in the district of Piotrkow.

M. Grodzicki used the right which the law conferred upon him, as mayor of his parish, to tyrannize for many years over the peasants living on his domains; his wife was especially remarkable for her cruelty to the women who took care of the cattle. For the least motive, the peasants were imprisoned or cruelly flogged (the mayors only having by law the right of giving twenty blows at a time, elude this provision by administering the punishment several times a day); the least complaint they uttered he called rebellion; and summoned the bailiffs to quell the revolt. The peasants, crushed under the weight of excessive labour, passed the whole day working in the proprietor's ground, having no time to attend to their children, who were literally dying of hunger in the abandoned huts. In 1859 the misery of the peasants reached its height; reduced to the last extremity, they demanded that their labour should be replaced by an annual money payment, of which the amount should be fixed by the Government.

This request was represented by M. Grodzicki as open revolt against his authority as proprietor. Inquiry was made

* Lelewel, vol. ii. pp. 288, 289.

into the affair, and it was shown that the peasants, reduced to despair, had, after many years of suffering, refused to labour, but that this refusal could scarcely be regarded as one in reality, as they only demanded that the labour illegally exacted by the proprietor should be commuted for a money payment, the amount of which should be fixed by the authorities, so as to avoid making it the subject of daily contention and constant injustice. The inquiry proved that M. Grodzicki had, since 1840, deprived the peasants of their best land; that he had forced them to work for him for a longer time than he could legally demand, and paid them at a very low price; that he, his wife, and his intendant, treated them very badly, and inflicted corporal punishment on them in a most illegal manner; and that he had already driven out and defrauded of their land eleven families, some of whom had taken refuge in Prussia, whence they sent representations of their case to St. Petersburg and to the Prussian authorities. In the mean time the ground taken from these unfortunate peasants was distributed among German colonists.

After the insurrection of 1830 the Russian Government made several attempts to ameliorate the condition of the peasants, and relieve them from the arbitrary oppression of the proprietors; but the civil administration of the kingdom, combined with the Polish nobility, paralyzed its efforts, and laws instituted for the relief of the peasants were often ingeniously perverted to their injury.

Occupied almost exclusively in the maintenance of material order, the Russian Government too often abandoned the administration of civil affairs to the Polish nobility; thus it came to pass that their feeble efforts on behalf of the peasant were always checked, and that to the close of the administration of the Marquis Wielopolski scarce anything was effected on their behalf.

The population of the Congress kingdom is 4,800,466; of these about 77,000 are nobles; 6,400 are ecclesiastics; and about 180,000 are Schliacta (poor noblemen). This minority of 263,000 centre in themselves all civil and administrative power, and it has ever governed the nation most arbitrarily under shadow of the Russian law. The Emperor Nicholas could not control this confedcracy; he had wronged Poland, he had deprived her of her ancient immunities and of some of her treaty rights; she had rebelled against him and suffered the bitter penalty which tracks abortive treason; and now she was at rest, and that was all he asked. The bent of his haughty disposition would dispose him rather to side with the noble than the peasant; a constant interference with constituted authorities would serve to render them despised; and the Emperor having won, as he fancied, a lasting victory, was unwilling to encourage a policy so subversive. Although, therefore, the intentions of the Russian Government were fair and just, so far as the peasant question was concerned, they were frustrated by the powerful opposition which the Polish nobles made. An example of the mode in which the efforts of the Government were thwarted is to be found in the results attained by the law of 26th May (7th June), 1846.

By this law the possession of the land held by the peasants was secured to them so long as they paid the rents and fulfilled the duties imposed by their contracts with the proprietors, and these contracts were signed in presence of and approved by a public officer appointed for that purpose. In order to elude this law, the proprietors, with the assistance of the Polish authorities, persuaded the Government that its promulgation during the season when work in the fields was practicable would lead to considerable excitement among the labouring classes, suspend the operations of industry, and occasion great material loss; they therefore suggested that the publication of the law should be postponed till the following September, and this proposal was acted upon.

The proprietors profited by the delay. In many places the peasants were expelled from the soil they had occupied for generations; their lands were converted into farms, and whole villages were removed, and their inhabitants received in return new and uncultivated land. This system extended over the entire kingdom; almost everywhere the rent and other services were increased, and thousands of the peasantry were reduced to misery and pauperism.

Nevertheless the law of 1846 was received with gratitude by the peasants, and, despite the partial success of the nobles, was a decisive step towards the settlement of the land question. Having at length some inducement for industry, the peasant laboured hard to improve his condition.

Since 1846 the position of the peasants has sensibly improved; the contracts between them and the proprietors have curbed the avarice of the latter; pecuniary payments have, in many places, superseded obligatory labour, and Government has endeavoured to make this change universal. Notwithstanding, however, all the efforts of the peasants and the Government, out of 198,000 peasants' huts, situated on private estates, there were, in 1861, 131,753 families (about 700,000 souls) subjected to obligatory labour; giving the proprietors annually 18,998,806 days' labour gratuitously (or nearly three days' labour a week per family), besides extraordinary and supplementary labour, and payments and oblations consisting of provisions, capons, eggs, butter, grain, flax, &c. &c.

In the crown domains, in the property belonging to public establishments, in the majorats conferred on Russian functionaries; in short, in all the properties where the efforts of Government were not thwarted by the selfishness of the Polish proprietors, the condition of the peasant is comparatively satisfactory; for the Russian Government, in proclaiming the absolute necessity of these reforms, gave, on its own account and exacted from the Russian proprietors, an example of prudent disinterestedness.

Thus, on the land belonging to the Crown, the peasants occupy 1,265,088 morgs (1,750,067 acres) and pay 620,700 roubles rent (£99,312), or 49½ copeks per morg (1s. 1½d. per acre).

In the properties attached to public establishments the peasants possess 51,758 morgs (71,604 acres) and pay a rent of 26,476 roubles (£4,236), or 51 copeks per morg (1s. 2d. per acre).

Lastly, in the majorats belonging to Russian proprietors, the peasants pay still less; for 447,634 morgs (619,274 acres) they pay an annual rent of 166,901 roubles (£26,704), or 37¼ copeks per morg (10¼d. per acre).

The peasants dwelling on the land of the Polish nobility were very differently circumstanced. It might have been anticipated that from men of the same race, from their natural and hereditary leaders, they would have met with liberal treatment and wise encouragement. Such, however, was not the case. When the Government by the law of $\frac{4}{16}$ May, 1861, gave the peasants the right to substitute a money rent for their labour, the labour was valued at a sum which the proprietors complained of as too low. When, however, the matter was investigated, it was found that the money value of their labour amounted to 2,961,368 roubles (£473,819) for 1,848,936 morgs (2,557,892 acres), or about 1 rouble 60 copeks per morg (3s. 8d. per acre).

Even this sum, enormous as it is, considering the state of agriculture in Poland, and out of all proportion to the rents imposed by the Government and the Russian proprietors, is not the whole of the charge which the peasants have to defray. There are many other extraordinary and supplementary charges which they have to meet: these bring up the total rent to about 4s. 6d. per acre.

In the North and South-western provinces the condition of the serfs was unaffected by the changes which took place in the Congress kingdom. Servitude was preserved intact by the Russian Government, and neither personal freedom nor the liberty of removal was introduced there. The proprietor, therefore, having nothing to gain by depriving the peasant of his land, allowed him to continue in undisturbed possession of it from 1772 to the time of his enfranchisement, and during this long period he gradually acquired a larger and larger interest in it.

The first step taken by the Russian Government for the protection of the peasants was the introduction in 1849 of the so-called "Inventories." These "Inventories" were returns made by the proprietors to the Government, setting forth the quantity of land held by the serfs, the rent they had to pay for it, and the labour and other services they had to perform. Since these inventories were made, the landowner has had no power to deprive the serf of his land so long as he observes the conditions of his holding, nor has he had the power to increase his liabilities, or in any way alter his tenure.

In the South-western provinces the returns made by the

proprietors were, to some extent, checked and reduced by the authorities; but in the North-western provinces this was not the case, and they were adopted without modification as correct.

The land mentioned in the inventories was by the law of 1st March (19th February), 1861 (the law by which the serfs were enfranchised), vested absolutely in the serfs, subject only to the customary rent and services. A slight deduction was however made from these liabilities in the North-western provinces, in consequence of the exorbitant character of the claims of the proprietors.

In the South-western provinces the peasants were allowed to commute the labour due from them for a money payment, of which the amount was fixed by law; but in the North-western provinces commissions were constituted to ascertain the value of the labour; and until their awards were made, the labour continued to be performed.

When, therefore, the rebellion broke out, there existed two different systems in the North and South-western provinces: in the latter the condition of the peasants was ameliorated; they were freed from the personal labour which had been a great subject of complaint and a most efficient weapon of injustice, and the money payments they had to make in commutation of it were much easier to meet than their former obligations. The peasants, therefore, of these provinces were hostile to a revolt commenced by the men who had oppressed them, and which was aimed at a government that had so recently improved their condition. In the North-western provinces, however, the peasants were more dependent on the will of the proprietors; they were safe from personal ill-treatment, and their land was secured to them; but the rents and onerous services to which they were liable rendered them more submissive to their late masters.

While such was the condition of the peasants, and such the policy of the Russian administration, there were many conflicting opinions among the Poles upon the land question.

The aristocratic proprietors wished to retain in themselves the absolute ownership of the soil; they were, they professed, willing that the peasants should continue to hold as tenants the land they had long been occupying; but they claimed rent from, and desired to stand in the same relation to them as the English landowner does to his tenant. This, however, would have deprived the peasants of all certainty of tenure; they would have been absolutely at the mercy of the proprietors, and have had no check on their avarice and rapacity.

On the other hand, the more liberal party contended that the soil belonged to the peasant; that it had been given to his ancestors long since; and that the time had arrived when any condition with which that gift had been clogged should be remitted. They did not propose that the landowner should lose his rent, or the services to which he was entitled, without compensation, but such compensation they considered should be paid by the Government, and not by the peasants; others, again, contended that the land should be vested in the peasants, subject to their performance of the customary services, or to their redeeming them by a money payment.

The relations between landlord and tenant in England are utterly dissimilar to those existing in Poland or the Western provinces. The only analogy which will apply is one of a far older date, and we must seek it by looking back into history, and tracing there the gradual enlargement of villain tenures into absolute ownership. Those who are conversant with the early history of our real property law will recall the steps by which, from the great feudatory to the humblest serf, the ancestors in title of the present proprietors of the soil converted their conditional or precarious tenures into absolute estates. Originally holding them so long only as they could perform certain feudal services, or so long as it was the will of their lord that they should retain them, we see in our early history how soon the rights of the owners of limited interests and of mere occupiers became enlarged. The hereditary principle crept in, and then the only advantage the feudal superior derived from the death of his retainer was the payment of a stipulated fine, and perhaps the wardship of an heir. Gradually the rights of the lord were reduced to a money payment, and the interest of the vassal became absolute in the soil of which he formerly was the precarious tenant.

The feudal system was unknown in Poland, and so far no

parallel exists; but the gradual recognition of the rights of the holder of the soil was somewhat similar, and generation by generation, and year by year, those rights acquired a stronger hold and more general acquiescence. All parties acknowledged them in some sense, and admitted, at least in the Western provinces, that so long as the tenant paid his rent and performed his services, the landlord had no right to eject him. But the personal freedom granted in 1807 injured the position of the peasants in the Congress kingdom; it altered their relation to the lord, perilled their possession of the soil, and gave the Polish proprietary a colourable title to treat them as mere tenants at will.

The conduct pursued by the Austrian and Prussian governments towards the serfs of Galicia and Posen confirmed the view taken by the peasants of their claims. In both provinces the rights of the lords had been gradually diminished by custom and legislation, and when in 1848 the land was absolutely assigned to the Galician peasants, the claims of the proprietors upon them were in many cases reduced to two, or even to one day's work in the week. The value of the labour to which the lords were thus entitled was estimated, government bills were given them, supposed to represent it, and a tax was laid on the province to pay the interest on the bills. The Austrian Government therefore fully recognized the rights for which the peasants in the Congress kingdom as well as in the Western provinces contended.

The Prussian Government adopted a different course; they enfranchised the serfs, giving them their land subject to payments to the proprietor of one-third of the estimated money value of the labour (*corvée*) which they hitherto had performed. This arrangement was altered after the insurrection of 1848; the Government then gave state bills bearing interest, and equal in value to the capital sum the rents were worth, to the proprietors, in liquidation of the rents the peasants had to pay, and the peasants were subjected to a tax of sufficient magnitude to extinguish principal and interest in 1871,—at which time, accordingly, they will be completely free from all claims in respect of their land.

The Russian Government had always considered that the

serf and the peasant had qualified interests in the soil; they had in many instances refused both in Russia and the Western provinces to allow the proprietors to enfranchise their serfs unless they gave them land for their support, and they had always peremptorily rejected any general scheme of emancipation by which the lands held by the peasants would become the absolute property of the lord.

The Polish nobility had on several occasions manifested a readiness to emancipate the peasant and retain his land for themselves; such an arrangement would doubtless have been very profitable to them, but, under the circumstances, would have been unjust. In 1857 this suggestion was made by the nobles of the provinces of Wilna Kovno and Grodno; but it was opposed altogether to the principles of the Russian Government, and was without result. Indeed the proposition argued as little political wisdom as it did generosity, for it was certain of rejection, and was sure to irritate the people, on whose aid in a future insurrection that very nobility would have mainly to rely.

The political economists of Russia have contended that the theory of their Government is wrong; that the right to occupy the land ceases when the peasant fails to perform his task-work, and that it is a mistake to create a number of pauperized proprietors, instead of a prosperous class of tenant farmers.

The abstractions of political economy must yield sometimes to other and more powerful considerations; questions of justice must sometimes be answered before the dogmas of economists are obeyed; and it is on the ground of justice as well as of the highest expediency that the claims of the peasants rest.

They have no charters to boast, no elaborate deeds to exhibit from which their title may be deduced; but they till the same fields, occupy the same dwellings, and regard as their own the same little properties which their ancestors held for centuries. Generation by generation their immunities have increased and their liabilities dwindled away, until at length Government and the popular voice alike regard them as the limited owners of the soil. Precedents from our own history confirm that view, and the statesman who disregarded it would be the most dangerous revolutionist of his age and country.

Moreover, in the long account between proprietor and serf, the balance surely does not incline in favour of the former; the slavery of centuries, the cruel and debasing injuries with which it was accompanied; the scourge, the dishonour, and the nameless wrongs under which the Polish serfs ineffectually writhed, have left behind them a bitter remembrance, which, if they were prudent, the proprietors would strive to obliterate.

Allowing the land to be absorbed by the landlords is not a step which would lead to the formation of a class of prosperous tenant farmers; no such class can be created without capital, and that capital must be either imported or saved; it is admitted that its introduction from abroad is not looked for, and therefore it is by saving that it must be created. It will not be contended that the freeholder is likely to be less industrious than the tenant who is at the mercy of his landlord; that property paralyzes his efforts, and renders him sluggish and inert. On the contrary, it seems probable that freedom and the possession of his land will stimulate his exertions and arouse his ambitions. The system the Polish nobles proposed to introduce in the Western provinces is the same that has been so unsuccessfully tried for more than half a century in the Congress kingdom. Far from producing wealth or stimulating improvement, the peasant is as miserable now as he was when the *Code Napoléon* was introduced. Nowhere in Russia is his condition more pitiable, and nowhere is he more completely at the mercy of the great proprietors. This plan, therefore, has been already tried, and has failed in producing those benefits which are alleged to be its certain accompaniments.

There is yet another reason for ceding their land to the peasants. In a vast and thinly-peopled country, the effect of mere *personal* emancipation would be to set loose all those whose condition as serfs had hitherto kept them on one spot, unless attached to their former home either by compulsion or some peculiar advantage it afforded them. Why should the peasant remain there? Why should he stop in the North, where for six or eight months in every year the frozen ground forbids his industry, while he could find constant employment in the sunny plains of the South, or occupy himself amid the corn-fields and vineyards of the Crimea? Mere personal emancipation would have given the signal for a vast migration, which would have rendered valueless immense tracts of country and displaced important industries.*

* The difference in climate between various parts of Russia is strikingly evidenced in St. Petersburg. On 15th December, 1863, I saw Crimean grapes of excellent quality hawked about the streets at 3*d.* a pound, while the ground was covered with snow, and the thermometer stood at 17° Fahrenheit.

CHAPTER IV.

Commencement of "Unarmed Agitation" in Warsaw.—Meeting in the Old Square.—"The Warsaw Massacre."—Address to the Emperor.—Indecision of Prince Gortschakoff.—The Delegation.—The Funeral.—Conduct of the Delegation and its Dissolution.

IT will be seen from the statements contained in the previous chapters, that the years which immediately followed the accession of the Emperor Alexander were marked by great prosperity. There was every prospect that as commerce developed and wealth increased, Poland would gradually rise in importance, and win self-government and constitutional freedom from her conqueror. The inclination of her new sovereign gave probability to the most sanguine anticipations, and to the casual observer the future promised to atone for the misery of the past.

Unfortunately for Poland, the restless conspirators of the Emigration, the returned exiles, and the malcontents at home, were not content with the spectacle of present prosperity and the prospect of constitutional freedom. The only liberty in which they trusted was that which is won by the dagger or the sword, and they determined to pave the way to it by an organized and most extensive agitation. For this end, national celebrations of all kinds were resorted to, and every means was adopted of stirring up popular feeling against the Russian authority.

In June, 1860, the funeral took place of the widow of a General Sobinski, who had been killed in 1831, while defending the fortress of Wola against the Russians. The funeral passed over quietly, but at its conclusion the students and rabble, who had attended it in considerable numbers, proceeded to the

burial-ground of the Greeks, which is near that of the Roman
Catholic church where the ceremony had taken place, spat on
the Russian tombs, and tore up the shrubs and flowers which
were planted round them.

This circumstance was at the time regarded as an isolated
outrage, and not as part of a premeditated plan, and was
therefore left unnoticed by the authorities.

Early in October, however, a marked change took place in
the demeanour of the people. A meeting at Warsaw between
the Emperors of Austria and Russia and the King of Prussia
had been arranged, and the walls were covered with placards
calling on the inhabitants to receive appropriately the three
ravens who had torn in pieces the body of Poland; the theatres
were less frequented, and on one occasion when the Emperor
was to attend, asafœtida was sprinkled through the house
before the performance began; illuminations which took place
at the summer palace were only attended by the dregs of the
people, and caricatures and squibs of all kinds were circulated
against the Emperor of Austria.

An uneasy feeling was gradually setting in against the
ostentation and luxury of the rich; against costly amusements,
and lavish expenditure on ladies' dresses. This feeling was art-
fully encouraged, and as an example of the extent to which it
was carried, on the occasion of the foundation-stone being laid
of a new bridge over the Vistula, boys threw vitriol on ladies'
dresses and cut them with knives.

In November these excesses became more systematic; in
houses where balls or evening parties were given, windows
were broken; and Russian and foreign signs were forcibly
torn down from the shops and houses which displayed them.

The town-post was completely taken up by the delivery of
libels, anonymous and threatening letters forbidding amusements, and letters insulting the Russians and their friends.

Thus passed the months of December, January, and the
early part of February, and these disturbances were occasionally varied by demonstrations, or funeral services commemorative of the rebellion of 1830, and the Poles who had
fallen in it.

In January, a rumour circulated through the town, that on

25th February, the anniversary of the battle of Grockovo,* a funeral service would be solemnized on the field of battle for the Poles who were slain there, and that all the population of Warsaw would be summoned to attend this celebration; the Russians, also, it was alleged, would join in it, and for that purpose troops and Greek clergy would be sent to the field, and would take part in a funeral service in memory of the Russians who fell there.

Little by little, this rumour died away, and public attention was entirely fixed on the coming meeting of the Agricultural Society, which took place on 23rd February. Simultaneously with the opening of its session, placards were scattered in the churches, and subsequently in the streets, in which the people were invited to meet in the Square of the Old Town, instead of on the field of Grockovo. The plan originally determined on was changed on account of the temporary removal of the bridge over the Vistula, and because a demonstration held in the town might be made more effective, and might point more directly to the objects the malcontents had in view, than one held some miles away.

The crowd was to follow the procession past the palace of the Lieutenant of the kingdom, to the house called the Namiestnikowski, where the Agricultural Society assembled. There they were to demand the attendance of the members present, in order that they might be requested by the crowd to present an address to the Emperor requiring a constitution.

At half-past five in the afternoon of the appointed day, the people commenced assembling in great numbers, and refused to disperse, though summoned to do so by the police. At seven o'clock many students of the Academy came out of the Pauline church, close to the Old Town, and with them were youths from various schools, and workmen.

The Square in the Old Town is a relic of ancient Warsaw; it is small and surrounded by lofty houses, apparently erected in the sixteenth and seventeenth centuries; and occasionally these houses are overtopped by others at their rear, which are more

---

* One of the battles in the insurrection of 1830-31, where the Poles defeated the Russians.

lofty still; so, in addition to the house immediately facing the bystander, he sees, by looking upwards, the quaint gables and little windows of another dwelling, whose inmates may observe unnoticed the busy crowds below.

On that winter night the Square was the scene of a picturesque gathering. It was filled by an excited throng of men, whose minds were possessed with dim and shadowy aspirations after changes they were never to achieve. Some of the crowd bore banners which were blazoned with patriotic emblems—the white eagle of Poland, the portraits of her martyrs, the symbols of her faith, the names of her battle-fields, and the pious ejaculations which she addressed to her tutelary saints. Others carried torches, and the light they gave glanced fitfully on the banners above and the agitated crowd below; it flashed on the thousand windows filled with sympathizing spectators, and threw an angry glare over the police, who stood aloof in grim and silent expectation.

The crowd resolved to carry out their programme, and to proceed from the Square to the house of the Agricultural Society, and obtain from that powerful body the assurance of its sympathy and aid; but the authorities determined that the demonstration should terminate. An additional squadron of gendarmes arrived, the people were commanded to disperse, and, after a show of opposition and some angry demonstrations, they sullenly departed to their homes. The only resistance which was made proceeded from the students of the Agricultural School; eight of them were arrested, and upon them were found proclamations of Louis Mieroslawski, revolutionary addresses, and portraits of the patriot leaders of former insurrections.

On the following day the town was quiet, but the streets were more than usually crowded, an air of gloom and expectation prevailed, and as a symbol of mourning it was remarked that the men had the lower part of their hats brushed the wrong way. To this date no lives had been lost, and it is therefore evident that mourning formed part of the revolutionary programme.

On the 27th of February occurred the first of those events which were subsequently styled by the revolutionary press "the Warsaw massacres." In the morning of that day many members of the Agricultural Society, students of the Agricultural School, workmen, and mechanics, assembled at the Carmelite Church. A solemn service was celebrated there in honour of the Poles who fell in the insurrection of 1830, and religion was again invoked to aid the struggles of a revolutionary cause.

This demonstration was intended as a protest against assurances which Count Andrew Zamoyski was reported to have given to the Lieutenant, to the effect that the Agricultural Society had nothing to do with the meeting of two days before. It was thought that these assurances would prejudice the society in the estimation of the party of action, and that some overt act, some solemn covenant, should be entered into binding the people to the society, and the society to the people's cause. It was therefore resolved that a procession should be formed, which should pass through the Sigismund Place, and proceed thence to the house of the Agricultural Society.

The Sigismund Place is a square in the centre of the town, and contains the column and statue which commemorate Sigismund and give his name to the spot. On one side of the square is the castle, the palace of the former kings of Poland, and now the residence of the Russian viceroy; separated from it only by a road stand the Church and Monastery of the Bernardines, a large heavy-looking mass of building, without architectural beauty or any external evidence of antiquity.

In execution of their design, the leaders of the people formed a procession, and, preceded by a large portrait of Kalinski,* marched at the head of the crowd into the Sigismund Place. The assemblage was then summoned to disperse, and as the order was not obeyed, a detachment of Cossacks was sent to meet it, and form a chain in front of the palace, so as to prevent all access to it.

The crowd paused in uncertainty. In their front were the Cossacks, on their flank stood the church, and if they per-

---

* A shoemaker and patriot leader in 1794.

severed in their intention, they would have have to force their way past the Cossacks and across the square to reach the house of the Agricultural Society. A hearse was at the door of the church, and at this critical moment a priest left the building accompanied by the coffin and the mourners. A minute later stones were thrown at the troops by some unknown persons, who are believed to have been on the tower of the church, and one of them felled a Cossack to the ground. His comrades, believing that the stones were thrown by the funeral cortége, endeavoured to disperse it with their whips; but the crowd stepped forward and resisted them with stones and sticks. By this time a rumour had circulated through the people that the Cossacks had broken the cross and beaten the priest, and, infuriated at this report, they resisted the Cossacks, who were powerless to disperse them.

General Zablotsky, at the head of a company of infantry (200 men), marched against the crowd, who received them with threats and pelted them. The soldiers loaded their rifles and prepared to fire, but the people did not believe they would do so. An absurd idea appears to have prevailed among the lower orders in Warsaw, that the Emperor of the French had forbidden the Russians to fire upon them, and that the latter dared not disobey him. While, therefore, the soldiers loaded their rifles, the people cursed and spat at them. The troops were ordered to fire: they obeyed, and at the first volley five men were killed, and the insurrectionary movement received its baptism of blood.

The multitude withdrew, and the evidence of bystanders greatly varies as to their demeanour. It is stated, on the one hand, that they were terrified and subdued by the rigour which had repressed them; and on the other it is alleged that they departed in wrath, but not in fear, resolved to wreak ample vengeance in the future for the wrongs they then endured. It, however, is admitted on all sides that they carried their dead away with them, and that in their retreat they were unmolested by the soldiery or police. Strange, indeed, was the termination of the solemnity of that day. The agitators had failed to carry out their programme. They had not forced their way to the halls of the Agricultural

Society, and they had had no noisy scene of patriotic fraternization with its members; yet they had succeeded in creating an irreparable breach with the Government whose overthrow they were plotting to achieve, and they foresaw that the events of the day would enable them to hold up their Russian masters to the opprobrium of Western Europe.

The five corpses were placed on hastily-constructed litters, and were carried openly through the town. The students who accompanied them compelled all who met them, whether civilians or military men, to stand uncovered as they passed; and thus, followed by a great crowd, and with the appearance rather of a pageant than a flight, the bodies of four of the slain were carried to the Hôtel de l'Europe; the fifth was taken to the house of Count Andrew Zamoyski, and laid in state in one of his reception-rooms.

The inside of the gate of the Zamoyski Palace, and the rooms there and at the hotel where the other bodies lay, were draped with black. The approach to these rooms was jealously guarded by students; and even military men and officials who entered the palace and hotel on public business were only permitted to pass the door after they had satisfactorily answered any questions those guardians of the dead put to them.

A photographer took portraits of the slain, which were sold and distributed in immense numbers. They were represented with their wounds exposed, and with crowns of palm intermingled with thorns upon their heads.

The following day (the 28th of February) a great crowd collected before the hotel, and the rooms on the ground floor were thronged with people. Some one proposed to send an address to the Emperor, and it was written on the spot, and numerous copies were instantly distributed. It is evident that this address had been prepared beforehand. By its terms the Schliacta appeared willing to abandon their traditional claims, and to recognize the rights of other classes; the disturbances at Warsaw were explained to be the result of deep-seated and universal discontent; and the principles of Polish nationality were strongly insisted on. All who could write were invited to sign this address, and it was subscribed by a large portion of the population of the town.

The agitators determined to use their opportunity to the utmost. A solemn funeral was resolved on, and many and anxious were the consultations as to its details. All classes in Warsaw were to be represented there; deputations from other parts of the kingdom and from the Western provinces were invited to be present, and great efforts were made to secure the attendance of the peasants.

Minor distinctions of party, creed, and even race, were for the moment forgotten, or only remembered to give occasion for bridging over by some scheme of fantastic liberality the gulf which had hitherto divided them. Thus it was discovered that a reconciliation must be effected with the Jews; and as a first step towards it, the very name of their race was changed, and in substitution for their ancient designation, they were styled "Poles of the Mosaic persuasion"! A committee was constituted, under the name of "The Committee for the Erection of a Monument in memory of the slain of the 27th of February, as well as for collecting money for their families." The formation of this committee and its object were publicly announced in the papers of the following day, and a subscription was immediately commenced in a room at the hotel. The wealthy crowded there with costly gifts; the poor, out of their poverty, cast in their mites; and the women of Poland, ever foremost in patriotic sacrifice, poured their jewels, their ornaments, and whatever else of value they possessed, into the common fund.

While the leaders of the people were thus prompt and united in their action, the course adopted by Prince Gortschakoff was weak and indecisive. He was a soldier, and not a statesman. Calm and self-possessed at the head of an army, unmoved amid the perils of the great game of war, he was unequal to the guidance of a state in troubled times, and could not distinguish between the occasion where lenity is admissible and the license which demands restraint. To a man of this stamp the position of Lieutenant of Poland must ever be embarrassing; he has that half-confidence reposed in him which is fatal of success, and, at the mercy of telegrams and orders dictated by the impressions of the moment, he must ever prove unequal to imagine and carry into effect a bold and successful policy.

The crisis was one which would have tried the strength of a stronger hand and the nerve of a more equable spirit, and the Lieutenant of the kingdom broke down under it. Contrary to the anxiously expressed commands of the Imperial Government, blood had been shed in Warsaw, and yet, though blood had been shed, order had not been maintained. The enemy had been repulsed, but he had carried his dead away with him, and his retreat was a funereal triumph, and not an ignominious flight.

Perplexed, astonished, irresolute, uncertain of the approval of his sovereign of any course he might adopt, Prince Gortschakoff took refuge in the last resource of the irresolute, and determined to temporize. He permitted, therefore, the formation of the committee, though its purpose was certainly illegal, and was prepared to allow any license to the leaders of the people which was compatible with the preservation of order and the outward maintenance of his authority.

Keenly appreciating the character of the Lieutenant and the concessions to be won from it, the popular leaders grew yet bolder. They represented to him that the indignation excited by the massacres of the 27th was so great and overpowering that no ordinary measures would suffice to curb it; that the Russian Government, their soldiery and police, were for the moment regarded with abhorrence, and that there was danger of the population of the city breaking out into a riot, which might give the signal for insurrection throughout Poland. They proposed, therefore, that the government of the city should for some days be committed to an independent body, the members of which they should themselves nominate, subject to the approval and sanction of the Lieutenant. This body, which was to be styled a Delegation, was to consist of twenty-four members, and would make itself responsible for the good order and quiet of the city; it would appeal to the people through arguments which the Russians would not employ; it would rule them by the aid of national sympathies, by the strong influence which confidence in them would naturally evoke, and by instilling into them the conviction that, if they now showed their capacity for self-government, their conduct would be the most powerful argument which could subsequently be employed when they sought a constitution and administrative autonomy from a just and enlightened sovereign.

This strange demand was granted. The Delegation was constituted, and contained representatives of every class,—nobles, clergy, officers, Jewish Rabbis, merchants, shopkeepers, and peasants. It met daily at the Town-hall, and the control of the city passed into its hands. At their first meeting the members resolved to request the Lieutenant to concede six points to them: they were,—

1st. That they might organize a public funeral, and bury the dead with all honours.

2nd. That the Delegation might be continued in office, and be recognized by the Government until after the funeral was over.

3rd. That troops might not show themselves during the funeral.

4th. That General Marquis Paulucci might be named head of the police.

5th. That the Delegation might proceed to St. Petersburg and present an address to the Emperor.

6th. That all those who had been arrested on 27th February might be liberated.

These requests were preferred to the Lieutenant by a committee of the Delegation, accompanied by Count Andrew Zamoyski, and all, with the exception of the fifth, were granted.

The Delegation used to the utmost the concessions it had wrung from the Government. Students in the academies and higher schools were sent as couriers through the country; they bore tidings of the events which had occurred at Warsaw, and aroused in all classes of the community the deepest sympathy in the sufferings and aims of the revolutionary cause. Everywhere religious celebrations and solemn rites were resolved on, and it was determined that on the day of the funeral one universal wail of lamentation should swell through the mourning land.

On 1st March the corpses were taken to the church of Holy Cross. The streets through which the procession passed were strewn with sand; the windows and balconies of the houses were hung with black cloth edged with white borders and embroidered with crowns of thorn and other emblems of martyrdom and glory; white ribbons and other signs of mourning were worn by the people, and the ceremonies of the day were conducted in an orderly and peaceful manner, under the immediate control of officers appointed by the Delegation.

On the following day the shops, magazines, and public offices were closed; signs of general mourning were everywhere displayed, and the funeral bell filled the air with its fitful and melancholy throb.

The procession from the church of Holy Cross to the cemetery was one of unprecedented solemnity. At its head rode the Marquis Paulucci in the full dress of a general in the Russian service; then followed the monastic orders (and they were numerous and wealthy in those days) in their various habits, with slow and stately tread: they had among them men who had suffered much for their country's cause; and some who subsequently rendered up their lives in her defence. Then came the secular clergy; less able and more scrupulous than those of the regular orders, they were yet men who firmly and consistently loved their country, and strove to work her good. The various guilds succeeded, each with the banner of its craft. Then came the pupils at the academy and schools, too many of whom were at a later date to reap the bitter fruits of the sedition that day sown. To these again succeeded the clergy of the various Protestant creeds, and after them the rabbis and inferior priesthood of the Jews.

The coffins of the dead were made of black wood; on the lid of each was a white cross, and above the cross a crown of thorns was laid. The bearers were men selected from all ranks, for it was the desire of the Delegation to evidence to the Government that all classes sympathized in the demonstration of that day. Following the coffins, the inhabitants of the town and neighbourhood came in long array, and conspicuous among them was Count Andrew Zamoyski, who was walking arm in arm with a peasant. As the procession passed the guardhouses, the sentinels presented arms, paying homage to those whom they had deprived of life only six days before. The cemetery was reached, the corpses were lowered side by side into their narrow graves, and as earth was given again to earth, the multitude of mourners rushed forward to obtain one last look at the coffins of their martyred countrymen; they flung flowers and crowns of thorn into their graves, and with wild passion wept, or vowed deep and speedy vengeance against their murderers. The earth closed over the coffins of the dead, and then, one after another, the priests of the Catholic Church preached funeral sermons above their graves. They were not the dull and commonplace discourses which we so habitually hear; but they were powerful and eloquent appeals to the patriotism of an awaking race; they dwelt upon the past, in order that its renowned memories might animate the men of to-day; they commented on the present, as the age of trial and of strife; and they foretold a future which should revive the glories of ancient Poland, and reward for all their trials her steadfast but persecuted sons.

Photographs of the dead were circulated through the crowd; fragments of the crowns of thorn and pieces of linen dipped in their blood were distributed with lavish hand; and men were invited to swear vengeance against Russia on the graves so newly filled.

After the funeral ceremonies had ended, handbills were given to the people urging them to wear mourning as a sign of national grief.

On the 5th March the Lieutenant acknowledged, in the Government paper, the laudable efforts of the Delegation to preserve order; and, after expressing his approval of their conduct, he temporarily continued them in their office. They therefore met at the Town-hall, under the presidency of the Marquis Paulucci, and commenced their proceedings on the following day. The result of their first meeting was that they requested the Lieutenant to allow counsel to prisoners charged with political offences, to which he replied that the request should be considered; but that it could not be granted at the moment, as it changed the existing order of things. They also asked that the names of parties arrested and the charges made against them should be published, and that their trial should take place with as little delay as possible; and these requests were granted. They next desired to form an unarmed body of police for securing the public safety, and asked that the existing police should report to them every important occurrence. Powers were granted them to appoint constables for the preservation of public order, and subsequently two of their number were appointed to attend the political inquiries.

On the 8th March the Delegation issued a proclamation calling on the inhabitants to continue to preserve good order, and assist them in the execution of their arduous duties; three days later, becoming more exacting as the weakness of the Lieutenant grew more and more apparent, they demanded that prisoners who were charged with promulgating inflammatory proclamations, with scattering asafœtida, placarding walls with revolutionary addresses, sending anonymous and threatening letters, and assaulting the police, should at once be liberated: these trifling offences they deemed had been adequately punished by the few days' imprisonment which the accused had suffered while awaiting trial.

On the 13th March the Lieutenant announced to the Delegation that the Emperor had granted the liberal institutions which will hereafter be mentioned; and on the 23rd he summoned them to the castle, thanked them for the services they had rendered, and informed them, as an elective municipal council was about to be constituted, that it was needless for them to continue their labours.

The Delegation, however, having once tasted power, were unwilling thus to relinquish it, and even after their official dissolution they continued to hold their meetings. Large numbers of people crowded them, and frequently as many as 2,000 auditors were present, and the speeches made were of a violent and revolutionary character.

While the Delegation continued in power, the town was in a very excited state; the police nominated by them were utterly inefficient; lists were spread among the people of so-called Russian spies; and Russian officials were constantly assaulted and insulted by the mob.

The religious ceremonies continued, and many revolutionary sermons were preached; none of them, however, attracted so much notice as one by the Rabbi Cramstuck, who discovered certain texts in the Bible that were solely applicable to Poland, and proved from them that the Jews were bound to second the efforts of the patriots! At this time a strong disposition to combine in political exertions was evidenced by these incongruous allies, and the Jews presented the Roman Catholics with a richly-ornamented cross, while the latter, not to be outdone, gave the Jews in return a silver candlestick with seven branches.

CHAPTER V.

Embarrassment of Government.—Suppression of the Agricultural Society.—Liberal Institutions granted.—Polish Demonstrations.—Suppression of Disturbances.—State of Warsaw.—Death of Prince Gortschakoff.

THE Government was greatly embarrassed by the state of public feeling and the conduct of the agitators in Poland. The disorders which had terminated so fatally in Warsaw were a decided triumph to the revolutionary propaganda. At the cost of a few lives, they had held up the Russian tyranny to the opprobrium of Europe; they had spread reports in the capitals of the West, of sanguinary excesses and wholesale arrests; they had vaunted the noble behaviour of a suffering race; they had enlisted the sympathies of the world in the success of their cause; and all this time, under an exterior thus quiet and resigned, the Government knew that the work of sedition was being carried on, and that an excuse and an opportunity were alone wanting for a revolt to be commenced.

It was difficult to know by what line of action to resist the invisible foe. A religious celebration might be discouraged, a political demonstration might be arrested, but steps such as these in no way really checked the activity of the agitation; besides which, such occasional blows were necessarily aimed at men who were mere tools, and left untouched the ambitious leaders by whom they were secretly prompted.

The only institution about which the revolutionary parties obviously gathered was the Agricultural Society. The meetings of this body had long ceased to be confined to the subjects which nominally occupied its attention; every question affecting, however remotely, the welfare of the people was discussed there; and it was obvious that the party of action hoped to use it as a centre and rallying-point of disaffection. A society such as was contemplated by the Government when the authority to form it was first accorded, would have been very useful in improving the agriculture of Poland; there was great need of such improvement, and among its members were several enlightened men, from whose efforts and example the happiest results were anticipated. It was, however, quickly seen that political change rather than agricultural improvement was the object of many of its most influential members. The alteration in its constitution, by the admission of members from Galicia, Posen, and the Western provinces, has already been named, and it was sufficient to excite the suspicion and provoke the interference of the Administration. By this time, however, the Society had gone much further: its meetings were constantly invaded by factious men not enrolled among its members, who made revolutionary speeches, and advocated measures utterly irrelevant to the questions properly under discussion. In short, the mob of Warsaw broke in upon its deliberations whenever they pleased, and the halls of the Society were rapidly degenerating into a Jacobin club.

Rumours had for some time been circulated that the Government intended to suppress the Society, and having but little time to live, it resolved to mark its last hours by unusual exertions. A committee of its members had for some time existed, whose province it was to inquire into and report upon the condition of the peasants, and suggest a scheme for the settlement of the land question. The tendencies of the Society upon this head had not hitherto been liberal, but the events of the moment hastened their action and altered their views. The peasants could only be influenced through the land question, and if the proprietors required their aid in any future contingency, they well knew it must be won by large concessions now. Besides this, the Society perhaps remembered that very little real sacrifice was involved in any plan it might suggest; for the Government had settled principles on which it was certain to act, whatever might be the views or wishes of the committee.

Thus resolved on immediate action, there was another motive for making it as decided as practicable. In a short time the Government project would be announced, and a plan

F

put forward by it would certainly carry more weight than one promoted by the Society. To counterbalance this disadvantage, therefore, it was essential that the Society should greatly outbid the Government.

An attempt on the part of any institution to dictate a policy to the Government of its country, is in all states and under all circumstances to be deprecated. More than once in the last half-century we have seen, even in England, the dangers that too powerful combinations may create; sometimes they have been successful, sometimes they have forcibly been checked; but experience teaches us that these attempts at creating an *imperium in imperio* are always dangerous even to the best and most stable Government. If such a combination be dangerous among a free people where the citizen obeys the law because he feels that it secures him liberty, how much more perilous is it where the Government is despotic and unpopular! The Agricultural Society attempted to arrogate to itself legislative functions: it was the centre round which all the intrigue and all the disloyalty of Poland revolved; its propositions in respect of the peasants were an obvious bid for popular support; it counted among its members the most influential of the nobles and great proprietors, and it had assumed proportions which made its existence inconsistent with the safety of the State.

The Government had always foreseen that its measures of enfranchisement in the empire must be followed by an amelioration of the condition of the peasant in the kingdom. Accordingly, inquiries had long been on foot, having for their object such an arrangement between the two parties as should be beneficial to both, and free the peasant from all except the monetary claims of the proprietor.

While measures of this character were in course of elaboration, the revolutionary party felt the necessity of action. Any such arrangement as was contemplated by the authorities, would deprive the party of action of its last hold upon the peasants, and its policy, as some alteration was inevitable, was to originate it instead of waiting for the Government to do so; a scheme of settling the land question was therefore proposed and adopted immediately before the Society was dissolved, which was supposed to be more favourable to the peasants than any project which would meet with the sanction of the Government.

For some time previously the Poles had taken every possible opportunity of marking their disaffection. Anniversaries commemorative of events and men most distasteful to the existing authorities, and most obviously pointing to their desire for complete independence, were kept with the greatest ostentation. The patriotic hymn, to which reference has been already made, was constantly sung in their churches. Poles would not mix with Russians in society, or treat them with ordinary courtesy in the streets. If a Russian and a Pole chanced to meet in the same coffee-house, and the former used a glass, it was no unusual occurrence when he placed it on the table, for the Pole to take it up and dash it to pieces on the floor, and then pay for the damage he had committed, observing that another Russian should have no chance of again polluting the vessel he had broken; if Russian ladies travelled in company with Poles, they avoided the use of their own language, knowing that its employment would expose them to gross insults; in public places the Russian officers had long been instructed to show the utmost forbearance to the Poles, as it was the earnest wish of the Government to avoid all collision with them. The fact was, however, everywhere apparent, that the educated population throughout the kingdom, and the town population of all grades, were banded together in opposition to the Government, and would not be satisfied with anything short of absolute independence, or a trial of strength which would probably terminate in absolute subjection.

Whatever may be the views of an individual as to the justice or expediency of the continuance of an established system, it is certain that so long as it exists, those who are interested in its continuance are entitled to resist illegal attempts at its overthrow. The English rule in Ireland very likely was extremely bad in the last century, and during nearly one half of the present; and very probably the great majority of the Irish sincerely wished its overthrow when O'Connell summoned meetings at Clontarf and Tara. Very likely that spirit-stirring ballad in which it is predicted that "Ireland shall be free," and many another revolutionary chant which has in later times found a responsive echo in the hearts of millions, may have been as entirely national as the sad and supplicating hymn of the people of *Poland. And I believe they were. But does any one blame the British Government for putting down the rebellion of 1798 with the strong hand of power? and does any one question its justice at a later date, when, under the guidance of Sir Robert Peel, it suppressed the "monster meetings"? No! every one will admit that power cannot confer with agitation; that the latter must be quelled before the former can conciliate.

The Government resolved to dissolve the Agricultural Society, but they determined to precede that act by the publication of their intention to grant more liberal institutions to Poland than she then possessed.

Accordingly, by an oukase of 26th March, the Emperor directed projects of laws to be submitted for ameliorating the institutions of the country. These projects were subsequently matured, and assumed the following form:—

1. The re-establishment of a council of state in Poland.
2. The re-establishment of a commission for the regulation of religious matters and public education.
3. The separation of the different branches of Polish from those of the Russian administration.
4. The separation of the civil from the military administration of Poland, and the appointment in the civil administration of persons of Polish birth.
5. The decentralization of the administration and the formation of local self-government by the institution of local councils chosen by election.
6. The elaboration of a liberal system of public instruction. The foundation of a university in Warsaw, and the adoption of the Polish language in all the schools in the kingdom.

The Council of State existed in Poland from 1832 to 1841, when it was abolished by the Emperor Nicholas. When re-established by the oukase just cited, it became a superior legislative body, holding the same position in Poland that the Council of the Empire holds in Russia. Its duties are to examine and modify all projects of law sent to it by special commissions nominated for that purpose, and having approved them, to submit them to the Emperor. It has also to examine the budget of the kingdom, the accounts of its officers, to investigate complaints of abuses, and perform many other important functions.

At the outbreak of the rebellion in 1863, all the Council were Poles except the Grand Duke Constantine, its *ex-officio* chairman.

2. The Commission of religious matters and public instruction existed in the kingdom till 1839, when it was abolished by the Emperor Nicholas, and the administration of the schools were confided to the Russian Ministry of Public Instruction. The Emperor in re-establishing the commission intended to secure the independence of public instruction in Poland.

3. The Post-office and administration of Public Works and Highways were in the reign of Nicholas placed under the same authorities in Russia and Poland. They were now separated, so as to give complete independence to the latter.

4. The civil was entirely separated from the military administration of the kingdom. The office of General Governor of Warsaw was consequently abolished, and a chief of the civil administration substituted. The Marquis Wielopolski was the first person appointed to this dignity, and all the civil offices in the kingdom, with very few exceptions, were filled with Poles, so that at the end of 1862 there were only six or eight functionaries of Russian birth holding offices of any importance in the kingdom.

5. For the purpose of decentralizing the administration, and of gradually introducing self-government, provincial councils were instituted, the members of which were elected by the nation. The right to elect and be elected was given to persons of all religions and conditions, of a certain age, who could read and write the Polish language and possessed property in the kingdom.

To these councils were committed the development of agriculture, trade, and public communications; the care of hospitals, prisons, and the poor; the administration of the local affairs of the towns; the raising and expenditure of local taxation; and the superintendence of public establishments.

The establishment of local provincial councils, freely elected by the people, was intended as the first step to a general representation in Poland, and, so soon as the nation had in any degree accustomed itself to representative institutions, would have been followed by the convocation of the Chamber of Deputies.

6. At the accession of the present Emperor to the throne, education in Poland was at a very low ebb. The suppression of the University at Warsaw has already been stated, and there was no establishment in the kingdom where a superior education could be procured. In all the kingdom there were only eight gymnasiums or institutes for nobles, where a second-class education was given; and by law the professors in these institutions were obliged to teach the sciences in the Russian language, though practically this enactment was not always observed, for it was difficult to find professors who could speak Russ, and still more difficult to find scholars to comprehend them.

The elementary public instruction was in a better condition. The number of elementary schools was 1,000 in 1861, and there were 20 district and "real" schools.

In a former chapter the effect of this want of a superior education in the higher classes of the Poles has been pointed out, and the extent to which it drove them for education to the universities of Moscow, Petersburg, and Kieff.

In 1857, the Government took the first step towards the establishment of a university in Warsaw, by endowing a faculty or academy of medicine there. A further step was taken in 1861, when the Emperor directed the Commission of Public Instruction to elaborate a project of law in order thoroughly to reform the organization of public instruction in the kingdom: the aim of this scheme was to enable men of every religion and condition to study special sciences there, and allow the common people to acquire all elementary knowledge necessary for them.

The law consequently elaborated was sanctioned by the

Emperor, and put in force from 20th March, 1862, and consisted chiefly in the following particulars.

Catholic priests and proprietors of towns and villages were allowed to found, at their own expense or at that of the place where they were established, elementary schools for teaching the Catholic religion, reading and writing in the Polish language, and arithmetic; and they could appoint as masters of such schools all individuals having the qualifications required by law for enabling them to take such office. In addition to these, one or more elementary schools were to be founded in each commune, at the expense of Government; these schools were to be placed under the surveillance of the Catholic priests and certain inhabitants of the commune, elected by the Commune itself, and to be subject to their inspection and local administration.

The district schools were to be divided into "general" schools, for general instruction; "training," for preparing masters for elementary schools; and special or "real" schools, for teaching agriculture, trade, and other special subjects.

In addition to the seven existing gymnasiums, six more were directed to be added, and instead of the Institute of Nobles, a lyceum was founded, as an establishment where a supplementary or superior class to those existing in gymnasiums might be taught. The scholars might belong to any religious denomination, and the cost of instruction was only sixteen roubles (about £2. 10s.) a year.

A Polytechnic institute was founded in Pulova, and the plan of the University of Warsaw was sketched out. It was to be composed of four faculties: medicine; philosophy, or physics, and mathematics; jurisprudence; and history and philology. To the University two seminaries were to be attached for preparing masters for gymnasiums and district schools. The Polytechnic institute was to be composed of five sections—mechanics, civil engineering, mining, agriculture, and forestry. Students of all religious persuasions were admitted to the University, and the cost of instruction was only twenty roubles a year.

The national language, history, and literature were to be

taught in all the schools; the Polish language was alone employed in giving instruction; and the Russian language was only taught in the superior and secondary schools.

Such were the institutions founded in consequence of the decree of 14th March, 1861; institutions which were intended to pave the way to others of a yet more liberal tendency, and to the eventual introduction of a system of constitutional government in Poland. They seemed well adapted for that purpose; for local self-government is the best prelude to national representation, and extended education is the surest preparation for the responsibilities of power.

Having thus evidenced the principles upon which it intended that Poland should in future be ruled, the Government of the Emperor proceeded to vindicate its contemned authority. The Agricultural Society was dissolved, and the house where its meetings had been held was closed.

For some time past—in fact, ever since the events of 27th February—public feeling had been greatly excited in Warsaw; disturbances were constantly created, which ceased before the police could reach the spot whence they proceeded; great masses of the people assembled at the graves of the so-called "martyrs," and there, as well as before the image of the Virgin in public places, chanted the national hymn.

When the suppression of the Agricultural Society was effected, the feelings of the masses of Warsaw found more decided utterance; the Society was to them the only embodiment and representation of the aspirations and will of the people, and they resented its dissolution as another national wrong. A multitude of all classes thronged to the house which was now closed, they crowned its doors and windows with flowers, they chanted seditious hymns, and then proceeded to the Sigismund Place, and drew up before the residence of Prince Gortschakoff. The Prince, accompanied by his aides-de-camp, endeavoured to persuade the people to depart, but they refused to obey him, and remained there undisturbed until night. The crowd was so great that the Prince was unwilling to employ force, which, had it been resorted to, would have entailed the sacrifice of many lives.

On the following day the demonstration was repeated;

dense masses assembled in the same place, and when legally summoned to disperse, refused to do so, and their conduct became turbulent. The Government had, on the previous night, decided that it would be necessary if the crowd re-assembled, to disperse it forcibly, should all milder expedients fail; and, pursuant to this determination, after the legal summons had been often repeated, the cavalry charged and scattered the people; but it was to little purpose; for the masses quickly re-formed themselves.

It is very difficult to ascertain with precision the events which subsequently took place. The accounts published in the journals representing the "Emigration" are utterly untrustworthy. To lead to these disorders, and subsequently make political capital out of them; to exaggerate and spread abroad the falsest and most damaging reports of Russian excesses, was the policy inculcated by their leaders, and insisted on in their state papers. It is impossible, therefore, to recognize such accounts as possessing in themselves the smallest historical value. More moderate* enemies of the Government affirm that the crowd was "so excited, though perfectly peaceable, that threats alone, or the employment of force against a few, would never have broken it up."

* Mr. Edwards gives, as the result of inquiries made by him in Warsaw, shortly after these occurrences, the following statement:—

"To begin with, however, it is quite untrue that the troops rushed into the town from the citadel and the various camps, and, taking up their positions, began the attack without warning, and without the people being repeatedly summoned to retire.

"In spite of a few assertions to the contrary, I am convinced, from abundant and most reliable testimony, that the crowd in the Sigsmund Place, in front of the Castle, was so numerous and compact, and the persons composing it, though perfectly peaceable, so excited, that threats alone, or the employment of force against a few, could never have broken it up. It might have been prevented from forming, or have been left unmolested until night, and the proper precautions taken against its re-assembling the next day, which was not, like the day of the 'massacre,' a holiday. . . . It is said that the Poles laughed at the soldiers, and threw cigars at them with a generosity which the Russian generals apparently thought could not fail to shake discipline. These contempt-breeding familiarities were checked by the wanton slaughter of some forty men."

Speaking of the time during which the firing continued, Mr. Edwards

The Government accounts are more consistent and probable, and from inquiries it has been in my power to make, I am satisfied they are believed in official circles in Russia to be true. I have also inquired from those who were present on the occasion, and found them substantially confirmed. They state that, on the crowd re-forming, stones were flung at the troopers.

The soldiers were then ordered to fire, and some few discharges dispersed the crowd. The number of the killed was ten.

The wounded were carried to the hospitals, or to their own homes, and there appears no reason to suppose that any unnecessary rigour was employed after the demonstration was suppressed.

The revolutionary press took advantage of these events. Hundreds of persons, it alleged, had lost their lives, and to conceal the greatness of the slaughter, the troops had thrown

---

states : " The discharges of musketry were not kept up with anything like continuity. The first rank fired. The second rank advanced, and collected the killed and wounded. Then there was a pause until after a certain interval, the crowd not dispersing, the order to fire again was given. Persons who witnessed this bloody scene declare that, instead of producing terror and dismay, the volleys of the Russians at first only excited the indignation of the Poles, and roused in them a species of enthusiasm, which may be called the enthusiasm of martyrdom.

" Many went down on their knees, but not to their enemies. In some parts of the crowd the more timid were entreated in the name of their country to remain firm, and these appeals were not without effect. Afterwards, when numbers had been shot down, and brute force was beginning to triumph, the most determined and desperate among the crowd still cried out that there must be no retreating, and some were seen to join hands, so as to prevent those before them from falling back."—*The Polish Captivity*, by Sutherland Edwards, vol. i. p. 61.

This account comes from an enthusiastic supporter of the cause of the insurgents, and is the result no doubt of careful inquiry; but that inquiry was evidently, from the whole tenor of the work, made from men excited by party passion, and maddened by the scenes through which they had lately passed. The author does not appear to note the inconsistency which exists between the highly-wrought feelings which forbade the mob to separate unless dispersed by force, and the sentiment which led them "to laugh at the soldiers, and generously throw them cigars :" yet the two moods are hardly reconcilable.

their bodies into the Vistula; the town of Warsaw had been given up to pillage, and the soldiers had only been recalled from this shameless occupation at five o'clock in the evening by the peal of the trumpet and the beat of the drum. The workmen in the town had to draw lots to see who among them should suffer death; a war contribution was levied on the inhabitants for the support of the troops; and a Major Penker (who committed suicide the day before these events happened) killed himself to avoid participating in the cruelties consequent upon them.

These are only some of the reports which were circulated constantly and with zeal; they were extensively copied by the press of Western Europe, and tended to excite hostility to Russia, and admiration of the party by whom she was defied.

During the ensuing six or seven months, Warsaw continued in a very agitated state. The Russian authorities were nervously anxious to avoid further bloodshed; they resolved to submit to almost every indignity rather than have recourse to it; and orders were secretly issued to the officers in the town, directing them in silence to submit to insults which they would at another time have repressed with promptitude and severity. Encouraged by the sufferance it met with, the frivolous element in the Polish character displayed itself in all its vanity; civilians were seen strutting through the streets arrayed in what they called the national garb, and thus equipped they would stroll along with their arms akimbo, treat every Russian they met with marked incivility, and be followed by admiring crowds of boys and lads, who enthusiastically cheered them. This national dress consisted of a white shirt, blue trousers, top boots reaching to the knee, a belt from which copper rings were suspended, which jingled when they were moved, and a red cap with a fur brim; on the shirt was a long red collar, hanging down over the shoulders, and embroidered with gold. The town looked extremely gay when half-filled by these dramatic costumes, and the gentlemen who indulged in them wore them with a proud consciousness that they were thus performing a great act of patriotic duty. There were constant gatherings in the streets and disturbances were hourly expected.

The Russian soldiers and officers were beyond measure exasperated at the insults to which they were compelled to submit: it was no uncommon thing to see them followed by a crowd of men and boys whistling and hooting at them; and their orders compelled them to bear these insults in silence. There were at this time in Warsaw bands of the lower orders, who made it their business to hire themselves out to whoever desired to annoy an enemy. A regular tariff of prices was established, and one charge was made for a mere *charivari*, another for a *charivari* which was accompanied by breaking windows. The pretence of patriotism was still kept up, and photographs of the head of the *charivari* band were extensively sold.

It was during this period that Prince Gortschakoff died. He was an able officer and an estimable man, but it was the misfortune of his life to be appointed to the vice-royalty of Poland under circumstances which afforded him no scope for the display of his military abilities, and required the exercise of administrative talents which he did not possess. An anecdote is related of him which strikingly illustrates the perplexity of his mind after the events of February and April. Talking to a gentleman who was supposed to be a leader of the disaffected party, he walked up and down the room in an excited manner, and told him he was much harassed by the policy of his coadjutors. "Why don't you rebel?" he asked; "I should know how to treat you then, but this system of unarmed agitation is killing me; why don't you take up arms and fight for the realization of your views?" "We have no arms, Excellency," was the reply. "Is that the only difficulty?" answered the Prince; "if so, I will gladly supply them; and shall be rejoiced to settle this question by such an appeal, instead of having to deal with this miserable system of unarmed agitation."

This anecdote well portrays the character of the Lieutenant. He was a soldier, and against a foreign foe would have acquitted himself manfully and with zeal; but he understood little of the art of administration, and nothing of the means by which civil intrigues are to be met. Vacillating between extreme harshness and unwise concession, there was nothing certain in his policy or consistent in his conduct; and the conspirators who plotted the overthrow of Russian supremacy took courage when they found the Lieutenant struck not at them, or only struck with a wild and wavering aim. A settled policy is absolutely necessary to curb revolutionary passions in anxious and troubled times, and the conduct of Prince Gortschakoff proved that he had no policy whatever. To fire on the mob on 27th February, and subsequently to follow up that measure by acts of stern repression, would have possibly been severe, but at least it would have been intelligible; but to fire on the mob, and, two days afterwards, to consign the peace of Warsaw to its care, was to act in a manner altogether irreconcileable with reason and common sense. Inconsistencies so startling gave hope and encouragement to the revolutionary movement, for they led to the impression that Russia regarded her position with impatience and dislike; and that if the agitation were continued she might be content to emancipate herself from the embarrassment it caused, by rendering back at least the Congress kingdom to the control of the Polish race.

CHAPTER VI.

Count Lambert.—Declaration of State of Siege.—Demonstration of 15th October.—The Blockade of the Churches.—Mourning.—Attempted Murder of General Luders.—Appointment of Grand Duke Constantine as Viceroy.—The Marquis of Wielopolski; his character and policy.—Attempts to assassinate the Grand Duke and the Marquis.—Distinction between the Kingdom of Poland and the Western Provinces.—Address of Polish Proprietors.—Count Andrew Zamoyski; his exile.

COUNT LAMBERT, the successor of Prince Gortschakoff, permitted the system of his predecessor to continue for some time, until at length the anarchy in which the city was plunged became utterly inconsistent with the supremacy of the law. Not only were the outrages to which allusion has been already made of constant occurrence, but revolutionary proclamations and appeals to the people were daily circulated, and on the occasion of the funeral of the Archbishop of Warsaw, religious emblems expressive of the union of Poland and Lithuania, accompanied the funeral *cortége*. The churches were transformed, by the complicity of some members of the Catholic clergy, into theatres for the display of manifestations of hostility to the Government, and in many places the *Te Deums* celebrated on certain days by command of the Emperor were stifled by the chant of the national hymn. That hymn, too, was chanted in church and cathedral on every occasion where it was possible to introduce it. It was heard at daytime in the crowded street, and its swell faintly reverberated at night in every quarter of the silent city. Money also was being collected for purposes said to be patriotic, though the objects were unavowed; and the Russians saw that a mine was preparing beneath their feet to be exploded on the first occasion when the revolutionary leaders had courage or opportunity to fire it.

The Government considered that it was necessary to resort

to determined measures, and in order to stop a political manifestation intended for the 15th of October, Count Lambert, by a proclamation issued the day previously, declared the kingdom of Poland to be in a state of siege. In this proclamation, after noticing the acts which in his opinion made the step a necessary one, he continued, " I invite the peaceable inhabitants of the kingdom not to be influenced by the promptings or threats of the agitators, which from to-day have lost their value, and to afford their co-operation to the Government, so as to preserve the public well-being. I exhort fathers of families to watch over their households, and particularly their children under age, who may accidentally incur the penalties of a state of siege, which extend to every person, without regard to age or sex, when it represses by force tumults in the public streets."

The celebration intended for the following day was that of the anniversary of the death of Kosciusko, and for some time past placards had been hawked about, inviting the inhabitants to consecrate it by assisting at the funeral services to be performed in all the churches; these placards also urged that all shops and magazines should be closed.

A special notice to the inhabitants of the town was issued simultaneously with the proclamation of the state of siege, by which it was pointed out that at such periods it was forbidden to chant revolutionary hymns, to celebrate *fêtes* not recognized by the law, or to close shops and magazines. A fine of 100 roubles, it was stated, would be imposed upon any one who broke the last-mentioned rule.

These proclamations brought the Government face to face with the revolutionary party. On the one side concession had been carried to its utmost limit; on the other, the recollection of many acts of successful insubordination gave encouragement to schemes of yet more determined resistance. The party of action resolved to persevere. To draw back now, to abandon their celebration at the mandate of the Russian Governor, would have been to surrender the hard-won fruits of a prolonged and anxious struggle; it would have obliterated the memory of the Delegation, it would have thrown dishonour on the martyred dead—above all, it would have flung Poland again at the feet of her conqueror, and permitted him to despise the people he never yet had spurned. Such were the motives which urged on the disaffected party to a fatal trial of strength with the Government. The answer given to the proclamation and notice of the state of siege, was the issue of fresh placards, urging the people to disregard them, and to persevere in the celebration of the anniversary.

On the morning of the 15th the shops and magazines throughout the city were wholly or partially closed, and immense multitudes of every age and rank and of both sexes thronged to the churches to take part in the religious services. The cathedral and the church attached to the Bernardine monastery were especially thronged, and when the services commenced, it was estimated that the two congregations numbered about four thousand.

To prevent any unseemly disturbances, it had been determined by the authorities that the military should in no case enter the churches, but that after they were filled, the troops should surround them, and that when the congregations left, all the men who formed part of them should be arrested, while the women and children should be permitted to leave unmolested.

By half-past ten o'clock it was ascertained that the revolutionary hymn was being chanted in all the churches, and the military were ordered to surround them. The congregations, however, were informed of their approach, and when the troops reached them, all the churches were empty except that of the Bernardines and the cathedral.

The congregations in these churches soon learned that they were surrounded, but they continued their services, chanted their national hymn, and did not allow the approach of the troops to disturb their devotions.

Such of the women and children as wished to leave were allowed to do so, but very few availed themselves of the permission; the great mass resolved to share the fate of their kindred, and remained. Then the inner doors were closed, all communication with the troops was cut off, and nothing was to be heard save the voice of exhortation and of prayer.

Meanwhile the city was occupied by troops. Cavalry and

infantry patrolled the streets; groups were not allowed to congregate together, and the excitement of the populace was curbed by the stern hand of military law.

Thus passed the day. The night was approaching, yet from within the churches arose no sound of vacillation or of fear. Unawed by the presence of the enemy, untired by the long continuance of a military blockade, the worshippers still bent before the altar of their God and implored His assistance to save their country from the chain. The weary soldiers, worn out with fatigue and unsustained by the religious excitement of the fevered crowds over which they watched, were relieved; their places were taken by fresh troops; the worshippers saw that the Government was determined to maintain its position, and yet they showed no symptoms of surrender, and refused to quit the beleaguered churches.

The Government was greatly embarrassed. Judging from the constancy they had hitherto displayed, there seemed little chance of the people leaving the churches, and the dangers that would probably arise from allowing them to remain were very considerable. For twelve long hours authority had been set at nought, and this in face of warnings and proclamations of the severest kind, and at a period when a state of siege justified the utmost rigour. The country was trembling on the verge of rebellion, and this was the moment the populace of Warsaw selected to measure itself against the Lieutenant of the kingdom. Then, too, among the thousands pent up within the churches were probably many who could ill endure protracted confinement and a prolonged fast; if there were any sufferers from these physical causes, the revolutionary press would inscribe their names in the list of political martyrs, and the Russians keenly remembered the scenes of 27th February, and deprecated their recurrence.

There was another danger in delay. Intelligence of a positive kind had been received that the disaffected were preparing a great demonstration for the following day, one feature of which was to be a procession of clergy and people towards the beleaguered churches. To avoid the consequences which it was feared this gathering might give rise to, and to terminate a contest of which they were very weary, the authorities directed the churches to be entered and the people forcibly expelled.

About midnight an officer entered the Bernardine church, from the monastery, and endeavoured to prevail upon the crowd to retire, and declared, should his solicitations be ineffectual, the troops would enter the church and arrest every man they found there. His efforts were fruitless; some persevered on principle, and others because they feared maltreatment from the soldiers if they left. None listened to his entreaties, and some threatened to defend themselves if the soldiers were sent to arrest them.

The officer retired for the moment, and then returned at the head of thirty soldiers, who entered the church without shakos or arms, and making the sign of the cross. The men grouped inside the church near the door for the moment endeavoured to defend themselves and to assault the soldiers with benches, chairs, and any other object which they could convert into a weapon of offence; but the slight struggle which ensued was unimportant: the soldiers had no weapons to employ, and a few bruises were all the injury that either side sustained. All the men in the church were arrested in groups of 100 each, and were escorted, first to the fortress, and subsequently to the Alexander citadel.

Towards three o'clock in the morning all efforts to induce the congregation to leave proving unavailing, twenty soldiers entered the cathedral with bare heads but carrying their muskets. It was expressly forbidden that, under any circumstances, they should fire; and only in case of extremity were they to employ the butt end. They compelled the men to leave one by one, and as they left they were arrested. The total number of arrests in the two churches was 1,678.

Some of the women and children left during the night, and at their own request were conducted to their homes by the police; the remainder were allowed to remain in the church till morning.

In the cathedral a priest was observed who, cross in hand, violently incited the people to resist; he, too, was captured and as he left the cathedral he assumed the air of a martyr, fervently clasping the cross and evidently anticipating that his sufferings would excite the greatest sympathy.

Count Lambert was on the spot, and his carriage was in attendance; he was much distressed at the whole proceeding, and the capture of this ecclesiastical martyr embarrassed him more than any other incident that had occurred. By his directions the astonished priest was courteously escorted to the carriage of his Excellency, and the people who a moment before had regarded him as their champion changed their minds when they saw him comfortably seated in the carriage of the governor, and supposed he had betrayed them. After a few hours' detention, the priest was released and allowed to return to his duties.

Reports were quickly circulated through Europe alleging that the Russians had committed the greatest atrocities on this occasion; they were charged with cruelty, unnecessary violence, and wicked profanation; excesses of every description were alleged against them, and, all the antecedents of the revolutionary party being ignored, the occurrence was represented as a wanton inroad of barbarians on a peaceful congregation engaged in the performance of religious duties. Yet no one who has ever travelled in Russia can have failed to remark the reverence shown by all classes to churches and shrines, whether of their own or of another faith. At Wilna, from the prince to the common soldier, I have seen them walk bareheaded under the image of the Virgin of Ostrobrama, although that is a Catholic and not a Greek shrine, and in other places their devotional feelings are evidenced with equal distinctness.

Now, as the Government felt that all occurrences such as those of the 13th of October were calculated to damage their influence both in Poland and Europe, it is most improbable that they would have neglected to preserve the churches from profanation, and the orders which they allege were given and obeyed are exactly such as we should anticipate to have been issued under the circumstances.

The information upon which my narrative of these events is founded is partly documentary; but I have also had direct personal communication with a gentleman who took a prominent part in them, and upon whose memory, accuracy, and good faith I can implicitly rely.

The establishment of a state of siege changed the whole aspect of affairs in Warsaw; all outward manifestations of disaffection ceased; the revolutionary hymn was no longer permitted to be sung, political celebrations were suppressed, and to all outward appearance the supremacy of the Government was restored. Yet the state of affairs was really unchanged; public feeling had been too successfully roused to be now lulled by superficial defeats, and the machinery of secret agitation continued to work unchecked.

There is little to chronicle in the few months that succeeded the declaration of the state of siege. The Catholic clergy, however, manifested their hostility to the Government by closing all the churches in Warsaw under the pretext that they desired to save them from profanation; the administrator of the see was summoned before one of the Commissions of Inquiry to answer for this offence, and, finding that he had committed a fault which during the existence of a state of siege had rendered him liable to capital punishment, he alleged that he desired to avoid the singing of the revolutionary hymn in the temple of God. The great doors of the churches remained closed, but the smaller doors were kept open, and the religious services were resumed, so that no great practical inconvenience arose from the course adopted by the clergy; they, however, discontinued ringing the bells of the churches, and took advantage of every safe opportunity that offered to show their enmity to the Government.

From the time that the state of siege was proclaimed mourning was universally worn; no lady could appear in the street in a coloured dress without being grossly insulted in case she had no protector with her; Russian ladies were subjected to so many indignities that they generally adopted mourning, that their nationality might not be remarked. To such an extent were these outrages carried, that a French lady residing in Warsaw, who had weak eyes and wore a green shade to protect them from the sun, had the shade violently torn from her because its colour was inconsistent with mourning.

In June, 1862, an audacious attempt was made to assassinate General Luders, who succeeded Count Lambert in the government of Poland. He was an old man, and for the benefit of his health was in the habit of going early every morning to drink mineral waters in a small park in the centre of the town, known as the Saxon Garden; while walking there he was fired at by a man who was fourteen yards behind him; the ball entered the back of his neck, broke the jawbone and passed out through the cheek; the General fell, and was carried severely wounded to the palace.

About this time it was resolved that the government of Poland should be committed to the Grand Duke Constantine, a prince who possessed considerable popularity in Russia, and in whom the Emperor reposed unlimited confidence. With more than average abilities, possessing a refined and cultivated mind, and a disposition which inclined to conciliation and not to severity, the Grand Duke seemed a well-chosen instrument for carrying out an enlightened and liberal policy. His want of knowledge of the peculiarities of the Polish character, and the many intricate questions in which the interests and prejudices of the inhabitants of the kingdom were involved, was guarded against by the appointment as his chief minister of the Marquis Wielopolski. I shall have hereafter to allude to the policy and views of the Marquis. It is for the present sufficient to remark that with great ability, great knowledge of his country and the wishes of his countrymen, and being, as far as it is possible to judge, animated by sincere patriotism, he was nevertheless probably the most unpopular man in Poland. He had the reputation of having acquired his property by lawsuits successfully conducted against numerous opponents; and rumour alleged that he was a harsh, unscrupulous adversary.

A man of cold and haughty manners, silent and self-reliant, few sympathized with him, and in none did he confide. In youth he had identified himself with the unfortunate struggle of 1830, and saw his hopes blighted when that revolt was crushed. He turned to Austria, and dreamed that through her agency the national spirit might revive, and through her aid independence might at length be won; she answered him by the annexation of Cracow and the extermination of hundreds of the Galician nobles. Exasperated by her perfidy, his letter to Prince Metternich was the gage of a battle in which he strove to involve her—a battle with Polish nationality assisted by the Russian arms. In that remarkable letter he declared that he would no longer struggle for an independent Poland; combination with Russia would in time give her strength, happiness, and freedom, and the union of the great Slavonic races under one dominion was the object for which he would thereafter strive.

In that Slavonic doctrine there is much to attract the suffrages of theoretic politicians, and from books rather than from men had Wielopolski learned his state-craft. Able he was, brave and resolute as well, and his courage did not falter when opposition surrounded him on every side; still he adhered to his policy, still he had confidence in his plans, and was willing to commit his own personal safety and the security of the State to their ultimate success.

But the Marquis had no followers. He was not the idol of the people; he was not the champion of a class; and, amid Poles who hated and Russians who distrusted him, he stood alone. Confident in his own genius, a sincere believer in the ultimate success of his efforts, he asked no counsel and courted no assistance. "I am certain," he said to one who knew him well, "that my policy must finally succeed, and all I ask is to carry it through without interruption." He allowed not, however, for the abiding power of national hatred; he thought material and political interests would bind up the wounds and silence the complaints which were the growth of ninety years, and expected the Polish nobility to lay aside their hereditary enmities the moment autonomy was granted and a paper constitution announced. A practical statesman would have seen that something more was required, and that confidence would not exist till it was seen that the new constitution would be observed. It will be seen hereafter that, unfortunately for his own fame, an act dictated by this statesman shook the faith even of the most loyal, and confirmed the gloomiest suspicions of the disaffected and wavering.

Arrogant and unbending, there was about him a contemptuous disdain of others which told them he prided himself on his intellectual superiority, and that he was resolved to do his will notwithstanding all the opposition they might make to it.

He seemed alike unfitted to win the favour of the court or the people. When he entered the vice-regal apartments, men stood aside and shrunk from meeting him, for he had no following and was too proud to acknowlege any equal. When he went abroad, he was not safe from the hatred of the people, and a guard of eight gendarmes was constantly in attendance on him to save him and his equipage from insult and injury.

He viewed popular applause with fierce disdain, and an anecdote is told of him, which, whether true or false, has at least the advantage of showing the received estimate of his character. "The government of your Excelleny," said some one, wishing to flatter him, "is certainly more popular than it was." "Ah! indeed!" was the reply. "I'm sorry to hear it; I wonder what mistake I have committed."

The public feeling towards him was well expressed by a caricature representing him in his carriage surrounded by his guards, while the inscription beneath was simply, "Trust me as I trust you."

Without a party or a confidant, there was only one man in Poland who willingly accepted him as a guide, but that one man was the Grand Duke Constantine, and his trust in Wielopolski never faltered.

The Grand Duke arrived at Warsaw on the night of the 2nd of July, and on the night of the 4th an attack was made upon his life. A man, named Louis Jaroszynsky, had determined to assassinate him on his arrival; he accordingly went to the railway station to meet his victim, but did not upon that occasion execute his intention; he subsequently attributed his inaction to the fact that the Grand Duchess accompanied her husband, and he was unwilling to shock her with the sight of the assassination of her husband. It seems, however, more probable that it was due to the difficulties the occasion presented.

On the night of the 4th the Grand Duke went to the theatre, and as he left it he was surrounded by the officers of his staff, who accompanied him to his carriage; he stepped in, followed by his aide-de-camp. At this moment a man standing near clasped his hands as though he wished to present a petition to him; the Grand Duke bent forward to listen, the man produced a revolver and fired; the ball struck him on the left shoulder, and the pistol was so close that his whiskers were singed; the assassin was arrested. The wound of the Grand Duke was examined and pronounced not to be dangerous, and he returned to the Summer Palace, where he was then residing. The ball with which the pistol was loaded could not be discovered at the time, but on undressing it was found in his clothes, with part of the gold wire of his epaulet attached to it. He evidently owed his life to the altered direction given to the ball by the epaulet, and to the fact that the pistol was insufficiently loaded.

The Grand Duke expressed his conviction to the municipal council that this was an isolated circumstance and was not the result of any conspiracy; but this opinion appears to have been erroneous, as two daggers were subsequently found at the door of the theatre.

It is believed that the culprit had poisoned himself previously to the commission of this crime, for when arrested he was violently sick, and it was found necessary to give him milk in large quantities to counteract the effects of the poison; one of his first acts was to throw himself on his knees and return thanks to God for his success; for he had seen the Grand Duke fall, and thought he had killed him.

On the 7th of August an attempt was made to assassinate the Marquis Wielopolski. On leaving the Treasury on that day he was twice fired at ineffectually by a man named Ludovic Ryll; and on the 15th of August a second attempt was made upon his life by a man named Rjontza, who attempted to stab him as he was passing in his carriage along one of the boulevards of the town.

These attempts were attributed by the Marquis to a desire,

on the part of the ultra-revolutionary party, to prevent the grant of the free institutions the Government was determined to confer. In making this statement, he announced that the Government would not be deterred from adopting such measures as it believed to be useful and necessary to the country.

Accordingly, the works of reform went on; the various liberal institutions granted by the Emperor were gradually elaborated, and every evidence was given which should have served to convince the Polish nation that the Government was acting in sincerity and good faith.

Nevertheless, instead of accepting the privileges granted to them, and consolidating the advantages thus obtained before they sought to acquire more, a large party among the nobles and proprietors determined, by assuming a defiant attitude, to win further concessions from the Government.

It is scarcely necessary to remind the reader that there is a great historical and political difference between the kingdom of Poland, often called the Congress Kingdom, and the so-called Western Provinces of Russia. The kingdom of Poland is substantially identical with the grand duchy of Warsaw of former times; wrested from his enemies by Alexander I., he was found in possession of it when the Congress of Vienna re-settled the limits of the empires and kingdoms of Europe; he claimed it as his own by right of conquest, and intimated with tolerable clearness that nothing would induce him to surrender his prey. At the close of a war which had already lasted a quarter of a century, the diplomatists of Europe declined to risk its renewal, in order that the grand duchy of Warsaw might become an independent state; therefore the duchy was, by the treaty of Vienna, confirmed to the Emperor Alexander, under the title of the kingdom of Poland. He on his part undertook, in effect, to give it such liberal institutions as he in his discretion thought fit. The result was the granting of that constitution of which diplomatists have written so much and apparently known so little; and this constitution was cancelled by the Emperor Nicholas, who declared that the Poles had forfeited it by the revolt of 1830.

The Western provinces of Russia, however, including the whole of ancient Lithuania, as well as the provinces of Volhynia, Podolia, and the Ukraine, had been won from Poland in the successive partitions which took place during the last century. These provinces had been thoroughly incorporated in the political system of the empire, and were regarded by every Russian as forming integral parts of it. As we have already seen, however, the proprietors and educated classes in these provinces were Poles by sympathy and descent, and regarded them as by right belonging to the kingdom of Poland.

Early in September, a proprietor who was anxious that the nobility should take an active part in the revolutionary movement requested a large number of them to meet together in Warsaw. They met, and he produced the draft of an address which he proposed should be presented to the Grand Duke, containing a statement of grievances and a demand for their removal. The tone of this address was unwise, and it was not drawn up with ability. Those who signed it, although not refusing the reforms conceded by the Emperor, expressed their conviction that no measures whatever would succeed in pacifying the country or reconciling it to the Crown until the Government was a Polish one, and until "all those provinces which form our nation are united in one by means of organic and free institutions;" in short, they required the union of the Western provinces of Russia to the kingdom of Poland.* This address was debated long and angrily in a conference which lasted several days. According to the Russian law, such an address was illegal, and many of the proprietors also deemed it to be unwise. A considerable proportion of them, therefore, refused to sanction it, and left the assembly; the remainder signed it.

A deputation of twenty-six of those who were parties to it waited on Count Andrew Zamoyski, and requested him to present the memorial to the Grand Duke. He read it, pronounced it an "imbecile" document, threw it into the fire, and refused to have anything to do with it.

* A Russian hearing the address read, piously made the sign of the cross, and said, "Thank God, they leave us at least Moscow."

A few days later the deputation again waited on him with an unsigned copy of the address, and begged, if he did not himself coincide in its views, or think it wise so to express them, he would at least mention the subject to the Grand Duke, and tell him what was the purport of the document. This he consented to do, on the distinct understanding that he was to choose his own time and mode of doing so, postponing the communication to any period, however distant, when in his opinion it would be wise to make it.

Rumours of this petition spread through Warsaw; the official paper of the 15th stated that the Government would never permit a private assembly to arrogate to itself the power of an organized body, or allow any subject of the Emperor or king to step forward, either as the leader of such a body, or as its organ; it concluded by saying that the step taken was contrary to the established order of things, and Count Andrew Zamoyski would have to answer for it to his sovereign.

The authorities had misconstrued the fact; they regarded Count Zamoyski as the instigator of the address, and resolved to put a stop to a manifestation which they considered dangerous to the public peace. The Grand Duke sent for and questioned him on the subject, and he replied that there was now no address in existence; but he produced the copy, and stated the circumstances as they occurred. The Grand Duke replied, he must refer the matter to the Emperor, whom he desired Count Zamoyski to see. He added that the Count was not to consider himself under arrest, but that he wished him immediately to repair to St. Petersburg and explain his conduct to his sovereign. In the existing state of the country, the Grand Duke declined to assume any responsibility in the matter.

A few days later, an interview between the Count and the Emperor took place; the former explained at length his view of the requirements of his country, and its present condition, as well as his own conduct. He was listened to with attention and consideration; but the audience was closed by the Emperor intimating to Count Zamoyski that in the present disturbed state of public affairs he thought it desirable that the Count should travel abroad for a short period, until the popular agitation had calmed down, and his presence could be permitted without danger of treasonable manifestations being provoked.

This act has in Poland been widely attributed to the influence of the Marquis Wielopolski, and the same spirit seems to have animated it that subsequently prompted the conscription. At this time Count Andrew Zamoyski was the avowed head of the resident proprietors of Poland. He and other members of his family enjoyed great estates and the inheritance of an illustrious name. He was one of those who believed the regeneration of his country would be better effected by industrial than political means. In all questions, therefore, by which industry could be developed or agriculture improved he took a leading part; and while, on the one hand, he organized and was principal proprietor of the steamboats which plied upon the Vistula, on the other he had introduced great improvements on his own estates, and endeavoured to assimilate the condition of his peasants to that of the class of small tenant farmers in our own country. His tendencies were indeed so greatly in favour of our civil and political institutions that he was at one time known as " the English Count." With the exception of his connection with the Agricultural Society, he does not appear to have taken part in any of the more violent proceedings of the disaffected parties, and in his great estates and easy temperament the Government had efficient guarantee for his not allowing himself to be involved in treasonable practices. He was by force of circumstances placed in antagonism to the Marquis Wielopolski, and if he had been ambitious of political distinction, there was a great field open for him. The mob who hurrahed for " Zamoyski, the first nobleman of Poland," only echoed the popular sentiment, and he could easily have given direction to any national movement. His disposition, however, was not adventurous, his views were conservative, and if, instead of intriguing for his exile, the Marquis Wielopolski had endeavoured to enlist his active aid in the service of the crown, he might have gained an adherent whose active assistance could perhaps have prevented the subsequent outbreak of the insurrection.

His compulsory withdrawal gave an apparent advantage to

the Marquis Wielopolski; there was now no rival to contend with him for power, or to thwart the development of his plans. The nameless masses had no leader; the unruly nobles had lost their chief, and, high in the confidence of his sovereign, with a distinct policy and unbending will, the future of Poland was apparently in his grasp.

These advantages were dearly won. The dismissal of Count Zamoyski brought the Marquis face to face with the revolution. Its unbridled passions, its tireless exertions, its unscrupulous mendacity, and its assassin zeal were no longer under any control. The nobles, who could have checked its excesses had they been united, were now without a head; counsels of timidity and rashness alternately swayed them; the conservative influences of property and rank were paralyzed; and though the Marquis ruled, it was over a disaffected land, which he governed by the power of the Russian sword.

CHAPTER VII.

Revolutionary Press.—Plan of an Insurrection.—Increase of Agitation in Western Provinces.—Demonstration at Wilna.—Repressive Action of Government.—Celebrations at Kovno, and throughout Lithuania.—General Disaffection.—Wavering Policy of General Nazimoff.—Its Effects.

THE revolutionary press was gradually increasing in violence, and in the autumn of this year it began to draw comparisons between the relative strength of Russia and Poland; everything pointed to the determination of the party of action quickly to risk the struggle upon which it had so rashly resolved. One of the articles which appeared about this time will serve to show the nature of the views it held out to its dupes. It affirmed that Poland could bring 500,000 men into the field; she contained, it alleged, 22,000,000 inhabitants, of whom 4,500,000 were men between the ages of eighteen and forty-five; half of these might be roused to revolt, by which means upwards of 2,000,000 recruits would be obtained. Selecting from them those only who were familiar with the use of arms, 100,000 would be ready to take the field, and of these 50,000 would form the active army, while the others would constitute an army of reserve. With such materials any enemy might be baffled; but the means by which this force was to be kept in the field and how it was to be fed and clothed were subjects upon which no suggestion was offered. It being, however, evident that these troops must be armed, the author was upon this point more explicit, for he stated that they must provide themselves with axes, lances, scythes, and oaken sticks, and endeavour to seize the weapons which their enemies possessed.

The number of Russians, Austrians, and Prussians (for the 22,000,000 inhabitants included Galicia and Posen) which might be brought into the field against the insurgents was stated at 360,000 men only.

Rules of action were laid down for the insurgents, which appear to have been subsequently acted upon. Thus it is recommended that some time before the breaking out of the rebellion the country should be agitated by false news, that proclamations should be circulated, that disorders should be created in the towns, and religious celebrations organized in the villages. As soon as the revolt began, the civil and military functionaries were to be seized, and the lodgings of officers and the barracks of soldiers attacked when part of them were absent or asleep. This attempt we shall find was made on the night of the 22nd January, 1863.

In the villages the revolt was to be organized by the landowners, who were to send unarmed men into the towns to win partisans there. In the towns a local militia was to be embodied and drilled.

To obtain arms, the insurgents were to place themselves in ambuscade and assail soldiers passing alone or in very small detachments. If the attack failed, recourse must be had to flight, arms must be thrown away, and any one who happened to be captured must deny having fired, and ascribe his flight to his terror at hearing the shot. The authorities would thus be compelled to release him or punish by death an unarmed man, who would be pronounced innocent by the public voice, and such a judicial murder would serve the cause of the insurrection.

The events at Warsaw were ably taken advantage of by the leaders of the insurrection. On the Continent and in England the press teemed with accusations against Russia, and every endeavour was made so to excite public opinion against her as to insure the intervention of the great powers of Europe.

In the Western provinces,* where, as already stated, the educated classes are all Poles by birth or sympathy, the revolutionary propaganda met with rapid success. It was impossible that a contest so strikingly commenced, and which was so deeply interesting to every individual of their race, should be viewed by them with indifference.

* This and the following pages are partly a translation of a secret state paper of the Russian Government, the accuracy of which is undoubted.

A feverish excitement pervaded the public mind, and this excitement was specially remarkable in the Polish youth. A sullen haughtiness was observable in their bearing towards the Russians; there was a strained attention to events passing in Poland, an anxious watching for tidings from thence, and an ill-concealed triumph at the success which had attended the opposition in the first conflict with the Government.

The leaders of the movement availed themselves of the excited state of public feeling, and redoubled their endeavours to inflame the popular passion; they deluged the country with the revolutionary proclamations of Mieroslawski and Czartoryski; they exhorted the inhabitants to oppose the authorities, to sympathize with the movement, and to emulate the scenes of Warsaw; they required them to devote a certain portion of their income to the liberation of their fatherland from the yoke of the stranger, and they insisted on the necessity of a good understanding with the peasants and the lower orders, that all classes might harmoniously work together in opposition to the Government.

The results of this agitation were quickly visible. Funds were transmitted through secret channels to the foreign leaders of the movement, mourning and emblems of national grief came gradually into use; revolutionary verses, speeches, and proclamations of every kind soon made their appearance, evidently the work of moveable as well as secret presses.

Political demonstrations multiplied. They were expressed by funeral services for the victims who fell at Warsaw; by chanting patriotic hymns in churches; by the celebration of anniversaries commemorative of the principal events and of the leaders of former revolutions in Poland; by noisy and numerous processions; by disrespect to the authorities and disobedience to their orders; and by insults to the military.

These manifestations were accompanied by the continuous raising of funds for treasonable purposes, by the increased activity of the secret press, and by the systematic efforts of the educated classes to draw the people closer to them, with the evident object of destroying the loyalty of the latter by placing a hostile interpretation on those legislative acts of the Government in which their interests were involved.

These efforts to secure an unaccustomed popularity in some localities induced members of the higher classes of society to mix in crowds of the lower orders; ladies were seen to dance with drunken or only half-sober peasants,* and gentlemen with peasant women. In such cases mourning was replaced by the most vivid colours. On separating, the common people were presented with revolutionary verses, songs, and hymns, and with emblems of grief, to be thereafter constantly worn. There were instances, also, of tumultuous and numerous gatherings, prepared with such ostentatious manifestations of violent intent as to force the conclusion on the Government, that the ill-affected desired to drive them into shedding blood, and thus arouse the people.

One of the demonstrations about this time was produced by the stay of Count Andrew Zamoyski in the neighbourhood of Grodno. The crowd, assembled on his departure, took off their hats, threw bouquets of flowers, and shouted "Hurrah for Zamoyski, the first nobleman of Poland."

Demonstrations continued to be made during May, June, and July in the governments of Wilna, Kovno, Grodno, and Minsk.

These demonstrations consisted generally in funeral services, mourning, and national dresses. On the 8th (20th) of May, however, the festival of St. Stanislaus, the patron saint of one

---

* Among the efforts made by the nobility to win the sympathy of their inferiors, the following incident has been recorded. Count Zichchavitch, a young man of large property near Wilna, desired to enact there the part so successfully played in Warsaw by Count Andrew Zamoyski, and he left his pedestal to make visits to shoemakers and tailors, and invited them to his splendid dwelling.

The young count paid a visit to a tailor, took him into his carriage, and drove him to his mansion, in order to introduce him to the Countess.

When they entered the splendid hall, filled with servants in livery, the latter rushed to their master to assist in taking off his overcoat; but he waved them away, and pointed to his honoured guest. The servants stopped in amazement and vacantly stared at the tailor, and the Count was compelled to repeat his order.

The servants would stand it no longer: "How," said one of them, "are we to help a fellow who is just such a servant as ourselves? But last week he sat a whole hour in this passage, waiting the orders of your Excellency."

of the Catholic churches in Wilna, the church was crowded. The bishop was performing the service when he was suddenly interrupted by singing among the congregation. The national hymn was sung by five youths, while a friend accompanied them upon the organ: the hymn was repeated several times. On the congregation leaving the church, the five singers were arrested. Immediately after the arrest, some twenty women besieged the palace, saw the General-Governor, and demanded the release of the prisoners.

The five young men who had been arrested were students from Warsaw, sent from thence to instruct the people of Wilna in the national hymn. Previously to the manifestation in the church, several meetings took place in private houses, where the intended proceeding was discussed. The majority were entirely opposed to the scheme, for they anticipated but too accurately its fatal issue; old men implored their juniors not to embark in it; but violent counsels were advocated by women and priests, and the young men were misled by them.

On the day following the arrest, crowds of people assembled in the Ostro Brama street; they consisted principally of women, schoolboys, and young men. The crowd knelt down and sung a hymn; then all the women, clad in deep mourning, marched through the steep and narrow street to the palace of the Governor; the men walked at their side, but did not otherwise mingle in the manifestation. This black mass surrounded the palace, and about a hundred entered it. The doors leading to the great hall were then closed; the ladies who were admitted were mostly of the better class, such as tenants of houses, governesses, and wives of proprietors. For some time they sat in the hall, and then several were called into the Governor's room, and explanations were given. After the conference was ended, they were let out by a side-staircase.

Meanwhile the crowd without became tumultuous, and a detachment of soldiers arrived, together with the fire-engines; their intervention, however, was not required, and after two hours' disturbance the crowd dispersed.

To arrest the progress of these manifestations the Government resorted to energetic measures; but they were taken without any system, only against single individuals and in single instances, and therefore they failed in their aim of securing the permanent tranquillity of the district. Marshals of the nobility who had joined in funeral services for the souls of the slain in Warsaw, were reprimanded by the Emperor; some of the nobles who had taken an active part in those celebrations were temporarily banished, and a priest who had preached a revolutionary sermon was exiled to Omsk.

These severe measures, coupled with the unceasing prosecution of those who had joined in the demonstrations, for the moment paralyzed the agitation. Occasionally, indeed, individuals were found to commit offences against the Government; but their action was desultory and unsystematic, and resulted from no common principle or connection.

By the month of August the Southern provinces seemed pacified, and the occasional Polish demonstrations which took place there were of little moment. The Governor-General of Kieff so little anticipated immediate troubles (though he was alive to the danger of their recurrence at a future period, from the preponderance of the influence of the Polish nobility in the governments under his charge), that in a report dated so far back as the 4th (16th) of June, 1861, he represented to the Government the necessity for insuring the permanent pacification of the country by developing the Russian element, and sketched out a series of measures involving many considerations, a protracted execution, and a remote result. The Governor-General of Wilna (Nazimoff) was so thoroughly deceived as to the true character of the situation, that he suggested nothing but a few administrative changes for tranquillizing the provinces committed to his care.

The secret police were not so readily deceived, and projects for the establishment of special courts for the trial of political offenders were drawn up and submitted to the Governors of the provinces.

While these reports were yet under consideration, events occurred which proved how great a mistake it was to fancy the lull in the political agitation betokened that the storm had passed away.

On the 31st July, 1569, Lithuania had been united to Poland, and on the anniversary of that day in the year 1861, the leaders of the revolutionary party resolved solemnly to commemorate it. In the town of Rossiny, about forty miles from Kovno, a crowd of young men and women took down some banners from the walls of one of the churches, formed themselves into a procession, and, singing patriotic and revolutionary songs, proceeded to a cross near the town on the road to Kovno, performed their devotions there, and then returned.

At Kovno a demonstration of a more important character took place. This town lies on the Lithuanian bank of the Niemen, which here divides that province from the kingdom of Poland. Although the Polish element in the government of Kovno is not numerous, forming, indeed, not three per cent. of the entire population, it will be seen by the tables in the Appendix that there is in this province a vast preponderance of Roman Catholics; the Letts, who make up the bulk of the people, being here almost universally of that persuasion, and therefore much under the influence of their educated co-religionists, and particularly of the Roman Catholic clergy.

Kovno was certainly an appropriate spot for the intended celebration. The Russians had often admitted their claim to the kingdom of Poland to be one of conquest or of treaty; they had ever allowed that the Poles were an alien and a hostile race; of late they had spoken in a hesitating manner of the justice, or even expediency, of holding the kingdom in their grasp, and it seemed to require but little persuasion to induce them to relax it.

But Lithuania they asserted was their own. Carrying back their researches through long ages of contested history, they alleged that the records of the past were the best title-deeds to this recent acquisition; they claimed Lithuania as formerly Russian, and as wrung from them when that country was ruled over by a turbulent nobility.

The Poles, on the other hand, contended that Lithuania was theirs; that the Russian theory of their original title was inconsistent with fact, and would be immaterial even if true, and that while the Lettic preponderated over the Russ and the Polish element, so far as numbers were concerned, the sympathy which existed between the Roman Catholic races established the equitable title of the Poles beyond all question or dispute.

This place then was a spot well chosen by the Poles for proving that the sympathies of Lithuania were with them rather than with their opponents, and they arranged that a procession similar to that at Rossiny should take place on the same day, and that it should consist both of the inhabitants of Kovno in Lithuania, and of those of the village of Alecot, in the government of Augustino, on the Polish side of the Niemen.

The authorities, desirous of avoiding a contest which might probably involve loss of life, withdrew the floating bridge which connects Kovno and Alecot, and placed a guard, consisting of a platoon of Cossacks and a garrison battalion, along the river.

Nothing daunted by these preparations, a great multitude of both sexes, to the number of about 5,000, collected on the morning of the 31st July at the Augustinian Church in Kovno.

Forming themselves into a long procession, they marched towards the Niemen. They were unarmed, but their banners were blazoned with many a device, and appealed to many a sympathy. High above the enthusiastic throng was carried the sacred cross; around it were clustered standards, images, and every other emblem which could recall the ancient history and triumphs of Poland; while at their head were the pastors of the flock, the zealous and unshrinking priests of the Roman Catholic Church.

Simultaneously another procession sallied forth from the village of Alecot, and also marched to the banks of the Niemen; so now the self-constituted representatives of Poland and Lithuania stood fronting each other, divided only by that broad and rapid stream.

Then both assemblies assisted at the celebration of the mass, and received the blessing of their Church.

The religious ceremony ended, and the crowd on the Kovno side of the river advanced towards the bridge. The scanty guard of Cossacks, unable to contend with the multitude without using their arms, and having no instructions which warranted recourse to so decisive a step, fell back, and the people by their own united efforts began to put up the bridge. Vainly the authorities warned them to desist; they persevered; they declared that at all hazards they would cross the river; they completed their task and accomplished their intention; then, uniting with the assemblage they found on the other side, they proceeded with solemn chants and patriotic hymns to the village of Alecot, and there celebrated the anniversary of the union they desired to restore.

In other parts of the North-western provinces similar commemorations took place, and in many of the churches revolutionary hymns were sung; while, to give additional meaning to them, the ladies who assisted at them, for the time abandoned their mourning, and appeared in brilliant colours, as though in this manner to mark their sense that their dormant nationality was awaking; and the men arrayed themselves in the historical costume of their race.

A few days later a religious ceremony was performed with great solemnity at a church in the district of Lepel. After service, some of the land-owners, dressed in white robes, carried banners round the church, and then the whole congregation fell upon their knees and chanted the revolutionary hymn.

About the same time a report spread through the town of Wilna that a procession was to reach it from the kingdom of Poland, which the inhabitants of the town were to join. Day after day, therefore, a crowd of persons assembled, waiting anxiously the arrival of the expected pilgrims, and repeatedly sung revolutionary hymns over the grave of the patriot Kanarsky.

On the evening of the 7th August a crowd of about 5,000 persons proceeded from the town towards one of the suburbs; they were stopped at the barrier by a company of infantry and two hundred Cossacks. A part of the crowd halted, while the remainder attacked the foot-soldiers with the evident intention of disarming them and passing the barrier.

The women carried paving-stones in their pockets and in the skirts of their dresses, which they gave to the men, who showered them upon the soldiers; the men also broke down a fence and converted the stakes into pikes with which to carry on the struggle. The Cossacks then dispersed the crowd by force, and the people having fled from them, repaired to the sacred gate where the image of the Holy Virgin of Ostrobrama stands; sung before it their supplicatory hymn, repeated it before a crucifix, and then separating, went home.

In this affray several persons were wounded, but none were killed. Nevertheless, in Warsaw, Cracow, Lemberg, and Paris, funeral services were celebrated in honour of the Wilna martyrs, as it was said that numerous persons had been killed and their corpses thrown into the river in order to conceal the fact.

It was singular, in the presence of these demonstrations, to find governors of provinces and men high in authority deceive themselves as to the character of the movement by which they were opposed. To any bystander of ordinary observation it would have been evident that the processions, the commemorations, and the prayers which on all sides were witnessed, were the evidences of wide-spread disaffection to the Russian rule. A statesman trained in the history of constitutional kingdoms would have recognized that there was something deeper agitating the minds of the people than temporary discontent, petulant vanity, or trifling ills. A great man, cognizant of the history of Poland for the last hundred years, would have divined that the proudest memories of a high-spirited race had been desecrated, their most cherished institutions trampled in the dust, and their hopes for the future cruelly marred by a long period of grinding oppression.

There comes, to nations and to men alike, a time when every hope in the justice or the mercy of those placed in authority above them perishes; when, sick and worn out with a prolonged series of injuries, hope fades utterly away in the dulled and broken heart, and, weary with prayers that are not answered, and representations that meet with no redress, the spirit, thrown back upon itself, will darkly ponder, and resolve to win by force the justice that monarchs and governments refuse.

Thus it had been with the Polish race: there may have been much of intrigue and much of the machinery of modern agitation in the scenes I have chronicled; but below that degrading surface there lay a profound national sentiment; the thoughts may have been stirred into action by agitation, but they had existed for many years, and when the stern hand of Nicholas, who alone had curbed them, was removed, it was natural that those stifled feelings should find vent.

Nor let us too severely blame them for the moment they selected. True, they saw in the Emperor Alexander a prince whose policy was diametrically opposed to that of his predecessor; they witnessed his emancipation of the serfs and his advances in the path of constitutional freedom; but in none of those things, desirable though they were, did the Pole see any approach to the realization of his favourite dreams. On the other hand, he saw Russia in the throes of a social revolution; he heard wild theories of all kinds discussed, and he thought the great empire was doomed to fall a sacrifice to her own internal feuds. He believed, therefore, it was better to strike for independence than to speculate on the effect of liberal institutions or the result of a social revolution.

The very spread of the liberal movement made it his interest to act with promptitude; the only hold he had on the wavering allegiance of the serfs was the institution of servitude which that movement threatened to destroy; and if it were once destroyed, he well knew his power would be gone; for they differed from him in language, in race, and above all, for the most part, in religion.

The effect of enfranchisement would necessarily be to destroy all connection in the nature of master and servant between the two classes, and to turn the thoughts and the hopes of the peasants exclusively to the Russian Government instead of their existing lords.

The Pole knew too well that no love existed between himself and the serf over whom he tyrannized, to be deceived into putting the smallest trust in him when once his shackles were unbound, and he was driven, therefore, into immediate action, while a chance yet remained that he could array a numerous and ignorant population in hostility to the Government.

Nevertheless these manifestations of disaffection so widely spread through the Western provinces, do not seem to have roused the governors to whom they were committed to a sense of the peril surrounding them, and at a council held about this time, General Nazimoff appears to have confined himself to pointing out some minor grievances of the Roman Catholic Church, and suggesting their removal.

The Imperial Government, however, were more alive to the perils which they ran, and, after a full discussion, the following, among others of less importance, were the resolutions agreed to.

That the number of troops in the North-western provinces should be increased; that the dangerous classes should be disarmed, and the possession of arms (after a certain time had been given for their rendition) should be treated as an offence; and that political demonstrations and gatherings should be forbidden. That the clergy favouring demonstrations in churches, and the leaders of such demonstrations, should be arrested. That special commissions for the trial of political offences should be constituted and temporary police courts opened. That untrustworthy officials should be removed and tried. That, where requisite, districts should be proclaimed in a state of siege, and be placed under the command of military governors.

These various measures were promptly carried into effect, and certain regulations were published for lightening the burdens of the peasants, in order probably to bind up their interests more closely with those of the Government. But these measures had scarcely any other than an existence upon paper, for the police and the administration in the Western provinces were in the hands of the Polish nobility and petty employés, who were also Poles, and who in most cases were not only indifferent to the interests of the Government, but who even in secret favoured the agitation.

Events now rapidly developed themselves. On the 9th August, General Nazimoff telegraphed to the Emperor in the Crimea that the Western provinces were tranquil. On the 24th a state of siege was already proclaimed by him in Wilna, Grodno, and four other towns, and in the whole province of Kovno, with the exception of one district.

In the province of Kioff, the town of Jitomir was declared in a state of siege at the end of September, and about the same time the population of the South-western provinces was disarmed.

The adoption of these measures was due to the continuance of the political demonstrations. On the night of the 20th September, in the cathedral square of the town of Jitomir, a black cross was erected, with the inscription, "To the memory of the Poles murdered in 1861." The cross was removed by the police, but a turbulent crowd led by ladies demanded its restoration, and a company of infantry and gendarmes was called out, which dispersed the people.

Although the declaration of a state of siege for a short time checked the outward signs of disaffection, the condition of affairs was in truth but little altered; mourning was everywhere seen; the national costume was everywhere worn, and on all sides the youth of Polish origin took part in political demonstrations, and closely leagued themselves with the leaders of the revolt.

The measures of repression adopted by the Government became more numerous and severe. The Agricultural Society at Kieff was dissolved; the Governor-General of that province was authorized to dismiss functionaries in all branches of the public service; to constitute commissions for trying prisoners by martial law; and to expel from the university such Polish students as identified themselves with political demonstrations. In the North-western provinces General Nazimoff was authorized to remove even the marshals of the nobility in districts declared in a state of siege. A military governor was appointed in Minsk, owing to the increase of disorders in that province; the nobility elections in various provinces were from time to time postponed; a special house-tax was laid on the Roman Catholic proprietors of Wilna; penalties were imposed on persons guilty of political disturbances; and a considerable number were deported to places of residence within the empire, more or less remote.

But there was, for the reasons already stated, a want of system in the acts of the legislative Government, and a variance in the mode of executing the law in different districts, which to a great extent deprived measures, rigorous only in sound, of their intended efficacy. The judgments of the courts-martial were often not carried into execution; the disaffected, whether priests or proprietors, were banished for a prolonged period to a distant province, and a few weeks or months afterwards, the banishment was ended, at the will of the Governor of the province where the offence was committed. When the Minister of the Interior proposed to General Nazimoff the banishment of certain priests who had taken part in funeral services for assassins executed in Warsaw, the worthy man replied that banishment was attended with considerable expense for post-horses, and that it would be far cheaper to select a few monasteries, where such men could be sent under surveillance! The instructions of the Minister to the police courts were not acted upon; he desired that prosecutions should be instituted, not for the singing of revolutionary hymns, but for compelling others to do so, or insulting them if they refused; and that where irregularities were committed in the procedures in those courts, the superior tribunals should be appealed to. Instead of obeying these orders, prosecutions were constantly set on foot for singing hymns in churches, and, no matter how inefficiently the police courts acted, appeals were but rarely made. Under these circumstances, there ceased to be any cordiality between the Minister at St. Petersburg and the provincial governors; the administration of the law was confused, and its penalties unequally dealt; while the unknown disturbers of the tranquillity of the country encouraged their partisans to persevere, not only in their secret organization, but occasionally in open demonstrations.

I have said that the proclamation of a state of siege was followed temporarily by a diminution of the outward signs of disaffection; this, however, was not the sole cause of this change. Winter was at hand, and the season for out-door processions and public meetings was passing away; in some minds there was growing up a weariness of demonstrations which led to no result save occasional punishment; and the leaders of the popular faction discouraged the longer maintenance of this agitation.

The revolutionary proclamations now advised the discontinuance of further demonstrations; enough had been done by the people of Lithuania and the South-western provinces to prove to Europe their fixed determination to throw off the Russian yoke, and to be united as of old to Poland, when the day of her resurrection should dawn. Now it only remained for them to watch their opportunity; Italy or Hungary would ere long be in arms, or Russia herself be torn in pieces by her own revolutionary parties. Meanwhile there was work to do. The rural population were to be won over to the national cause; the love for Poland, her traditions, her history and her monuments, should, by education, be instilled into the lower orders, and the popular mind should be elevated, with a view to prepare for the struggle and the sacrifices of the future.

The priests at the confessional instructed the people to commit perjury at the police courts, and actively instigated them to counteract the views of the Government.

The proprietors secretly consulted together as to the possibility, by territorial sacrifices, of winning over the people to their cause, and extensively instituted schools for their education, in which the Polish language was alone to be used.

Revolutionary sheets and proclamations in all shapes and in every local dialect were circulated by unknown hands. They were scattered upon the roads; they were left at houses; they were sent through the post; but not one of the distributors was ever discovered. There was a close and evident concert between the North and South-western provinces; whatever was done in the one was forthwith known in the other. From the shores of the Baltic to the banks of the Dniester there was manifested the same general impatience of the Russian yoke; the same memories were invoked, the same anniversaries were commemorated, and the same signs of mourning were everywhere to be seen.

Whenever there was an opportunity of making known their wishes to their sovereign, the proprietors took advantage of it. The nobility of White Russia showed a wish to be united with Lithuania, on condition that the Lithuanian statute should be restored and the Polish language officially recognized; the Polish language also was proposed to be used in a Land-bank intended to be established for the North-western provinces; and at the provincial assembly of the nobles of Podolia an address to the Emperor was agreed on, asking the separation of all the western Ukraine from the administrative unity of the Empire, and its union with Poland.

CHAPTER VIII.

Conflicting Views of the various parties among the Poles.—The Conscription.—Outbreak of Insurrection.—Massacres.—Despatches from the Consul-General at Warsaw.—Proclamation of the Central Committee.—Conduct of the Proprietors.—Revolutionary " Order of the Day."—Attempt to poison the Marquis Wielopolski.

At the beginning of the year 1863 there was a great difference in the views of the two branches of the revolutionary party in Poland. The "unarmed agitation" had lasted for more than two years, attracting, doubtless, considerable attention in Europe, but practically producing no definite result. This agitation had succeeded in reviving a very strong national feeling; it had excited the minds of the youth of the country, by recalling the remembrance of past history and sacrifices; it had influenced the population of the towns by spreading among them vague hopes of great advantages to be derived by throwing off the Russian yoke; it had enlisted on its side the petty nobles who thronged the towns and villages, and who were also scattered in no inconsiderable numbers throughout the country.

The materials for a future insurrection were thus prepared, and the question arose, What use was to be made of them? Now that the weapon was ready for the conflict, was it to be employed, or was it to be hung upon the wall for an indefinite period, till time and rust had worn away its edge and deprived it of its power?

It was an anxious question, and one which was differently answered by those who had something, and by those who had nothing, to lose.

The great nobles trembled for their estates; they called to mind the bitter recollections of 1830, the spoliations that had resulted from that unhappy struggle, and feared a repetition of those scenes of confiscation and bloodshed. It was well for "the party of action" to endeavour to goad the people into a revolt, but what had the party of action to lose? Those men had no great estates on which the vultures might fatten when the strife was done; they had no proud ancestral names which disaster would for ever obliterate; they had no stake and no influence in the country, and would never be missed if they fell in the strife they were so anxious to precipitate. But it was fit that the nobles of Poland should be prudent, and not insanely throw away their chances of independence at the bidding of political adventurers; it was their province to watch and wait, and to take advantage of the first event which offered a reasonable prospect of success.

The history of Europe for the last fifteen years was full of hope for them; in that short period how much had been done to shake despotic power, and to secure freedom for those who had patience to wait a favourable moment, as well as valour to take advantage of it! There were complications of all kinds on the Continent; many wars seemed impending, and the moment one was commenced, Poland might have her opportunity. It would be madness now, while Europe was tranquil, to defy the power of Russia, and to rush into a struggle with her without preparation and without an ally.

The Republican party denounced this reasoning as mistaken and cowardly. What is it that you fear? they asked: the army of Russia is weakened by six years' neglect; it is demoralized by recent changes,—the abolition of corporal punishment, its loss of respect for its officers, and many other causes; the Russian Government dare not trust it, it knows how deep-seated is the disaffection which pervades it, and it knows, among the officers it is compelled to employ, that opinions the most liberal and the most hostile to itself are widely prevalent. Again, they urged, look at the political condition of Russia, and it is evident she is herself in the agonies of dissolution; the addresses of her nobility, the clamours of her liberal press, the disaffection which is everywhere apparent, clearly demonstrate it; far from wishing to curb our liberties, she is intent upon extending her own, and she will hold out a helping hand to us, because in our freedom she will see some guarantee for her own enfranchisement. If additional evidences were required of the condition of Russia, the outbreak among the students at the various universities, the incendiary fires with which St. Petersburg had been lighted up, some laxity of discipline which had been punished at the military schools, and finally the alleged existence of a "Revolutionary Committee of Russia," were cited as the near and sufficient evidence of the correctness of these extreme views.

While these different opinions were in agitation, and while it was yet uncertain whether violent or moderate councils would prevail, the act of the Government turned the scale, and precipitated the long-pending insurrection.

Since the conclusion of the peace, there had been a suspension of the conscription both in Russia and Poland, and the army had been weakened to an extent which was deemed imprudent. It was determined to have recourse to a levy, and the number of men to be raised in Poland was about 8,000.

From the year 1815, the mode in which conscriptions were carried out in Poland* had been exceptional and arbitrary. Instead of being chosen by lot, the recruits had been selected by the police, who in their selection had been influenced almost entirely by political considerations. Year after year the most high-spirited, or, as the authorities deemed them, the most insubordinate of the youth of Poland, had been draughted into the Russian army; and thus the conscription was converted into a political engine for weeding the country of its dangerous classes.

The conscription having been suspended for five years, during which period a strong national feeling had evidenced itself, it was naturally to be expected that an unusual number of the youth of the country would be found on the black list of the police; and the conscription would thus offer to the authorities a welcome opportunity of ridding themselves of their enemies.

But in the year 1859 a law had been passed abolishing the old system, and introducing a new one, under which future

* The system in Russia has hitherto been for the landowner to nominate the conscripts. The most idle and worthless among the serfs have, therefore, habitually been selected; but, consequent upon emancipation, the ordinary system of ballot has been introduced.

levies were to be made. By this law conscripts were in future to be chosen in the ordinary way by lot.

Unfortunately for his own fame, and most disastrously for his country, the Marquis Wielopolski resolved that the old system should be adopted, and the law of 1859 be ignored. He saw at a glance the power it would place in his hands; he failed to see the loss of popularity, confidence, and respect a course so illegal must infallibly entail. He knew there were extensive preparations for an insurrection, and he knew that a large number of young men, not of the lowest class, were mixed up in it; he knew also that they were not quite ready for a rising, and that the act he meditated would either break the power of the party of action, by subtracting its most active adherents from its ranks, or precipitate a struggle, which he foresaw must come, sooner or later, but for which that party was at present unprepared.

There was nothing in the details of this proceeding to lessen the gross injustice of its conception. The Marquis resolved that, with the exception of 2,000, all the conscripts should be levied from the town populations, because it was among the town population that the most active of the revolutionary party were to be found. The workmen and the lower orders were not to be affected by it; they possessed no political power or significance, and it was well that they should entertain a friendly feeling towards the Government; but the higher class of mechanics and artisans, the shopkeepers, the Schlachta, and lesser nobility, were marked out as fit objects for selection, and wherever an individual of these classes was regarded as disaffected, his name was certain to appear on the list of the conscription.

This plan of the Marquis Wielopolski was received with great disfavour; it was felt that the law of 1859 should be adhered to; that the act he proposed to perpetrate possessed no political advantages which could atone for its cruelty and injustice, and that it would entail on the heads of the Administration an amount of odium which would increase tenfold the power of the revolutionary party. The Marquis, however, persevered; he considered, as the head of the civil administration of the kingdom, as a Pole thoroughly conversant with the condition of his country and the character of his countrymen, that he was the proper person to judge of the expediency of the step to be now adopted. He pressed its acceptance upon the Grand Duke and the Emperor, and finding them unwilling to adopt it, he offered to resign his offices. Under pressure of the determined course adopted by the Marquis, the Government gave way, and resolved that the conscription should be conducted on the old principle.

The necessary lists were prepared by the police; but they were purposely kept secret, in order to prevent the escape of those who were named in them, and it was resolved that the conscripts should be seized at the dead of night, without warning given. The number to be obtained in Warsaw was 2,000; the population of the city was from 150,000 to 180,000.

Meanwhile the Central Committee, an anonymous body who assumed to govern the revolutionary parties, adopted a defiant attitude. It declared that it had at its disposal the means of resisting the Government, and that insurmountable difficulties would in due time be opposed to this measure being carried into effect. It also issued a circular, which was sent to the various local authorities throughout the kingdom, threatening with vengeance and summary punishment any person in the employment of Government, or any magistrate, who should assist in carrying out the recruitment.

At this time the system of terror, which at a later date was carried to perfection, had already been inaugurated. A man named Abicht, who was travelling with an English passport, having been denounced to the police by the Jewish waiter at an inn where he was staying, was arrested. The Jew applied on three successive days at the Treasury for a reward of 200 roubles, which he had been promised, and on the third day, on leaving the office of the Paymaster-General, he was stabbed by an emissary of the revolutionary committee.

On the night of the 14th of January the conscription in Warsaw was effected. The conscripts were seized by the authorities without any resistance or disturbance, and to all appearance the Government had effected their purpose and paralyzed the party of revolt.

This momentary triumph, however, lasted a very short time, and on the 19th Colonel Stanton, the English Consul-General in Warsaw, while writing to Lord Russell and announcing the entire success of the conscription, states: "Unfortunately a number of working men and others belonging to the secret societies, have been induced to assemble not far from this town, in obedience to the orders given them by the chiefs of the movement. Their numbers are, however, not supposed to amount to more than 500 or 600, the greater portion of whom are unarmed. . . . The weakness of the ultra party, and the impossibility of their resisting the Government, will, at least, be clearly demonstrated by this foolish attempt, and I believe, my lord, it is not too much to anticipate that the Polish movement will now shortly be brought to an end, and the country resume, if not a peaceful attitude, at least one of comparative quiet and freedom from revolutionary attempts."

Three days from the date of this letter the insurrection in Poland had commenced.

The Russian authorities had made no preparations to guard against a possible outbreak. When the conscription was decided on, the Grand Duke had been advised by several military officers of high standing to concentrate the troops, which were quartered in small detachments through the kingdom, as is usually done when danger is anticipated. The advice, however, was rejected, for the Marquis Wielopolski positively affirmed that no danger existed, and that no revolt would take place.

The insurgents alluded to in Colonel Stanton's letter were more numerous than he imagined. They consisted of two bands, one on either side of the Vistula, and were composed not only of the classes named by him, but of some of the townspeople who were named in the conscription, and who, having been warned in time, escaped it. They thought no fate could be worse than to swell the ranks of the Russian army, and preferred struggling for freedom on the plains of Poland to suffering years of unrequited toil in the Caucasus or Siberia. Bodies of troops were sent against these parties with the intention of surrounding and capturing them before they could unite; but the effort failed. The bands united, and retired in safety to the shelter of the vast forests that extend in this neighbourhood for a distance of more than sixty miles.

Simultaneously with the appearance of these rebel bands, two others appeared in the neighbourhood of Serotsk and Pultusk, against which troops were also sent.

These disorders were not regarded as the prelude to a serious insurrection. The Government continued to deceive themselves as to the state of popular feeling. They forgot, although the assembling of bands might not have been planned by the party of action, that it was most improbable they would fail to take advantage of them now that they were collected, and that in the then exasperated state of feeling in Poland it was only natural that men committed to an act of rebellion should quickly find leaders and organization. The violent and unconstitutional character of the conscription gave that stimulus to the national feeling which the Red Republicans had striven in vain to create. It enabled them to overpower the more moderate party, and it set fire to all the elements of mischief and revolution which had for so long a period been carefully collecting. Nothing was more easy than to persuade the town populations that there was now no security for them under the Russian sway; that one arbitrary measure would assuredly be followed by another, until the whole of the Polish youth had been kidnapped and carried away.

Moreover, this act of the Government was an excuse in the eyes of Europe for whatever the revolutionists might do. Insurrection, which was criminal without a cause, became right and just and holy when it vindicated personal freedom as well as national independence. The organs of the Emigration filled the world with exaggerated statements of an act which in itself was sufficiently reprehensible; imaginary scenes were portrayed of Polish sufferings and Muscovite barbarities; horrible details were invented by unscrupulous and rhetorical scribes; and a deed of arbitrary injustice, which had been carried out with perfect order* and tranquillity, was represented

---

* See letter of Colonel Stanton (already quoted) of 19th January, 1863.—No. 4 of Correspondence respecting the Insurrection in Poland, 1863, presented to both Houses of Parliament.

in colours worthy only of the persecutions of Alva, or the wildest excesses of a sanguinary war.

The ultra party took advantage of this great opportunity; they saw in it an invaluable apology for rushing to arms; they believed the more moderate leaders of the Emigration and the great resident proprietors must in time unite with them; from the one quarter they looked for the ultimate intervention of foreign powers; the other they reckoned upon for more immediate and substantial aid. The Emigration could hardly refuse to countenance them, for if they did, it would be an acknowledgment that they were unable to control the people they had long professed to govern, and then the influence they possessed in the great capitals of Western Europe would die out, and they would be powerless for evil or for good. The great proprietors could not for long refuse to unite with them, for they would certainly be objects of suspicion to the Russians; they would assuredly be subjected to the most close and jealous espionage, and be consigned to a state prison, and have their property sequestrated, the first moment the authorities chose to question their loyalty. Was it not, therefore, to be assumed that they would throw off the mask, and give in their avowed adhesion to a cause which was really theirs?

The first act of the revolutionary party was to organize an attack on the various Russian detachments scattered through the kingdom. These detachments were generally weak in number, and unprepared for any outbreak; and although their destruction might not, in a military point of view, be very important, the insurgents calculated on the moral effect it would produce among a peasantry who were almost certain to side with whichever party they thought the stronger. It is probable also that the arms, accoutrements, military stores, and treasure in the possession of the troops were a great temptation to the badly-armed, ill-provided, and impoverished levies which formed the army of the National Government.

The intended outbreak was entirely unlooked-for by the Russians: they believed the scattered bands which were being followed by the regular troops were the only enemies they had to fear; and, wrapped in a false and perilous security, they took no precautions against surprise.

At midnight on the 22nd of January, attacks were simultaneously made in all the provinces of the kingdom upon the Russian troops, with the intention of overcoming them by force of arms where they resisted, and of murdering them in cold blood where they could be surprised. It is alleged that, wherever they had the opportunity, the insurgents assailed the soldiers in their beds, and massacred them. In general, however, though unprepared for these assaults, the soldiers successfully repulsed them. In the town of Plock, a band of 1,500 insurgents attacked the forces that were stationed there; but after an action which lasted some hours, they failed to make any impression, and retreated, leaving some forty prisoners in the hands of their enemies. The attacks made in other places were, for the most part, less important, and in almost every instance they were repulsed with loss. The village of Stock, near Siedlee, however, was the theatre of one of those occurrences which envenomed this struggle from its very commencement, and led to its subsequent prosecution in a spirit of bitterness which was certain to lead to the commission of acts of cruelty and excess. A detachment of soldiers quartered in the village, being assailed by greatly superior numbers, took refuge in a house, in which they barricaded themselves; the insurgents were unable to overcome their resistance by force of arms, so they set fire to the house, and the soldiers were consumed in the flames.

Two companies of soldiers, stationed at Leckoff, were also treacherously murdered. An attack was made on a park of flying artillery at Kohen, and, although it was unsuccessful, the insurgents carried off fifty muskets and the military chest; while at Radsin, Loerbartoff, and Biala, unsuccessful attempts were made by them to seize cannon and ammunition.

In the province of Radom, the insurgents attacked the troops stationed at Szydlowick and Bodzetyn; in the former of these places, Major Rödiger, having a few minutes' notice of the intended assault, withdrew his men from the town, to which he did not return until the following day. At Bodzetyn, however, the insurgents surprised the sleeping soldiers, killed an officer and several men, and set fire to the barrack in which the Russians were defending themselves. Escaping from the flaming building, the troops cut their way through the insurgents, and retreated from the town, which, however, they reoccupied on the following day.

While these attacks were being made, the insurgents also tore up the rails in several places on the different Polish lines, cut the telegraph wires in all directions, and did everything in their power to impede the movements of the troops, and prevent the Government from taking such measures as might lead to the suppression of the revolt.

When, a day or two afterwards, the Russian troops arrived, for the purpose of reopening the railway and telegraphic communications, there was every sign that the railway officials were implicated in the movement. At the station, where railway carriages and plant were kept in large quantities, they had all been carefully destroyed, and everywhere mischief had been systematically done in the most complete and businesslike manner: at intervals, rails had been removed, and every precaution had been taken to render the march of the troops slow and difficult. At length the road was repaired, and a train sent from Wilna to convey the troops. As a measure of precaution, the engine was from time to time sent on in advance of the train, to test the safety of the line before the carriages were trusted to it. The train had left a station some miles behind it, the next station was many miles away, and the line, after running perfectly straight for a considerable distance, made a curve which hid it from sight. At this point the engine was again sent on, and as it proceeded slowly, the soldiers followed it with their eyes, and wondered how soon it would return. It reached the curve, and in another moment would be out of sight; when the engineer sprang up, and waving them in mockery a last farewell, departed, and they never saw him or his engine more!

The results of the operations of the night did not fulfil the hopes of the insurgents, or justify the exceptional measures to which they had had recourse. Many soldiers were killed, but not such a number as to tell in the smallest degree on the issue of the struggle which had commenced; on the other hand, the insurgents had been repulsed on almost every side, and had commenced their movement by a systemized attempt at assassination, which had not even the miserable excuse of success to gild the blackness of its cowardice and guilt.

About 300 prisoners were captured by the authorities, and among them were many Roman Catholic priests, who had been taken with the insurgents, whom they were encouraging and leading on; it was also remarked that in many places the church bells had been rung to summon the rebels to arms; "thus proving, were such proof required, the complicity of the priests with the movement."*

On the morning of the 22nd of January, the Central National Committee issued a proclamation addressed to the Polish nation :—

"The Central National Committee," it said, "the only legal government of your country, bids you all appear on the last battle-field—the field of glory and victory, where it pledges itself to give you success before God and heaven; for the committee knows that as you have heretofore been penitents or avengers, so you are ready to become to-morrow heroes and giants of strength. It knows you ready to achieve your liberty and independence by deeds of courage, and to make such sacrifices as no people have yet inscribed on the annals of their history. It knows well that you are ready to give all your blood, your lives, and your freedom, without regret, hesitation, or weakness, as an offering to your rising country.

"In return, the Central Committee promise to wield the sceptre of authority with an unflinching hand, so that your strength shall not be wasted. Your sacrifices shall not be in vain. It will know how to overcome all difficulties, to break through all impediments; it will pursue and punish every disinclination, nay, even every case of want of sufficient zeal in our holy cause, with the utmost severity required from a tribunal which metes out justice in the name of an offended country.

"This being the first day of open resistance, the commencement of the sacred combat, the Committee proclaims all the sons of Poland free and equal, without distinction of creed and condition. It proclaims, further, that the land heretofore held by the agricultural population in fee, for corvée, labour, or for rent, becomes henceforth their freehold property, without any restriction whatsoever. The proprietors will receive compensation from the public treasury. All cottagers and labourers who shall serve, and the families of those who may die in the service of their country, will receive allotments from the national property in land regained from the enemy."

---

* Colonel Stanton to Earl Russell, 25th January, 1863.

From the tenour of this proclamation it is clear that the Central Committee was then the exponent of the views of the "Red" party, which possessed neither means nor organization, and had little more influence than that which the conscription had for the moment given it. Veiling its weakness, it uses a tone of confident authority intended to impress its countrymen, and still more the Western nations, with a conviction of its supreme power. Its promise of protection to the patriot is introduced to heighten, by contrast, the terrors of its threats, and to drive into its ranks a reluctant proprietary who saw no choice between a reign of terror and dumb submission to its will. The last paragraph is a direct bid for the support of the peasantry, on whom it professes to confer property without payment or qualification; it demonstrates that the constitution of the committee must at this time have been thoroughly democratic, for the landed proprietors and the moderate party would never have given their consent to so rash a step.

Startled by this sudden outbreak, the proprietors crowded into Warsaw, and held many anxious consultations. Their position, indeed, was most embarrassing; they were distrusted by the Government, which for many years they had thwarted and opposed, and which knew that their hostility had given its original impetus to the revolutionary movement; no sympathy, therefore, could now exist between them; and even if the Government were disposed to exert itself to the utmost, it was doubtful how far it had the power to protect their persons and estates. They were proclaimed traitors by the Central Committee because they did not join in the national movement; and if they returned to their estates, their personal safety was in peril, for the peasants had long regarded them as their enemies, and the emissaries of the National Government might prompt them to outrage and murder. Their position, then, was anxious and critical: they were numerous, had large estates and many retainers. They had everything to lose by a Red republican revolution, and much to gain by constitutional reforms. But their vast estates gave them little influence, and their conduct deprived them of all personal popularity. Distrusted by the Government, hated by the peasants, regarded with jealousy by the Schlachta, and menaced by the Central Committee, they were surrounded by dangers they had neither the courage to face nor the ability to avoid.

The infatuated conduct they had pursued for two years reacted upon them. They had lent themselves to the schemes of the Red party, they had joined them in stirring up the national feeling till the people were goaded into revolt, and now, brought face to face with an armed insurrection, they feared to encourage, and were unwilling to oppose it.

They should have known that it was madness to goad men into action, and then to pause, to hesitate, to draw back, and to pronounce that they had no policy to pursue; such conduct was sure to throw the revolution into the hands of the violent men whose hatred to the Government was scarcely greater than their jealousy of themselves.

Two courses of action were now open to them; they led in very different directions, but either might have been taken with considerable prospect of success; they required, however, unanimity and courage, and neither was forthcoming.

They might have placed themselves at the head of the insurrection. By doing so they would have incurred great risks, and failure would have been attended with wide-spread ruin; but they would have given enormous strength to the revolutionary cause by committing it to the guidance of men of station and ability, by restraining its sanguinary spirit, and by placing before the world a moderate manifesto of its aims. Had they thus joined the movement, the revolution would have been regarded by foreign courts as a thoroughly national cause, and the chances of European intervention would have been multiplied tenfold. A movement guided by those whose names were recognized as the traditional leaders of their country, and whose adhesion to it was a guarantee for its policy and conduct, would have utterly differed from the Red Republican rising, which was inspired and directed by a nameless band of secret assassins. But why should the great powers of Europe interfere and incur the hazard and the sacrifices of a general war, when the men most deeply interested in the cause for which it would be undertaken shrunk from risking life or property in its prosecution.

On the other hand, the proprietors might have given their frank adhesion to the policy of the Government; they might have recognized its genuine anxiety to increase the liberties and develop the resources of Poland; and they might have pronounced, as the fact was, that they regarded the Red party with detestation and terror. Even a successful revolution, far from improving their position, would only have subjugated them to that dangerous faction; and the few who entertained hopes of the success of the revolt, believed it would be followed by a reign of terror and anarchy before any settled form of government could e rest ored.

Such an adhesion would have been consistent with their interests and their honour. Their leading men, and those best informed among them, were convinced the revolt would not eventually succeed, for they were satisfied that Europe would not intervene. The struggle, therefore, could only lead to ruin; and although they were not loyal to the Russian Government, the most patriotic among them would have deserved well of their country and their class if they had opposed the insurrection to the utmost.

There were, however, among them men of different dispositions and hostile views. The hatred of Russia which some of them felt would have hurried them into the ranks of the insurgents; the Conservative party, on the other hand, would have given in their adhesion to the Government. A large and important section wavered in their views, and favoured an expectant and ambiguous policy, which would have kept up friendly relations with both parties, and pledged them to neither.

Never was there greater want of a leader than at this moment, but none was forthcoming; for Count Andrew Zamoyski, who had alone been recognized as head of the moderate party, and who would almost certainly have done his utmost to preserve the peace of his country, was in exile, his rival was in power, and there was no one to take the place of the absent leader.

There was, also, a patriotic party among the Poles, who

insisted it was not to misgovernment that their struggles for freedom were due; they contended that an intense yearning for national unity and independence animated them, and that if the Russians had ruled them ever so wisely the same contest for freedom would eventually have ensued.

It was useful to point to cruelty and oppression, for by citing examples of these they secured the sympathies, and possibly the assistance of the nations of the West; but the great wrong done them was the partition of their country, and this was the grievance they were determined to redress.

Neither had the conscription ought to do with their revolutionary purposes; it had precipitated the outbreak, for it enabled violent men to summon the country to arms; but that outbreak was premature and unfortunate, it was opposed to the wishes of the White party, and was directly in contradiction to the settled policy of preceding years. The revolutionary committees had for a long time agitated the country, and summoned it to prepare for a great and approaching contest; they had circulated their ideas among all classes, they had won converts on every side, and had laid the deep foundations of opinions which must eventually upheave the supremacy of Russia.

But the struggle would not be one for the restoration of a kingdom defined by arbitrary caprice; it would be waged for the independence of Poland, as Poland was constituted of old,—of every province, town, or village in which Polish nationality was the prevailing element, no matter whether now oppressed by Russian, by Austrian, or by Prussian bayonets.

The insurrection was commenced in the Congress kingdom, because in that portion of ancient Poland the national element had the freest range. In Posen every official, from the governor of a province to the meanest clerk, was German by nation and anti-Polish by sympathy; German was the only language employed in public offices and courts of law, and, with an inconsiderable exception, in schools and colleges. In Galicia somewhat more liberty was apparently given to the Poles, because the peasants were so bitterly hostile to the proprietors, that such liberty could not be abused; the

Galician soldiers who guarded the Austro-Russian frontier were zealous anti-revolutionists, for they regarded the insurgents as the confederates of their late masters, and the natural enemies of the peasantry both in Poland and Galicia.

In the Congress kingdom, however, the Poles had many advantages. Severe as was the Emperor Nicholas, and anxious as he was to blot out their nationality, he yet always discriminated between the Kingdom and the Western provinces. The stipulations of the treaty of Vienna had not been utterly useless, and, though he oppressed the Poles of the Kingdom, their language remained to them, their nobles filled public offices throughout the Russian empire, and in many particulars their nationality was respected. The people, also, were of the race, and shared the religion of the landowners, and it was believed they would rally to the banner of their country when the hour of trial came.

The reforms introduced by the Emperor Alexander had a very different effect from that which the friends of the Poles in Western Europe attributed to them; instead of conciliating the disaffected proprietors, and inducing them to abandon their revolutionary designs, they simply made them more determined to rebel. It had this effect because they thought the substitution of Polish for Russian officials had enormously increased their power over the people, and facilitated all the operations by which an insurrection can be carried on; and because, in the intended settlement of the land question by the Government, they foresaw that their influence would be lessened, and, if the revolutionary movement were long postponed, would be utterly destroyed.

The singular want of political foresight which was the distinguishing characteristic of the Polish proprietors, was nowhere more apparent than in this great error. They should have accepted frankly the reforms introduced; they should themselves have worked the institutions accorded them; they should at an early period have solicited their extension; and, by the lead they took in the conduct of public affairs, have taught the people to recognize in them their natural leaders. In this position, and with the entire body of officials at their call, the kingdom of Poland would rapidly have become the centre of a new and more formidable organization; an organization which would have attracted Posen and Galicia to her, and would probably, in the end, have extorted from Germany and Russia the unity at which it aimed.

An "order of the day" of the revolutionary "chief of the town of Warsaw" was issued on the 4th February, which was couched in the following terms:—" As numbers of landed proprietors, instead of serving their country in their residences, are wasting their time and their money in Warsaw, they are hereby desired to return forthwith to their homes, unless exempted from their obligation by the chief of the town, and to fulfil their duty to their country, more especially those who are young. All functionaries of the organization are to carry out this order." After several meetings, the proprietors, unable to come to any conclusion, separated, and it was understood that each of them was to act as he thought right; many of them returned to their estates, and while they carefully avoided any open act of rebellion, they subscribed largely to the support of the insurrection, and afforded the insurgents all the shelter and aid they could possibly extend to them.

Immediately after the conscription had been carried into effect, the Central Committee had published a proclamation in which it had said, " a system of recruiting like this has never yet been seen. It is worthy of its author, of that great and vile criminal, that traitor to his country, Wielopolski. . . . 'The Wielopolskis,' the father, and his son Sigismund, and all the criminal band who have taken part in the recruitment at Warsaw, together with all those who have up to the present time assisted, or who are about to assist, these wicked attempts at usurpation, shall be outlawed, and it is permitted to every one to judge, and to execute them without incurring any sort of responsibility, either before God or before his country." Within three weeks of the publication of this manifesto, an attempt was made to give effect to the sentence it pronounced; poison was mixed with the provisions that were sent to the house of the marquis, and he, his family, and servants, all partook of it; but the attempt failed, and though it caused much suffering, no deaths resulted from it.

CHAPTER IX.

Excesses of the Insurgents.—Their Position, and Character of their Bands.—Battle of Wengrow.—Progress of Revolt.—Concentration of Russian Troops.

EVERY effort was made by the revolutionary party to continue the struggle. Various bands scattered through the kingdom, harassed the Russians by the guerilla warfare they carried on; the vast forests, and the difficult nature of a great portion of the country they occupied, made it extremely difficult for regular troops to act efficiently against them; and although, when an engagement took place, it almost invariably terminated in favour of the Russians, the dispersed insurgents quickly re-assembled and resumed the offensive. These bands constantly pressed villagers into their service, notwithstanding their unwillingness to take part in the struggle. In many cases they had recourse to violence and even murder to procure recruits, and one instance* may be cited as an example of the terrorism to which they had recourse.

A band of horsemen, under the guidance of a priest, rode towards a village intending to stir up the peasants to revolt. Stopping at the first cottage, and finding the owner of it absent, the priest inquired of his wife where he was to be found. She refused to inform him, and he, in a transport of rage, murdered her by stabbing her with a knife, and then set fire to the dwelling. The peasants thronging to the place, manifested the greatest horror at this unprovoked assassination, and the band, seeing how strong was the popular feeling against them, departed without carrying their intended conscription into effect. Determined to revenge this crime, the villagers sent the following day to the insurgents, to assure them they were ready to join them, if the priest would explain to them what they were to do, and where they were to march. Accord-

---

* See Lord Napier's letter to Earl Russell, 8th February, 1863.

ingly, the priest came; but he had hardly begun to speak, when they attacked and killed him on the spot.

It was by deeds such as these that the insurgents gradually changed the passive dislike with which the peasants regarded them into open enmity, until at length they actively exerted themselves to assist the Government and repress the revolt.

Instances of barbarous cruelties committed by the insurgents upon their prisoners, excited the strongest feelings of horror in the Russian forces. On the night of the 22nd January, fifteen soldiers were hung by the insurgents, after having been first horribly mutilated by them; and it is impossible to wonder, though one deeply may regret, that for some time afterwards the comrades of the murdered men refused to grant quarter to the insurgents, saying, "Remember the 22nd January," as they cut them down.

Another well-authenticated instance of the excesses which inaugurated the revolt, is the case of a soldier who was tied to a tree, his feet and hands were then cut off, and while he was screaming in agony, a cigar was put into his mouth, and he was asked whether he wished to have it lighted.

The events which marked the outbreak of the revolt roused the Government from its delusions and its apathy. It was no longer possible to mistake the nature of the rising. It was civil war, not a riot. It was the deliberate act of an organized party, who had long been meditating armed resistance, a party which must be met and crushed now and for ever. Even the Marquis Wielopolski was compelled to acknowledge that stern measures were inevitable; after some hesitation he admitted that acts of vigour were required, and gave a reluctant consent to the counsels of men of more practical ability than himself. His enemies exulted over him. The minister who, a few months since, had thought to govern Poland by trusting her people, had now twice acknowledged the worthlessness of his theories. He had vaunted the effect of the constitutional reforms he was pledged to introduce, and then (like the drunkard indulging in a last carouse the night before he intends to take the pledge) he had relied on an infamous conscription;—and now, only ten days later, he threw conciliation to the wind, and trusted for the triumph of his policy to the weight of the Russian sword. How could monarch or people confide in a statesman whose theories were so utterly thrown aside in the first hour of trial?

The kingdom of Poland was declared in a state of siege, and was divided into seven sections, each of which was placed under the charge of a military officer. These sections were Augustovo, Plock, Kalisk (including the Warsaw and Bromberg railway), Warsaw (including part of the Warsaw railway lines to Petersburg and Vienna), Radom, and Lublin.

In the Augustovo district the greater part of the insurgents appeared on the north, bordering on the province of Kovno, thus threatening to carry the insurrection into Lithuania; a portion, however, acted in the south-east, in a district which was well fitted for partisan warfare, and were not dispersed until they had injured several portions of the railway between Kovno and Konigsberg; they reunited a few days after their defeat, and passed into the province of Grodno, where they were again dispersed by troops sent against them from Wilna.

The insurrection spread rapidly in the district of Plock, which is chiefly inhabited by small proprietors and Schlachta, and several actions took place there which terminated in the defeat of the insurgents.

In the section of Warsaw, and the adjoining province of Grodno, the only acts of the insurgents deserving notice were the temporary destruction in several places of the railway, and the interruption of communication by telegraph.

It would be endless to particularize all the petty struggles which at this time occurred. Unimportant in themselves, and resultless in their consequences (for the defeated bands reassembled, by appointment, in a few days' time), it would only be to present to the reader the confused details of paltry skirmishes in an unknown land — skirmishes presenting no features of interest; not illustrated by any known act of heroism or magnaminity; and which, at most, never rose in consequence beyond the most ordinary incidents of a guerilla war.

In the encounters between the Russian troops and the insurgents the losses were very unequally divided, and many hostile comments were made upon the "lying bulletins," which stated some considerable number of the enemy were slain, while the troops lost "their invariable one Cossack." Without attempting to solve the question of whether or no the losses of the Russians were unduly lessened, I shall point out the explanations given me by those who contended that the bulletins were true, and then leave my readers to draw their own conclusion.

The insurgents were raw and undisciplined levies, no more conversant with war than are English yeomen and shopkeepers; and they had to contend against well-organized troops. Few of the insurgents had muskets; most of them were only armed with pikes, scythes, and sticks; the Russians were perfectly armed, and carried rifles.

An idea of the nature of the bands may be formed by a description of one which was defeated at Semititski, on the 8th February. It was said to have numbered 5,000 men. Every 1,000 men had a company of rifles, 200 in number, and that company was divided into four platoons. The riflemen were armed with double-barrelled guns and muskets, while the other 800 men of each 1000 formed four companies, and were armed with lances and scythes. The riflemen wore black (chamarkas) coats; while the other insurgents wore coats of similar shape, made out of rough grey cloth. So much organization was, however, seldom met with; in general the bands had practically none, and were miserably armed and clothed.

The bands were generally formed from priests, landowners, lesser nobles, petty officials, and such peasants as had no land, but were engaged as workmen by the landowners. The peasants who had land uniformly refused to join. Very often both the peasant workmen and mechanics from towns were induced through misrepresentation to join the insurgents. Thus they were told that the Government had determined to seize as recruits all men between the ages of sixteen and thirty, and were urged to fly into the forest and join the bands, to avoid this compulsory enlistment. When they did so, perfect strangers to them became their leaders, and explained to them that they now formed part of the national army, and promised them arms, food, clothes, and pay. These promises were, however, seldom fulfilled, and the ordinary food given to the insurgents was a piece of bread and a glass of spirits.

Many of them, finding how miserable was their condition, wished to leave the band and return home; but their leaders threatened them with death if they did so, and fear kept them to their colours. Many of the leaders, desirous of augmenting the numbers of their men, and wishing the rebellion to appear thoroughly national, endeavoured to secure the assistance of the peasants by acts of violence and cruelty. Their attempts were, however, vain; but fear sometimes prompted them to help the insurgents by giving them money and food.

The actions fought by the contending parties were of the character which generally distinguishes a partisan war. For the most part they avoided an encounter with considerable bodies of troops, while they plundered the posts, custom-houses, treasuries, and frequently the villages where no soldiers were stationed; they had neither the organization nor the arms to resist a regular force, and when they were forced to fight, they generally resisted only for a short time and then dispersed, seeking shelter in some adjoining forest, having arranged that on an appointed day and at a fixed place they should meet again. The only chance the Russians had of destroying a band completely was when they could cut off their retreat to the woods and compel them to fight.

The preceding remarks must not be considered to have an invariable application. Among the ranks of the rebels were to be found men of honour who would not stoop to deceive or misuse peasants; of true courage, who failed to recognize as patriotism the plunder of a strong-box or the robbery of a mail; and who tried with vain and hapless chivalry to wring from the armed hand of Russia the freedom which was the prize for which *they* strove.

The bands which operated in Lithuania generally came there from the Kingdom, and, except in the province of Kovno, where many of the crown peasants joined them, did not meet with much support from the lower orders.

The Roman Catholic clergy exerted all their influence in the cause of the insurgents, and, openly preached rebellion to the lower orders. Encouraged by the comparative impunity with which they carried on their operations, the insurgents abandoned the system which alone had secured it to them, and in three different quarters formed themselves into considerable *corps d'armes.*

The principal of these bands was concentrated near the town of Wachock, in the government of Radom, and consisted of from 3,000 to 4,000 men. They were commanded by Langiewicz, formerly a professor in a Polish military school in Italy, which had been recently closed by the Italian Government, who had now come to Poland with many of his pupils to assist in the insurrection. This band destroyed the bridge over the Pilica at Bialobrzegi in order to intercept the communications with Warsaw, and made every preparation to resist the enemy. The country held by Langiewicz was well adapted for the warfare he carried on, for it is one of the few mountainous districts which vary the otherwise monotonous plain of Poland; it is studded with vast forests and morasses, giving those who are acquainted with the neighbourhood great advantages over strangers, and affording the former ample shelter and opportunity for re-forming themselves in case of defeat. There are also in this neighbourhood many government forges for manufacturing iron, of which large deposits are found here, and the insurgents took possession of them, and fabricated scythes, knives, and other rude weapons, with which they armed themselves. The neighbourhood of the Galician frontier was another advantage this situation possessed, for it enabled supplies to be securely received from the Austrian territory; it facilitated the junction of exiles who desired to aid them, and it permitted the insurgents to establish constant communications with Galicia, and thus with the nations of Western Europe. The vicinity of the Austrian frontier also secured a safe refuge from the enemy in case of defeat.

In the first week in February, four of the eight towns in the government of Radom were in the hands of the insurgents, who established a species of provisional government there, appointed the old chiefs of districts to act in the same capacity for them, issued passports to traders who desired to pass their lines, and ordered a conscription amongst all classes, peasants included, of all males from eighteen to thirty-five years of age.

The second band had its head-quarters at Wengrow, in the

district of Lublin, near the Lithuanian frontier; it was estimated to consist of 3,000 men, among whom were many fugitives from Warsaw and a number of small freeholders.

A division of the Smolensk regiment was sent against them from Siedlee; its head, a Russian colonel, reconnoitred the ground, and halted about ten miles from Wengrow. When his report reached Warsaw, it was resolved to attack the insurgents at daybreak on the 4th February: the colonel, at the head of his regiment, with the aid of the artillery from Siedlec, was to attack it from the south, while Major-General Krudner, leading troops sent from Warsaw, was to attack it from the north. When, however, the troops under General Krudner approached the town, they found it already in the hands of the Smolensk regiment, who on the previous day had taken it, inflicting heavy loss on its defenders. This engagement was rendered remarkable by a charge which insurgents, who were armed only with scythes and pikes, made upon the artillery of the Russians. The attempt was unsuccessful; but it was a very gallant one. The residue of the shattered band retreated across the Bug.

The third band, about 2,000 in number, established itself in some forests near the town of Lovicz, in the neighbourhood of the railway from Warsaw to Vienna, and confined itself to intercepting the railway communication between the two places, and cutting the telegraph wires.

At the first outbreak of the revolt, the Russians appear to have been uncertain how to act; they had a large army in the kingdom, estimated at 100,000, and certainly in truth not less than 80,000 men, in addition to at least 50,000 more who were stationed in Lithuania and the Western provinces. The insurgents never amounted to 20,000 at any one time in arms, and they were undisciplined, badly armed, and unused to war; it seemed, therefore, that there should have been little difficulty in putting down the revolt. But although the Russians were numerous, their strength was wasted by being scattered over a large extent of country, where they garrisoned all the towns, and even every important village. Unless they withdrew from these places, they had not the power to bring any considerable force into the field, and if they withdrew from them, it was to allow the rebels to take possession of them, and apparently to gain great successes over the authorities. The choice was one of considerable difficulty; but it was eventually resolved to abandon the outposts which hitherto had been occupied by small bodies of troops, who were peculiarly liable to be attacked and cut off in detail; to concentrate the troops in the larger towns, and to form moveable columns which should pursue and attack the rebels wherever they drew to a head. This determination was not, however, arrived at before the Government had sustained considerable losses; for in many towns the insurgents had seized the public funds, together with arms and ammunition captured from the garrisons who held them; and such losses were not only intrinsically serious, they were far more important as giving confidence to the enemy, and as tending to persuade the peasants that the authorities were the weaker party, and were unable to protect them.

On 3rd February, a considerable force, consisting of foot soldiers, dragoons, and Cossacks, with two cannon, marched against Langiewicz. When they were about a mile and a half from the town of Winchock they were attacked by some insurgents, who were armed with scythes and pikes. The Cossacks, at the head of the force, fell back right and left to allow the artillery and the tirailleurs to open fire upon the enemy. At the first sound of the cannon the inhabitants of the town quitted it, and took refuge in the adjoining forest. The troops marched on the place, while the tirailleurs flanked them upon both sides. The insurgents, after a short conflict in the streets, fell back in confusion, and the troops occupied the town. The official journals at the time represented this action as a most calamitous defeat for the insurgents, and alleged that their forces were totally dispersed; but subsequent events did not confirm these statements; and while it is clear the rebels suffered a severe check, and were driven out of Winchock, it will be seen hereafter that they were not dispersed, but that they continued the struggle in which they had adventured themselves for some months longer.

CHAPTER X.

Policy of Prussia.—Her Government of Posen.—Convention with Russia for Rendition of Criminals. — Debate in Prussian Chambers. — English Despatches.—Policy of Austria.—Loyalty of Peasants and Clergy in Galicia.—Anti-Russian Feeling of Austrian, French, and English Press.

PRUSSIA and Austria had viewed the outbreak of the insurrection with great and reasonable anxiety. Accomplices in the original partition, ratifying and confirming the policy which dictated that act by their share in the treaty of Vienna and the territorial arrangements it effected, there was every probability, if the Kingdom were revolutionized, that the Poles of Galicia and Posen would fly to arms. Yet there was much in the position of the two great German powers which was likely to induce them to adopt a very dissimilar line of action now.

When Posen was first ceded to Prussia, the province lay waste and desolate. Its miserable inhabitants were reduced by prolonged wars and scarcely less disastrous peace to almost a condition of barbarism. Cities once populous and thriving were deserted; houses were tenantless, churches in ruins. Through the country the wretched peasants, wasted with famine, brutalized by war, without education, freedom, or enlightenment, were the helpless slaves of merciless masters. Those very masters were little their superiors save in the power they possessed to domineer over and oppress them, and they had neither knowledge nor refinement through which there was any hope that the country might be raised from her degraded state.

It was not, therefore, simply as a conqueror that Prussia came. Posen was necessary for her security; but it must be Posen humanized and strengthened—her people must be educated; her cities refilled; her blighted industry revivified; her altars rebuilt; and her prosperity restored. Frederick was not unequal to the exigency. Oppressed as Prussia was with costly military establishments, exhausted as she had been by sanguinary and long-continued war, still that great sovereign was to Posen a liberal and enlightened benefactor. Roads were constructed through forest and morass; in villages the most remote schools were introduced, and churches rebuilt and endowed; a postal service was organized, agriculture flourished, and an industrious population gathered in her towns. Posen, as Posen now is, has been the creation of Prussia, and she may well be proud of the triumph her civilizing arm has won.

The conduct pursued towards the conquered province by Prussia has for many years past excited the bitter indignation of the Poles. Anxious to ensure the continuance of the prosperity he had founded, it was the policy of the descendants of the Great Frederick to encourage the "noiseless Germanization" of Posen. In all directions a spendthrift proprietary wasted their fortunes in luxury and extravagance; reduced to poverty, they had forced their estates into the market, and the Germans were encouraged by their Government to purchase them. An orderly and industrious proprietary succeeded to a bankrupt and dissolute nobility; land long laid waste was cultivated with anxious care; comfortable houses, well-arranged farms, and a contented peasantry, changed the face of the country: though the Polish was still an important element in society, it had no longer a preponderating influence; and every year witnessed the developing prosperity and the increasing Germanization of Posen. The process which had been so thoroughly effected in Silesia as to leave no trace of its original Polish origin, was working here, and there was every reason to suppose that another half-century would obliterate all that was Polish in the province of Posen.

It was therefore natural that the Prussian Government should view with great alarm any insurrection in the kingdom of Poland which might by possibility extend to its own territories. War in the kingdom of Poland, so often devastated, so depopulated, and where civilization and improvement had made such scanty progress, might be of little import; but war in Posen, war which should destroy her peaceful villages, which should ruin her rising commerce and her thriving agriculture, would undo the painful work of fifty years, and obliterate that noble triumph which the slow and stolid industry of Germany had won over the light and reckless Poles.

In the year 1857 a convention had been entered into between Russia and Prussia, having for its object the rendition of political and criminal refugees. It related, first, to all individuals who deserted from the active service of the respective armies, and to individuals who had only obtained leave of absence, and who in fact belonged to the reserve; second, to all individuals who were prospectively liable to military service in the state which they had left; and, third, to criminals who had fled from the state in which they had committed crime in order to escape from the pursuit of justice. In this convention a clause was inserted, couched in the following terms:—"Neither deserters, nor individuals subject to military service, nor criminals, can, on the part of the State which claims them, be pursued in the territory of the other State, either by any act of violence or arbitrary authority, or clandestinely. It is, in consequence, forbidden that any detachment, military or civil, or any secret emissary, should pass the frontier of the two states with this object."

Early in February, confused rumours spread abroad of a treaty alleged to have been entered into between Russia and Prussia for affording each other mutual aid in the suppression of disturbances. The most exaggerated reports were circulated as to the stipulations of this treaty; and Sir Andrew Buchanan, the English minister at Berlin, writing to the Foreign Secretary on 14th February, stated, as the result of his inquiries, that he believed "it has been agreed that the commanders-in-chief of the two Governments will keep each other informed of the movements of the troops under their orders; that if the troops of the one Government should retire before the insurgents into the territories of the other, they will be allowed to retain their arms, and to recross the frontier as soon as they may be in a position to do so, and that the troops of either Government will be at liberty to pursue insurgents into the territory of the other."

These reports were strengthened by the terms of a proclamation addressed to the inhabitants of Posen by the president of the province, and the general in command there. It stated that "the armed insurrection which has broken out in the kingdom of Poland against the lawful authority of the Government, has changed our immediate neighbourhood into the theatre of bloody events; but whilst the cruelties perpetrated by the insurgents inspire the greatest horror, they at the same time afford the certainty that this criminal undertaking will bring about the destruction of those whose fanaticism has made them partakers in it. . . We fear that attempts will be made to seduce individual inhabitants of the province to a participation in the insurrectionary movement of the neighbouring country; a participation which, if even only an indirect one, but substantiated by any public manifestation, or by any act of support or assistance, of whatever kind, would have to be regarded (considering the notorious tendencies of the insurrection) as an undertaking against the laws of this country, and might therefore involve the heavy penalties of treason."

Under the influence of the prevailing rumours, a stormy debate took place on 18th February in the Prussian Chamber. The minister, M. von Bismarck, was asked whether any convention had been concluded between the two Governments for the suppression of the insurrection in Poland; and if so, what were its contents. He answered, that the Government did not intend to reply to the question. M. Waldeck denounced the convention, which he assumed to have been entered into, "as something so monstrous that it was difficult to find the proper category among public acts wherein to range it. It was nothing more or less than the sending over of gendarmes and armed police to a country whose existence had hitherto depended on police and gendarmes. And this was a part to be undertaken by a state that pretended to be at the head of German civilization. The man whose face did not flush with shame at such a thought was not worthy to be a Prussian or a German." The speaker protested that it was an absurdity to suppose that fugitives could endanger the security of Prussia, and declared that the true protection of the latter lay in the contrast the administration of her Polish possessions offered to the system of Russian rule. The only parallel he declared for this ignominious convention, was to be found in the sale of his troops during the last century, by the elector of Hesse, to the British Government for subjugating the revolted American States. "But," he continued, "the day for a policy of this kind is past, and kings can no longer treat the lives of their subjects as private property to be employed no matter on what frivolous or Quixotic adventures. An intervention on our part—let us not disguise the fact from ourselves—would be denounced by the whole civilized world. Austria condemns it, England openly condemns it, France rejoices at the opportunity offered her of making herself popular at our expense. Even in Russia the principles upon which such an intervention would be based have of late come into discredit, and the Emperor Alexander has himself endeavoured to adopt a more liberal policy. . ."

Lord Russell, on the same day that this debate took place, wrote to Sir A. Buchanan, instructing him to procure a copy of the convention; and on 21st February he saw the French ambassador, and learned from him, that although his Government was not in possession of the text of the convention, they knew enough of its purport to form an opinion unfavourable to its prudence and opportuneness; and that they considered Prussia had, by its conduct, revived the Polish question.

The reticence of M. von Bismarck had produced its natural result; the people of Prussia believed their Government had entered into some humiliating capitulation for hunting down the insurgents. France, only too happy to seize the opportunity she would gladly have created, was preparing by energetic protests to pave the way to future action; while the minister of England, unwilling to be left behind in the race of diplomatic liberality, thought it necessary that he too should write something, that he too should interfere.

On the 2nd March, the very day upon which Lord Russell wrote the despatch from which extracts will be presently made, a letter from Sir A. Buchanan reached him. In that letter he stated that M. von Bismarck had read to him the text of the convention; that it was of an informal character, was not divided into articles, and was to the following effect:—"That disturbances having broken out in the kingdom of Poland which might endanger property and tranquillity in the frontier provinces of Prussia, it was agreed between the two Governments that the troops of either should be authorized, *on the requisition of the military authorities of the other*, to cross the frontier, and, in case of necessity, should be permitted to pursue insurgents into the territory of the other: and it was further stipulated that either of the contracting parties should be at liberty to terminate this agreement." Sir A. Buchanan added that "not only was the convention incomplete from no ratifications having been exchanged, but, as its existence also depended on the will of the contracting parties, it could not be considered a binding agreement."

On the same day a despatch from Lord Napier reached the Foreign Office, in which he stated that he had seen Prince Gortschakoff, who had explained that the agreement was simply one for the maintenance of security on the borders of the two countries.

"The insurgents were in the habit of falling on the customhouse stations and other localities where public funds were deposited. It was necessary that the agents of Government should be enabled to withdraw with their funds from threatened posts to places of safety, if necessary, even on foreign territory. Such a liberty was assured for them; and if they were pursued by the rebels, the latter, in their turn, would be followed by the Russian troops over the frontier until they fell in with an armed force of Prussians."

It would perhaps be difficult to collect from these communications anything to justify the statements in Lord Russell's next despatch to Sir A. Buchanan; but on the very day he received them, he wrote as follows:—

"The convention which has been concluded between Russia and Prussia relating to the affairs of Poland has caused considerable uneasiness in this country.

"The powers of Europe were disposed to be neutral in the contest between the Russian Government and the Polish insurgents.

"Prussia has departed from this course.

"My inquiries, as well as a despatch from Lord Napier, have led me to believe that the convention contains—

"I. An agreement that Russian troops, upon crossing the

frontier of Prussia, shall not be disarmed, as would be required according to international usage, but shall be allowed to retain their arms, and to remain and to act as an armed body in Prussian territory.

"II. A permission for Russian troops to pursue and capture Polish insurgents on Prussian territory."

Sir A. Buchanan was directed to inform the Prussian Government, that it was clear that they thus made themselves a party to the "war raging in Poland;" that there was no necessity for their so doing; that it was an act of intervention unjustified by necessity; that it would alienate the affections of the Polish subjects of Prussia, and "give support and countenance to the arbitrary conscription of Warsaw."

In obedience to his instructions, Sir A. Buchanan saw M. von Bismarck on the 5th March; read him the despatch; was informed that no such clause as that first cited by Lord Russell existed in the convention; that the stipulation permitting, under certain circumstances, the entry of Russian troops on Prussian territory would have been restricted and defined by instructions issued to the frontier authorities, but that it had now been decided that in no case would such entry be necessary; that in no instance had Russian troops been allowed to cross the frontier and attack the insurgents; and that, in fact, the convention was a dead letter, as the instructions necessary for carrying it into effect had never been drawn up.

It was no longer possible for the Foreign Secretary to persevere in his demands or his comments, so on the 11th March he withdrew his request for a copy of the convention, and concluded with the remark, "the crossing the frontier with money from unprotected and insulated custom-houses, without any formal convention, must be considered as too unimportant to deserve serious notice."

While such was the policy of Prussia, which had something to lose by the spread of the insurrection, Austria, from the difference in the condition of her Polish possessions, was able to regard the future with equanimity and adopt with composure a rôle of unaccustomed liberality.

Galicia had never been Germanized, the Polish element preponderated there, and among men of education and property the Austrian Government was as much detested as was the Russian rule by the same classes in the Kingdom. But the peasants were devoted to their Emperor; they considered the freedom which they had obtained in 1848 as the guerdon for their loyalty in 1846, when they murdered a thousand of the Galician rebel proprietors; and they were prepared to give further proofs of their fidelity, in the hope that they thus might obtain fresh concessions and extended rights. The Roman Catholic priesthood also were the loyal upholders of Austrian supremacy; they preached submission to constituted authority, and exerted themselves to the utmost to prevent any revolutionary outbreak.

Austria had thus good reason for believing that there would be no successful insurrection in Galicia. It was, indeed, at least open to question whether she would not be strengthened rather than weakened by the reconstitution of the Poland of 1772, provided such a reconstitution made the kingdom absolutely independent of Russia. The intervention between her own and the Russian frontier of a strong military power, seeking nothing from her, regarding her as an ally, professing the same religion, and to a great extent having interests in common with her, would go far to counterbalance the loss of a province which gave her no real strength, and where she knew that her rule was utterly distasteful to all the educated classes of the population.

Swayed by these considerations, and by the exigencies of her own internal policy, which rendered it all-important to her to earn a character for liberality, the conduct of Austria was marked by impartiality and justice. All attempts to enrol men in Galicia were discouraged, and as far as possible repressed, and the meeting of the provincial Diet at Lemberg was adjourned to prevent revolutionary speeches being pronounced there, and also to prevent the younger members of it from compromising themselves and their friends; but the Austrian minister, Count Rechberg, discouraged any idea of a military convention between the two Governments, and resolved to be guided in his treatment of political fugitives by the ordinary usages of civilized nations.

The German Liberal press adopted a line of decided sympathy with the Poles. "If we would express the feelings which prevail in Austria," said the *Botschafter,* " with reference to the Poles, we should be guilty of an untruth were we to maintain that we do not wish them success. We speak of the feeling expressed in private and social life. It would be unnatural were it otherwise. . . . Austria has a right to protest before Poland and the world against the share ascribed to her in the iniquitous deed of partition. She has done whatever she could, and she will continue to strive against adding bad to evil. She will endeavour, by means of a liberal and humane government, to ameliorate the condition of the Austrian Poles, to save them from entering upon rash and foolish enterprises, and from a darker fate; the rest she will leave to Providence; and though reproach may be cast upon her for so doing, we are sure that a vast majority of the Austrian people will applaud her policy. No Austrian can for a moment entertain the thought of another holy alliance with Prussia and Russia, with Bismarck and Gortschakoff."

The anti-Russian feeling in England and France was carefully stimulated by the agents of the revolution. Extraordinary statements were circulated and believed, of unheard-of cruelties practised by the troops not only against the insurgents, but against peaceful and unarmed inhabitants. Equally improbable accounts were propagated of Polish heroism, magnanimity, and success. It was no uncommon thing to read of bands armed with scythes and pikes, putting to flight regular troops many times more numerous than themselves, and the only circumstance which appeared in the minds of thoughtful men to shake confidence in these strange recitals, was the fact that the insurrection seemed ever advancing, but yet never to make any way; and a hundred well-contested fields and brilliant victories failed to give them (after the defeat of Langiewicz) the command of a single province, fortress, or even town.

Examples without number of the gross exaggerations of the press might easily be adduced, but it will be sufficient to instance the reports which the Viennese correspondent of the *Times,* on 3rd February, judged sufficiently trustworthy to embody in his letter of that date. He stated that in Galicia it was said that more than 200,000 men had risen against the Russian Government, but that it was known in Vienna that not even a fourth of that number was actually under arms; that about 10,000 conscripts had been taken to the fortresses of Warsaw, Modlin, and Lublin; and, quoted from the Vienna *Presse*, that M. von Valbezen, the French consul in Warsaw, had said a few words to the Archduke Constantine in favour of the conscripts confined in the citadel; and the consequence of his interference was, that seventy prisoners were shot.

When it is remembered that certainly at no one time were more than 20,000 insurgents ever in arms; that the conscription was only carried out in Warsaw, and the number of conscripts did not exceed 2,000, of whom many had escaped, and that prisoners in Russia are only put to death after legal trial, and after sentence has been pronounced against them, the absurdity of the statements thus submitted to English readers will be sufficiently apparent.

It was, perhaps, an error in the Russian Government not to take care that these reports should be promptly and fully contradicted; but they regarded them as *canards*, weighing nothing with well-informed or educated persons, and therefore as too contemptible to be worthy of denial. If public opinion were only influenced by the intelligent and instructed, such a course might have been wise and prudent; but as it, unfortunately, is more frequently swayed by ignorant clamour and blundering good intentions, they allowed themselves to be greatly prejudiced by their haughty silence.

CHAPTER XI.

The Emperor Napoleon.—His presumed Designs on Prussia.—Exasperation of the French People.—Temporizing Policy of the Emperor.—Sympathy in England with the Insurgents.—Debate in the Lords.—Despatch of Lord Russell—Reply of Prince Gortschakoff.

THE policy of the Emperor Napoleon was constantly the theme of anxious inquiry and hypothesis. Men asked themselves what that mysterious silence, which nothing broke, portended, and over what thoughts that impassive countenance kept guard. Did the master of the army of France intend to launch its magnificent legions against the myriads of the Czar, to resume the strife which in 1856 he had so hastily abandoned, and to avenge the misfortunes, if he did not repeat the catastrophe, of 1812? Would he, the conqueror of Magenta and the victorious diplomatist of Solferino, now strive to arouse a second nation from its death-like sleep? And if he did, for what hidden purpose would that war be waged?

Men did not trust the Emperor Napoleon; they admitted his ability, wondered at his reticence, dreaded his power; they did not credit his professions, or believe in the integrity of his views; and now they anxiously inquired with what object he would draw the sword, and, looking round them, surveyed the Continent of Europe, and endeavoured to discover how France would indemnify herself for the cost and hazard of war.

At first the Emperor had avoided all interference in the Polish question; his ambassadors had expressed no sympathy with the struggling nation; the official journals had been silent, and the warlike tendencies of the French press had been restrained. Then came the alleged convention with Prussia, and immediately his policy was changed. He saw, men said, the germ of a great opportunity, and he would not let it pass. It was not Russia he desired to encounter, it was not Poland he panted to free; it was Prussia he longed to humiliate, it was the Rhenish provinces he desired to win.

There was colour for the inference, for to Prussia the Emperor attributed the revival of the Polish question, and from the hour he had done so he followed it up with perseverance and determination. When the provisions of that memorable convention had been explained, the English minister had deemed them so trivial as to be unworthy of further inquiry or comment. How then did it happen, when the stimulus was withdrawn, that the vane of French diplomacy pointed to war, and her press exhausted its bitter and unsparing energy in denunciations of Prussia as well as her northern ally? How did it come to pass that in official pamphlets she was significantly menaced in the name of peace, and threatened with conquest in the cause of European order?* These things are never done by accident in France; whence, then, did their inspiration originate?

Meanwhile the passions of the French people were fully roused; an European war was certain to give them new triumphs to celebrate, and a war for Poland appealed to some of their proudest recollections and most generous impulses. They remembered how nobly the Poles had fought in the battles of the great Napoleon, and they felt his betrayal of their cause as the one dark blot on the scutcheon of his fame; it was, they thought, a holy undertaking to redeem from bondage that chivalrous and patriot race; and they desired to lay the lance in rest against what they conceived to be the darkest and most barbarous tyranny that modern history had seen. Being disposed for decisive action, their feelings were

---

* In one of those historical references in which French pamphleteers delight, and from which they have the faculty of proving whatever suits their momentary purpose, Prussia is warned to be submissive; and then, as an intimation of what she might expect in case she proved contumacious, the author alludes, in the following terms, to the history of another age:—
"Posterity will one day ask why, during the last six years of his reign, Napoleon showed himself without mercy to Prussia. It is because Prussia is the power that injured him most, by compelling him to fight her, and destroy her when he wished to extend, fortify, and increase her."—"*L'Empereur, la Pologne, et l'Europe.*"

maddened by the tidings which daily reached them. Unheard-of atrocities, from which neither sex nor age, nor rank nor sacred duties availed to shield their victims, were chronicled with monotonous regularity; telegrams summarized them, correspondents dilated on their details, leading articles were passionately eloquent upon the same themes, and the people implicitly believed everything that was thus conveyed to them.

Amid all this excitement, diplomacy moved on with clockwork regularity, ever approaching nearer and nearer to the momentous hour when mere words would be of no more avail, and still the Emperor sat impassively gazing on the scene, and still he made no sign.

Sometimes in history, and frequently in every-day life, a silent man acquires a character he little merits for ability and knowledge. Perhaps, when years have rolled by, when the present generation has passed away, when the little incidents that look so great to us are all reduced to their true dimensions, the future historian may question the depth of that wisdom which it now so greatly embarrasses us to plumb. Is it not possible that the Emperor indicated no policy simply because he did not know what policy to pursue? Is it not possible that he was embarrassed by the efforts of former years, and by his own conduct, which had been often vigorous, often fortunate, but never straightforward?

His position was certainly difficult. The occupation of Rome embarrassed him, while it insulted Italy and contradicted every liberal aspiration and utterance of his life. His army in Mexico, instead of finding their march to the city of Montezuma a mere triumphal pageant, was thinned by an ignoble foe and decimated by a fatal climate; and this war, regarded by the French people with unmixed aversion, was costly, inglorious, and apparently interminable. His finances, known to be confused, were suspected of being seriously disordered, and those who were most conversant with them seemed to view them with the gravest alarm. Meanwhile the people, first tortured into silence by massacre and exile, then bribed into acquiescence by trophied monuments and two successful wars, were at length aroused; at length they bethought themselves that they were worthy of being more than a nameless mob, whose only destiny was to applaud their Emperor, or swell an unanimous vote whenever he appealed to a plébiscite to confirm his sovereign decree.

Thus encircled by difficulties, it needed a strong will to shape a policy and adhere to it without deviation or subterfuge. A war for the liberation of Poland would reburnish the tarnished popularity of the Empire, and if England and Austria were allied with France, it would be morally certain of success. The financial difficulties of the moment might be tided over, for in the lavish expenditure of modern war an existing deficit may be included in the loans it is necessary to contract; while the clang of the trumpet, the glitter and the triumphs of war, would divert the thoughts of the people from the dangerous path of liberty and self-government.

So far the course was smooth and very apparent. Strong remonstrances might be indulged in, if Austria and England concurred in them; a war might securely be waged if those two powers would lend their active assistance; and in the mean time the press might continue to excite the people; French officers might be encouraged or permitted to join the patriot levies, and contributions might be collected in their aid. If Russia yielded to diplomatic representations, France would claim the glory of reconstituting the liberties of Poland; if war were the result, she might arrogate to herself the prouder boast of reconquering her independence.

The danger was that France, by the vehemence of her representations and the passion of her people, might be hurried into the conflict, while the prudence of Austria and the pacific tendencies of England might sever her connection with the only nations whose joint action would ensure her triumph in such a war.

To protect himself against this eventuality, the Emperor tried, a few weeks later than the time which my narrative has now reached, to lure Austria and England into arrangements for joint action in case the six points, to be hereafter noticed, were not conceded; but those cabinets had then gone further than prudence would have counselled, and the Emperor tried in vain.

Other projects suggested themselves, and presented substantial advantages as an offset to the perils which environed them. The kingdom of Italy was yet imperfect, and its warlike monarch, a satellite revolving round the Napoleonic sun, was ready to assist a benefactor who yet had princely rewards to bestow. An Italian army might doubtless be marshalled in a new combination against Russia, under a king whose astutest and most successful action had been a similar alliance during the Crimean war. In the North, the hope of recovering her lost possessions might hurry Sweden into the field; in the East, the hardy tribes of the Caucasus, with French assistance, would give occupation to a large army; while Turkey might be incited to commence a holy war, and along her far-extended frontier find employment for the Russian sword.

France, we are told, alone among nations, goes to war for an idea, yet she would scarcely find in that of Polish independence compensation for the costly uncertainty of the strife. Whence, then, was profit to be extorted, and from whom were territories to be wrung? The Rhenish provinces was the answer; and Prussia, the inextricable ally of her mightier neighbour, was to be the prey. The war-cry of "the Rhine" would rouse the enthusiasm of France; it would strengthen that dynasty which is ever telling the world how much it requires "consolidation;" it would silence all opposition, and be a great and glorious realization of another Napoleonic idea.

Such, it would appear, was the position in which the French Emperor was placed, and such were the different courses open to him to pursue. Doubtless each had its advantages, and against each there was much to be alleged; one fact alone was evident, that something quickly must be done. The choice was full of difficulty. He could not withdraw from Mexico, and admit his enterprise had failed; on the contrary, he must support it with fresh troops, and continue the contest till success had crowned his intervention. He could not anticipate from day to day the extent of this drain on his resources, nor, in face of its possible requirements, could he prudently involve himself in European war. Meanwhile, his people were hourly becoming more impatient of inaction, were asking what the policy of the Government was to be, and were contrasting diplomacy at St. Petersburg with extirpation in Poland.

Unprepared to reply to these demands, anxiously weighing and balancing the merits of every scheme, it is little to be wondered at that the Emperor was silent; it is not surprising that he let events drift whither they would go, hoping ere long to discover the direction of the current, and resolved to guide the vessel of the State accordingly. His silence, while it did not complicate affairs, gave him one enormous advantage, for it enabled him, whenever he decided on a policy, to announce it like a thunder-peal. He knew the French passion for stage effect, he knew how certainly a *coup de théâtre* secures their admiration, so he folded around his irresolution a sibylline garb, and when he spoke, he gave his hesitating resolution the likeness of an oracular decree.

In England, also, a strong feeling in favour of the insurgents was manifested; day after day the press teemed with repetitions of the false reports with which foreign journals were filled, and incessant appeals were made, in powerfully written articles, to the former condition and future hopes of Poland, the hapless victim of a sullen and remorseless tyranny.

On 20th February, Lord Ellenborough, in the House of Lords, took occasion to make remarks of a very severe character both on the conscription, to which he attributed the revolt, and on some of the other acts of the Russian Government.

In reply, Lord Russell stated, that to those who knew what was the progress of events in Poland, the insurrection was not unexpected. He alluded to the demonstrations which had taken place in Warsaw, and stated, though apparently peaceful, their necessary result was concession on the part of the Government, or violence on the part of those who shared in them; and after a review of recent events in Poland, and an allusion to the conscription, he stated, "the feeling produced by such a measure may be imagined. The persons who were engaged in secret societies, who meant to rise in insurrection at some time, though probably they would never have carried out that intention, were driven to despair, and thought, if they must serve as soldiers, they would rather shed the last drop of their blood upon their native land of Poland, than waste their lives in distant lands in the service of Russia."

Urged on by the feeling thus excited in England, and by the fact that France announced her intention of remonstrating with Russia, Lord Russell, on 2nd March, addressed the following despatch to Lord Napier:—

"Her Majesty's Government view with the greatest concern the state of things now existing in the kingdom of Poland. They see there, on the one side, a large mass of the population in open insurrection against the Government; and, on the other, a vast military force, employed in putting that insurrection down. The natural and probable result of such a contest must be expected to be the success of the military forces. But that success, if it is to be achieved by a series of bloody conflicts, must be attended by a lamentable effusion of blood, by a deplorable sacrifice of life, by wide-spread desolation, and by impoverishment and ruin which it would take a long course of years to repair.

"Moreover, the acts of violence and destruction on both sides, which are sure to accompany such a struggle, must engender mutual hatreds and resentments, which will embitter, for generations to come, the relations between the Russian Government and the Polish race.

"Yet, however much Her Majesty's Government might lament the existence of such a miserable state of things in a foreign country, they would not, perhaps, deem it expedient to give formal expression to their sentiments, were it not that there are peculiarities in the present state of things in Poland which take them out of the usual and ordinary condition of such affairs.

"The kingdom of Poland was constituted, and placed in connection with the Russian empire by the treaty of 1815, to which Great Britain was a contracting party. The present disastrous state of things is to be traced to the fact that Poland is not in the condition in which the stipulations of that treaty require that it should be placed.

"Neither is Poland in the condition in which it was placed by the Emperor Alexander I., by whom that treaty was made.

"During his reign a national Diet sat at Warsaw, and the Poles of the kingdom of Poland enjoyed privileges fitted to secure their political welfare.

"Since 1832, however, a state of uneasiness and discontent has been succeeded from time to time by violent commotion and a useless effusion of blood.

"Her Majesty's Government are aware that the immediate cause of the present insurrection was the conscription lately enforced upon the Polish population; but that measure itself is understood to have been levelled at the deeply rooted discontent prevailing among the Poles, in consequence of the political condition of the kingdom of Poland.

"The proprietors of land and the middle classes in the towns bore that condition with impatience; and if the peasantry were not equally disaffected, they gave little support or strength to the Russian Government.

"Great Britain, therefore, as a party to the treaty of 1815, and as a power deeply interested in the tranquillity of Europe, deems itself entitled to express its opinion on the events now taking place, and is anxious to do so in the most friendly spirit towards Russia, and with a sincere desire to promote the interest of all the parties concerned.

"Why should not his Imperial Majesty, whose benevolence is generally and cheerfully acknowledged, put an end at once to this bloody conflict by proclaiming mercifully an immediate and unconditional amnesty to his revolted Polish subjects, and at the same time announce his intention to replace without delay his kingdom of Poland in possession of the civil and religious privileges which were granted to it by the Emperor Alexander I., in execution of the stipulations of the treaty of 1815?

"If this were done, a national Diet and a national administration would in all probability content the Poles, and satisfy European opinion."

When Lord Napier read this despatch to Prince Gortschakoff, the latter replied, that the insurrection was the result of a deep-laid conspiracy, widely organized in foreign capitals; that its explosion had only been hastened by the conscription. It was, he said, a democratic and anti-social movement, conceived in the pernicious notions of which Mazzini was the author and the symbol, and in these designs the Poles had been enlisted by flattering their natural illusions, which pointed, not to the objects indicated in Lord Russell's despatch, but to the severance of Poland from the Russian crown, to national independence, to the restoration of the limits of 1772. The insurrection only included the mechanics of the towns, the indigent nobles, and the clergy. The landed proprietors and great nobility had collected for security under the guns of the citadel of Warsaw; the peasantry were decidedly on the side of the Government, moved by a sense of the benefits which it had conferred upon their order, and disgusted by the exactions imposed on them by the roving band of marauding insurgents. Some, indeed, of the upper classes might join in the patriotic delusions of a restoration of ancient Poland, but their eyes were only scaled to the absurdity of such expectations, owing to the countenance extended to them by foreign governments.

Referring to the suggestion that the constitution of 1815 should be restored, Prince Gortschakoff said: "The constitution of 1861 embodied a complete autonomy. National institutions were granted by it, with a modified representation adapted to the form of political existence in force under the Imperial Government. Poland was now ruled by institutions purely Polish. There was a directing Minister, a Pole, entertaining national sentiments of the most decided character; a Council of Administration, composed of Poles; a Council of State, containing Poles taken from the several ecclesiastical and civil orders of the community, and embodying some representative elements, in which general laws for the welfare of the kingdom were elaborated; there were provincial, district, and municipal councils in descending order, all purely elective, charged with the local and material interests of the country. This national representation was not cast in the same mould as that which was designed by the Emperor Alexander I., or that which existed in England, but it formed, nevertheless, a system of national and representative institutions adapted to the condition of Poland and its relations with Russia. The kingdom of Poland enjoyed an absolute administrative independence. Even the department for Polish affairs in the Russian capital had been abolished, and the only institution common to the two countries was the army. The new institutions granted to Poland opened a wide field for activity and material prosperity to the country. With regard to the amnesty, he stated that, while a prompt and unconditional pardon could not be conceded to those who were actually in arms against the authority of their sovereign, it had always been the intention of the Emperor to grant a large measure of amnesty to his revolted subjects after the cessation of resistance, excluding only the principal authors of a movement which had caused so many calamities in the kingdom.

The ill success of English diplomacy has ever been proverbial, but on the questions to which the Polish revolt gave rise it was even more unfortunate than is its wont. Our statesmen, with few exceptions, have never been conversant with foreign politics, and almost every continental crisis has found them acting hastily, or unprepared to act at all; still we have a policy upon some great questions, and upon them, if our rulers do not act wisely, they at least act in accordance with precedent and the traditions of the past. Of Poland, however, they appeared to be completely ignorant; the discussions in the Houses of Parliament were scarce worthy of a debating club, while Lord Russell's despatches were hardly equal to school-boy themes. When the English ministry interfered between a powerful sovereign and his revolted subjects, it was at least to be expected that their spokesman and representative would understand the question upon which he wrote; that he would not betray, whenever he put pen to paper, an extraordinary ignorance of history, of the events passing before him, and even of the despatches he received from his own ambassadors. Something more was surely to be expected than the recapitulation of newspaper reports, the adoption of captious common-places, and the indulgence in boastful utterances, to be repudiated in the hour of peril.

Yet the perusal of Lord Russell's despatches must convince every impartial reader that their general character has not been mis-stated, and it must ever be matter of regret that where the honour and dignity of England were involved, they were intrusted to such rash and inadequate guardianship. In truth, however, Lord Russell was placed by the exigencies of our system of government in a position where his previous political experiences availed him nothing, and for which his habits of thought and action rendered him singularly unfit.

The great and solitary achievement of Lord Russell's life, the conduct of the Reform Bill, gave him a hold on liberal opinions in England, which even his subsequent career has failed entirely to loosen. Many excuses have been made for a time-serving, captious, and undignified policy, because the great revolution in our representative system, which was planned and carried out by abler men, was erroneously ascribed to his mediocre intellect and faltering tongue.

The knowledge of partisan tactics, learned in the House of Commons, was little qualified to aid Lord Russell in the conduct of foreign affairs; he had now to deal with a statesman of European reputation, whose great abilities had been conspicuously shown throughout an illustrious career. Trained from his youth in diplomacy and statesmanship, Prince Gortschakoff was fully competent to master the difficulties before him; his despatches are models of logical argument, and they breathe throughout a fixed determination to uphold the honour and integrity of the Russian empire. Always courteous in the tone adopted towards England, it will be found that he relied in the early part of his negotiations on common interests, treaty rights, and ancient friendship; to an ally he was willing to concede much, and his despatches were most temperate and conciliatory. As the negotiations, however, continued, and Lord Russell became more menacing in his tone and more exacting in his requisitions; as he lent the great name of his country to the cause of anarchy and European disorder, the replies of Russia made it clear that to threats she would never yield. Far from showing the cunning and chicanery which we too generally attribute to our Northern ally, there never was a series of state papers in which a national policy was more frankly avowed. Russia believed herself to be in the right, she knew that she was powerful, and while she desired peace, she did not shrink from war.

The great diplomatic triumph which the Prince achieved was, however, his celebrated despatches to the ambassador at the French court; despatches in which, with pitiless severity, he anatomized the diplomatic history of the past, ably vindicated the policy of Russia, and exposed the falsehood of the allegations upon which the French Government was preparing to draw the sword.

The effect of these despatches on the Russian people will not lightly be forgotten by any one who witnessed it; they regarded the prince as the noble and eloquent champion of his country, and responded with an unanimous voice to his words.

CHAPTER XII.

Langiewicz's Campaign ; his Defeat. — Resumption of Power by the National Government.

It is very difficult to follow with certainty the military events which succeeded the battle of Wenchock. It is clear, however, that the main hope of the insurgents consisted in the army under General Langiewicz. This force amounted to three or four thousand men ; but they were undisciplined, imperfectly armed, and unaccustomed to war ; and it was necessary for their leader as much as possible to avoid a general engagement. He harassed the enemy by a partisan system of warfare, keeping them ever in doubt where he would strike the next blow, and embarrassing them by the rapidity of his movements, and not unfrequently by their audacity. Thus gradually habituated to face regular troops, his followers learned steadiness and endurance, and, before long, bodies of men armed with scythes opposed themselves without shrinking to the Russian bayonets.

The system adopted by the Government gave the insurgents the advantage of being the apparent masters of the larger part of the country, for, in consequence of the Russian forces having been withdrawn from many of the smaller posts, they were able to boast that they had chased their foreign enemy into his fortifications, and that beyond them he did not hold one inch of Polish ground save that whereon his armies trod.

Gradually the new system adopted by the Russians enabled them to collect larger bodies to take the field against the rebels; but even then this change in their tactics produced at first no answering result. Heavy masses of troops might, indeed, slowly march through the disturbed districts; but the tread of their ponderous columns was heard afar, and they marched through a country dreary and desolate, but in which there was no sign of an armed and living foe. If, however, a small detachment ventured to separate from the main body, it was assailed and cut off by overpowering numbers; and then the revolutionary press rung with their triumph, and Europe was required to recognize an independent Poland because a few soldiers, and perhaps a *sous-officier*, had been vanquished in the forests or morasses of a country that was strange to them.

However much the revolutionary press might deceive others, it could not hide from the leader of the insurgents the desperate nature of the contest in which he was involved. A Central Committee sat at Warsaw, and nominally governed the whole movement. Its secret members were fluent writers, and inundated the country with flowery proclamations and sanguinary decrees; but they gave no sign of capacity for the work they had undertaken, if their actions were scanned by those who knew what were their sources of information and power: the tricks of the juggler astonish the ignorant boor, but the accomplice who has arranged the cards, or prepared the machinery, detects the faults and the blunders that the spectator never observes.

The movement, if it was indeed to become a national one, required a single mind to direct it. Through the whole country there were multitudes of independent detachments fighting without plan or purpose, and finally falling victims to their ignorance of the necessities of their position. It was necessary they should be controlled, that their rash valour should be utilized, that their selfish wishes should be checked, that their sanguinary excesses should be restrained; and all these ends could only be effected by placing the entire control of the movement in the hands of one competent chief. There was, perhaps, another motive for the work to be now undertaken; it was necessary to win the confidence of the great nobles; it was necessary to give them some pledge that a socialist propaganda would not direct the revolution, and no such pledge could be given while the Secret Committee reigned. The first act of that committee, an act by which the insurgents were now irrevocably bound, had startled and offended them; for they saw in the alienation of the peasants' land the carrying out of a policy to which they had ever been opposed, and they anticipated with gloomy forebodings the future acts of a party which had thus inauspiciously begun to govern.

Moved by these considerations, Langiewicz took a step which for the moment effectually superseded the power of the Central Committee. After some consultation with the officers about him, he published the following proclamation:—

" FELLOW CITIZENS,—The most devoted children of Poland have commenced, in the name of God, the combat provoked by the violence and oppression exercised by the Muscovite domination. They have commenced it against the eternal enemy of liberty and civilization, against the Muscovite intruder, the oppressor of our nation ; they have commenced it for the liberty and independence of our country. In the unfavourable circumstances in which the enemy has provoked the explosion of the insurrection by the excess of oppression, the contest, begun with empty hands against the armed multitudes of Russia, has continued not only for nearly two months in a great portion of our country, but increases and spreads further and further, thanks to the activity and devotion of the whole people, who are resolved to become free or to perish. Polish blood flows in torrents upon many fields of battle ; it flows in the streets of our towns and villages, which the Asiatic enemy is utterly destroying, massacring inoffensive inhabitants, and abandoning to pillage the remains of their possessions. In view of this life-and-death struggle, in view of the murders, pillage, and flames with which our enemy marks his route, Poland sees with grief, by the side of the grandest devotion and enthusiasm of her children, the want of a military and avowed leadership capable of preventing the scattering of the forces which have been called forth, and of arousing those who still slumber. It follows, from the general situation of affairs, as well as from the nature of the struggle which is proceeding, that outside the camp of the insurgents there is not to be found throughout the whole territory of the country a spot where a central power publicly avowed could establish itself ; and this is the reason why the Secret Provisional Government, which emanated from the former Secret Central Committee, has not been able to present itself in open day before the nation and the whole world. Although there are in the country men who are far above myself in capacity and merit, although I appreciate the extent and gravity of the duties which in a position so difficult weigh on the supreme national power, I assume, nevertheless, with the consent of the supreme National Government, the supreme Dictatorship, prepared to deposit it when we shall have shaken off the Muscovite yoke, in the hands of the representatives of the people. I assume it in consideration of the urgency of the circumstances which imperatively demand a prompt remedy, in consideration of the necessity of increasing the forces of the nation by the concentration of the civil and military powers in one hand, directed by one sole will, in this murderous contest against hostile troops. In reserving to myself the immediate direction of military operations, or in claiming the power of transferring, if necessary, the military command in chief to other chiefs in provinces which will be named, I deem it useful at present to confide all the civil administration of the insurrection, as well as that of the freed territory, to a private civil government which will act under my inspiration and control. The powers and organization of this government will be indicated in a special publication. In taking the dictatorship I commence nothing new, but simply finish the work of the National Government. I confirm, then, and proclaim again in all their entirety, the fundamental principles expressed in the manifesto of the Provisional Government, dated January 22nd, in the name of which the flag of the national contest for liberty and independence was raised, especially the liberty and political equality of all the sons of Poland, without distinction of belief, of condition, or of birth; also the giving, under conditions, of the landed property, subjected until now to rents or charges, to the rural population, with indemnity to the proprietors, who will be saved from harm out of the funds of the State.

"And now, peoples of Royal Poland, of Lithuania, and of Ruthenia—you who form one nation—in the name of God I call you once more to universal and immediate insurrection against Muscovite oppression and barbarity. The concord of all the children of Poland, without distinction of class or belief, the community and universality of efforts and sacrifices, and the unity of the object, will raise the scattered forces to a power which will be fatal to the enemy; they will procure independence for our country, liberty and happiness for our descendants, and will assure immortal glory to those who may meet the death of heroes in this sacred struggle. To arms, brothers! to arms! for the independence of the country.

"General MARYAN LANGIEWICZ, Dictator.

"Head-quarters, Goscza, March 10."

Intelligence of this decided step struck the Central Committee with astonishment; but it was better to submit to the usurpation than to disavow it; for the latter course would have disclosed to the world those dissensions which it was fatal at such a moment to avow. The Committee, therefore, wrote a secret letter to the Dictator, which curiously illustrates their embarrassments and internal feuds:—

"GENERAL,—The news of your proclamation as Dictator, notwithstanding it could not be considered by us otherwise than as a *coup d'état*, was at first welcomed by us with joy. All, without distinction of opinion, were ready to accept the revolutionary illegality, and to pardon a deed which might be regarded as the act of a man who felt the strong necessity of saving the country from falling. We also took into account the circumstances which would not permit of the formation of a political combination, however patent. It was almost without deliberation that it was decided to print and publish your manifesto; every means had been resorted to in order to gain for you in public opinion as general an adhesion as possible, and the Government, convinced that the direction of the movement had passed into strong hands, hailed with joy the approach of the moment when it could withdraw from power. In effect your voluntary declaration that you looked upon yourself as the heir of the revolutionary and national policy of the committee, was for it a guarantee that you would not overturn the bases laid by the committee, and was the strongest proof that you would not allow yourself to be guided by the Reaction, at all times the most sanguinary enemy of the rising and the men who have sprung from it.

"Nevertheless, at the moment when we printed your proclamation we learnt with unspeakable grief the circumstances which preceded your assumption of the dictature. Never did we suppose that the soldier of St. Croix and of Staszow, who needed no other consecration than the benediction of the revolution, sought support from political intriguers who deserved nothing but contempt. From esteem for yourself, and for the honour of the revolution, we were willing to admit that your good faith had been surprised in the most shameful manner, and we could explain at a future time with what object this was done. It was only from that conviction that we did not suspend the publication of your manifesto; we did not wish to depart from the course we had adopted before the reception of that news, and we did not refuse you our concurrence, of which you have had occasion more than once to appreciate the value and importance. We have nothing to say against the principle of the dictature, we have no feeling against you personally, as you have up to this time acted so as to merit our esteem and gratitude; we have, therefore, no objection to make against the exercise of the dictature by you, provided that you will exercise it vigorously and for the good of the country; but we declare frankly, once for all, that from regard for the good of the country and the rising, from esteem for ourselves and for you, we will never support, we cannot and do not wish to support, your present *entourage*.

"We ask you, General, to reflect coolly for a moment, and you will comprehend that our speaking in other language to you would be at the present time, on our part, an unpardonable crime.

"When on the memorable night of the 22nd of January, at a signal given by us, you placed yourself at its head in one of the palatinates, the men whose agents now crawl at your feet, in order to destroy you more easily and to cover the revolution with opprobrium—those men pronounced against the revolution, and with an impudence of which the Reaction alone is capable, proposed to bestow revenues upon you on condition that you would desert the ranks of the army, and that you would betray the country. Without doubt, the revolutionary party, represented by the Provisional National Government, was not then able to bring any military succour to aid you; but do not forget that, thanks to its previous activity and its labours alone, you found an inexhaustible material of devotion and patriotism, from which by your superior talent, which we have constantly appreciated, you profited for the formation of your valiant legion. Do not forget that, General, and do not conclude from the weakness of its military preparations, any weakness in the revolutionary party, which, reduced to rely on its own strength alone, and in spite of the obstacles thrown in its way by the Reaction, has brought about events that have increased your power.

"We have mentioned above the manner in which you treated with the department of landed proprietors. Nevertheless, when having profited by the moral dispositions of the country, you had, with indefatigable activity, organized a considerable armed force, then that department commenced carrying on around you a series of intrigues unworthy of a generalissimo—intrigues that we must absolutely lay bare before your eyes.

"Count ———, who giving himself out as the representative of the National Government, placed in the hands of skilful intriguers the cornerstone of the machinations carried on around you in order to insure your destruction, never was sent by this Government nor was provided with any plenary powers. In order that you may learn what this Count——— is, we refer you to General Wysocki, and from him you will learn the history of certain receipts fabricated by Mr. ———, for problematical sums. As to the political convictions of Mr. ———, who can have nothing in common with those of a revolutionary organizer like you, General, we refer you to the *Czas* of the past year. Mr. ——— is an adventurer whom a gentleman would be ashamed to speak to. The name of the honest Bentkowski has probably been mixed up with this intrigue in the same manner as yours has been, that is to say, by taking advantage of his good faith. These people, who represented nobody, who had nothing in their possession, could not offer anything to you, and from them you could not accept anything. According to our conviction, the dictature was conferred by Malogoszcz and Skala. You had no need of these men, nothing attaches you to them. Separate yourself from them, therefore, for that separation alone can save you, and with you save also the cause.

"Reflect, General, on the end to which they tend. The list of ministers and of divers other functionaries presented for your sanction, contains only the names of General Wysocki and some other worthy persons, who, it cannot be denied, will not on any account seat themselves on the same bench with intriguers, whose only aim in slipping into your camp was to ruin the revolution. The dictature has a right to make use of the services of men of all parties and all convictions; but it has not a right to sacrifice the principles from which it originated. We acknowledge accomplished facts, but no civil government can establish itself, nor shall it be established, without our consent; for all the portions of the country occupied by the enemy are in our hands, and can be governed by our permission alone. Do not forget that, in assuming the dictature you have taken upon yourself, before history, the country, and us, all the responsibility of the manner in which you exercise it, and that all complications resulting from your resolutions will fall on yourself alone.

"You have still our adhesion and our concurrence, as the hero of our revolution, the conqueror of Staszow and of Malogoszcz; they belong to you alone, for you have repulsed Mieroslawski. For us you are the representative of the new idea, for them only an instrument. Choose. We have still a firm conviction that a momentary mistake, which the greatest men have not escaped from, will be forgiven, and that in your political career you will show yourself, General, before the country and before us as pure as you were at Piaskowi Skala. If, against our expectation—for the misfortune of the country and of the rising—our hopes fail, do not forget that as surely as we now offer to you our support, we will commence proceedings against you. If the revolution should be defeated once more, it will be your fault, General. As to us, in the interest of the future of the country, we will preserve our principles unshaken and intact.

"And now we cry with all our might—'Hurrah for the dictature, and down with reaction.'

"Waiting for your reply, we are with profound esteem, &c.,

"Warsaw, March 16, 1863." (L.S.)

The time had, however, passed for these controversies; ere this letter could reach him, the Dictator was engaged in the struggle which was to prove fatal to his hopes and to those of his country.

The concentration of the Russian forces had enabled them to bring into the field a force of upwards of 12,000 men to act against Langiewicz in the province of Radom. Slowly, but very surely, they marched against him, leaving nothing to accident, but closing every avenue of escape as they advanced.

A strife so unequal could not long continue. Langiewicz did everything that an able and gallant officer could do to save a falling cause. At one time, swooping down upon some isolated detachment as it painfully threaded its way through the forests and morasses of Radom, he would defeat it. At another time he would rally his disorganized masses after they had been vanquished by the enemy, inspire them with fresh courage, and teach them how, for the sake of their country, to fight and suffer again. But the Russians gathered round him in all the strength of overpowering numbers, discipline, and arms. There was no prospect of success for his irregular levies, when they had to contend under such conditions with veteran and well-commanded troops. His men, armed with scythes and pikes, might win an occasional triumph over the irregular horsemen of the Don, but they had no chance against the men who at Sebastopol had made four nations feel their patient and abiding courage. And thus the storm increased, and the waters gathered round him, and little by little he found himself hemmed in, till in the increasing gloom all prospect of their subsidence vanished, and no ark of security was nigh.

Yet to the last he bravely bore up against the difficulties which were overpowering him. On three sides the dense masses of the Russian army encircled him. Opposed to his scythes and pikes were a powerful artillery, and regiments armed with rifles; while hanging on his flanks, skirmishing in his front, and spreading over the country on all sides, were clouds of Cossack horsemen. Nearer and nearer they came, and there seemed no way of avoiding the unequal contest they strove to drive him to accept, unless he retreated across the frontier and submitted to be disarmed by the Austrians. He evaded his enemies; their troops were within three miles of his little army, when by a sudden march he turned their flank, and freed himself from the toils once more. The respite was of short duration. From every direction troops were collecting to oppose him. Two days later, on the 18th March, he was attacked by a small Russian corps, which he defeated. On the following day he fought his last battle and gained his last victory. He was stationed at a little village named Busk, some twelve miles from the Austrian frontier, when he received intelligence that a strong detachment under Prince Schahoffskoy was menacing him from the south. Other troops threatened his right wing on the east, and to the north, at a distance of some twenty-five miles, the formidable ramparts of Keilee, and the troops who manned them, precluded all hope of escaping on that side. He retreated to a wood near the village of Grockowiska, and was attacked by the Russians there. In consequence of the nature of the ground, the Polish cavalry were unable to act, and the whole burden of the day fell upon the Zouaves and scythemen. The Russians charged them with the bayonet; but the charge was gallantly withstood, and repelled with heavy loss. Finding they met with a resistance so obstinate and effectual, the Russians retreated, leaving the field of battle in possession of their adversaries, and took up their position at Pynczow, some five miles to the north.

Surrounded by his enemies, who, although for the moment repulsed, were daily gathering strength; conscious that another battle, should it even be a victory, would only weaken his weary and diminishing army; perceiving that his position was fast becoming untenable, owing to the increasing power with which he was at length brought face to face; finding it impossible once more to break through the opposing force, and take up some fresh position; Langiewicz saw that the time was rapidly coming when he would be able neither to fight nor fly, and when, if he took no step to avoid a catastrophe so disastrous, he would be obliged to lay down his arms and surrender at discretion. That night he assembled the officers of his staff in a council of war, and consulted them on the critical condition they were placed in. It was determined, in presence of the overpowering forces which had taken the field against them, that it was hopeless to keep together a considerable army; that all that was possible was to resort once more to a guerilla war; and it was resolved that the force should be subdivided into bands, each of which was to act independently of the others, and to retreat from before their enemies in a different direction.

It was rumoured, and the report was confirmed by Langiewicz's proclamation, that dissensions in his own camp hastened the inevitable conclusion; that men were jealous of the Dictator; that they had their own objects to serve, and their own protégés to favour; and that they willingly saw the downfall of one whom they regarded as the representative of a party more moderate than their own.

After leaving his camp, Langiewicz drew up a proclamation, which was the next day circulated among his troops. In this document he stated it was necessary that he should now organize bands and detachments who were fighting in other parts of the kingdom, and that to do so he should leave them for a short interval. After recalling the struggles and victories of his troops, he continued:—

"The Russian agents, hiding themselves in your ranks, make it necessary for me to depart secretly, and without bidding you farewell. The same reason, also, prevents my informing you of my ultimate destination.

"Gathering round me some superior officers to be appointed to the command of forces worse officered than yourselves, I require no more than an escort of thirty lancers to accompany us a short distance on our way. Before leaving, the force under my immediate command has been divided into several corps, each under a separate general, and with special orders as to the march and work that lie before them.

"Companions in arms! in the face of God and the presence of my army, I took the oath to fight to the last. This oath I have kept and shall keep in future. You, too, have sworn to serve the country and obey my commands. The oath of the soldier is equally inviolable with that of the general. In the name, then, of God and country, continue the struggle, and fight the Muscovite, while fighting remains the only means of restoring the liberty and independence of the country.

"But a few hours after my departure calumny denounced me as a traitor, an embezzler, and a thief. The same infamous slanderers instigated desertion in the camp, and, while intending to destroy me, they only benefitted Muscovy and prepared an easy triumph for the foe. The adherents of the ambitious criminal I have to thank for all this are not aware, or, if they are aware, utterly ignore that my only object is to establish the liberty and independence of the country."

When the news reached the camp that the Dictator had left them, grief and terror took possession of the multitude. He was gone—the one master-mind which had given them victory, and found shelter for them in defeat; he was gone, and within sight were the threatening armies of their enemy, ready to renew a conflict which could only end in the discomfiture of the leaderless and broken Poles. To no purpose did the officers explain how the war was now to be conducted; to no purpose was the Dictator's proclamation distributed among them, for the only idea it conveyed to them was that their leader had deserted them. In their despair they listened to no counsel and obeyed no commands, but hastily retreating from the ground they occupied, they broke their ranks and fled for safety to the Austrian frontier. Some, however, were less dispirited, and instead of losing all faith in their country and their cause, united themselves to other detachments in the kingdom, and strove to carry on a guerilla war.

Leaving the camp with a few of his officers, Langiewicz attempted to reach Podolia, to take the command of a band of insurgents in that province; before, however, he had gone far, he met with a Russian corps whose numbers rendered it impossible for him to pass or successfully attack them. He avoided the danger by crossing the Vistula and entering Galicia, where he trusted that a French passport in which he was described as a M. Waligorski would protect him. Representing himself by his assumed name, he requested the Austrian commander to permit him to continue his journey unmolested. On being told that this request could not be granted without express permission from the higher authorities, he finally declared himself, and placed himself under the protection of the Austrian Government. And now, crowding over the frontier, poured the shattered fragments of the late insurgent army. Broken, dispirited, famished, shivering, and weary, the inhabitants of Cracow and Tarnow could scarce persuade themselves that this was the celebrated army whose deeds had been so widely told. Were these wounded boys who were carried to the military hospital the Zouaves and the scythemen of whom they had heard so much? And were these fugitives, who had not among them a weapon or an uniform, the men who a week ago were thought competent to annihilate the power of Russia and re-erect in Warsaw a national throne?

Yet so it was. The dictatorship of ten days was ended, and all chance of success in the struggle for national freedom seemed to have died with it. Doubtless brave and enthusiastic men might still be found to peril life and liberty in the cause of Poland; doubtless there yet remained able and daring plotters who would carry on their mysterious schemes for the revivication of their country; but there was nowhere to be found in the ranks of the insurgent party those combined qualities which the Dictator alone possessed,—a true patriotism unstained by selfish hopes and criminal ambitions; a dauntless courage which never swelled into boastfulness or sunk into ferocity; self-possession when perils of all kinds thickened round him; and a mastery and power over the minds of others, which converted a disorganized rabble into a phalanx of steady soldiers.

He fought no more for Poland; he was the guiding star

of the movement, and when his light was lost in the gloom of an Austrian dungeon, the insurrection dwindled into the ordinary insignificance of a guerilla and partisan war.

No sooner had Langiewicz failed in his enterprise than he was treated with the justice the world ever metes out to the unfortunate. Denounced, as we learn from his own proclamation, even while at the head of his army, what had a friendless prisoner to expect at the hand of his cowardly detractors? He was represented as having deserted his troops, as having sold them to the Russians, and as having only thought of his personal ease and security. To such an extent were the passions of some of the fugitives excited against him, that the Austrians were compelled to provide him with an unusual guard, not for the purpose of preventing his escape, but to secure him from the violence of the mob.

There was not only a character to be blackened, there was an inheritance to be won. A little while, and some daring hand might be stretched out to grasp the Dictatorship and assume the direction of the confused masses who were still in arms. Disorganized and broken, there might yet be found some one who coveted the dangerous pre-eminence and shrunk not from the risk that it entailed.

The Central Committee had yielded to the decided action of Langiewicz, but they were by no means disposed to pass by so fair an opportunity of recovering their lost dominion. A dictatorship they professed was a mistake, large armies were a mistake also, and in future the liberation of Poland was to be effected by guerilla bands. Probably they thought the isolated efforts of insignificant men would be more easily controlled by them than the movements of a captain whose ability was acknowledged, and who had under his command an effective corps. Their ideas seldom seem to have soared beyond the murder of an employé or the plunder of a strongbox, and it was natural they should seek to be secure from the irksome dominion of ascendant genius.

They published a proclamation, therefore, in which they styled themselves the Provisional National Government, and in the following terms resumed the authority they had so lately surrendered :—

"Fellow Countrymen,—The Dictatorship of General Laugiewicz having ceased on the 19th March, the chief authority of the country returns into the hands of the Provisional National Government at Warsaw, who have never left off their governmental duties, and are the only and sole legally constituted authority of the country. Fellow countrymen! the return of power into the hands of men who have called forth the rising, and perseveringly directed it, ought to be a guarantee to you that the movement will continue, and that it will not end without victory. Yes, we will fight without weariness, without being disheartened by ill-success or deterred by any obstacles. We will not concentrate the whole cause in one person, whose fall may occasion the destruction of the rising; and, strong in our possession of the confidence of the nation, we will boldly stand forth against all factions which might attempt to create, without our consent, any new power or authority. Fellow countrymen! we grasp again with faith and confidence the helm of the National Government, and, practical in devising remedies in cases of emergency, we are confident in being able to avert the danger which threatens us in consequence of the fall of the Dictatorship.

"Faithful to the cause the standard of which, upheld by us, sets aside every misunderstanding of party, we invoke the whole nation to obedience.

"To arms! In the face of the foe, in the face of our falling brethren, the place of every Pole is in the ranks.

"By authority of the Central Committee of the Provisional National Government.

"The Commissioner Extraordinary,

"Stephen Bobroski."

CHAPTER XIII.

The National Government.—The Peasants and the Government.—Public Feeling in Russia.—Addresses to the Emperor.—The Amnesty.—Its Reception by Insurgents.—English Cabinet.

PUBLIC attention had long been drawn to the self-styled National Government. It was alleged that two antagonistic powers ruled in Poland.

The first, legitimate only in name, was presided over by a prince of the imperial house, assisted by a long train of experienced councillors; was supported by a huge army; obeyed by a vigilant police; in its hands were all the honours by which ambitious spirits may be won, and all the emoluments by which mean men may be bought; everything was at its disposal, and it scrupled not to use its advantages to enforce its evil ends. Nor was its power bounded by its traffic in venality; it armed with unsparing severity and injustice the hand of the executioner against all it suspected of being its foes; it filled the dungeons of Warsaw and every other Russian citadel with men whose only crime was their nationality and the independence of their spirit; it sent those against whom it harboured the most paltry suspicions to waste their lives in ignoble warfare on the frontiers of Asia, or find a living tomb in some Ouralian mine. And yet, despite all this power, all this illimitable capacity to cajole, to bribe, and to punish, the Government could scarcely hold its own within its armed fortresses and military camps.

Beyond those narrow boundaries it was alleged that every one bowed in reverent submission to the orders of the National Government; that mysterious tribunal whose faintest wish was a command, but whose constituent parts were utterly unknown.

In the citadel of Warsaw the Russians ruled, in the streets of the same city the National Government were supreme.

The one power issued decrees for the levying of taxes; the taxes were paid, but they were paid to the collectors of the other. This secret administration was carried on with infinite daring and success. Admirably informed by its unknown agents, it was aware of every resolution taken in the vice-regal council-chamber ere the ink had dried by which that resolution was recorded, and consequently was often able to parry or anticipate an intended blow. Equally well informed of the movements of the Russian troops, the transport of provisions, and the convoy of arms, it had often the opportunity of intercepting a detachment or harassing a march, and thus obtained the successes which filled Western Europe with rumours of its achievements, and persuaded the world that the insurrection was maintained by powerful armies, who waged against the troops of Russia a not unequal war.

The explanation of the apparent mystery, so far as there was any truth in these exaggerated views, was, however, very simple. Almost without exception, the Polish officials were favourably disposed to the revolt; and it has already been seen that throughout the kingdom the civil officials were *all* Poles. They not only did nothing to check the schemes of the National Government, they did everything in their power to advance and further them. The information of which they became officially the masters, they placed at its disposal; the operations they were directed to carry out, they endeavoured to thwart and render useless; and, in short, all their efforts and all their opportunities were employed in undermining the Government whose rank they held and on whose salaries they lived.

The police, which, under ordinary circumstances, would have been certain to discover some traces of the conspiracy, were also Poles; many incidents, from time to time, demonstrated that they actively sympathized with the insurgents; there was reason to think, in many cases, that they directly obeyed the orders of the National Government; it was certain that in no case did they discover its emissaries or denounce its schemes.

The army was faithful: but what could the army do? they were in a hostile country, surrounded by spies, and many of their secret enemies were so placed as to be able to give them orders, instead of openly fighting against them in the rebel ranks. All the army could do was to act upon its instructions, and put down insurrection whenever the rebels drew to a head.

The peasants were helpless, passive, and expectant; their sympathies were mostly with the Government, for in the Government they recognized the only power which as yet had moderated the intolerable oppression of their lords; and they believed it would confer on them the land for which they now were compelled to work, and which in justice and equity, they conceived, long since should have been their own. But the peasants had no power to counteract the secret organization of their masters, and if they had had such power, they would have feared to exercise it.

Another cause of the success of the National Government was to be found in the scrupulous respect the Russian authorities paid to the Catholic Church. Although there was every reason to suppose that the priests of that Church were intimately connected with the leaders of the insurrection, although it was known that they encouraged their congregations to give it every aid in their power, and although for a long time past the pulpit had been little less than a revolutionary rostrum; yet the advisers of the Grand Duke, either from policy or weakness, instituted no inquiries into the relations existing between this clergy and the insurgents. The clergy, thus feeling themselves secure, took an active part in the insurrectionary organization; secret printing-presses were concealed in the monasteries, and the proclamations of the National Government were printed by them; arms and uniforms were sent thither as to a place of assured safety; and it was in the same precincts, at a later date, that the daggers and poisoned stilettos, with which the hired bravos employed by the National Government were to be armed, were found concealed.

The machinery, therefore, by which the National Government was carried on was very simple; it depended on the corrupt support of Polish officers, the treachery of the Polish police, the weakness of the Government, and the secure alliance of the Roman Catholic priesthood.

The proclamations of the National Government, its passports, and its orders, were issued anonymously, but were stamped with an official seal, and bore about them all outward signs of proceeding from some constituted authority. It appointed governors of towns, and all other officers, in rivalry of the Russian Government; it had command over many of the railway *employés*, its letters and missives were delivered with more than the regularity of the post; and it had a secret press which chronicled its acts, misled public opinion, and circulated fabricated news.

The National Government strove to prevent the proprietors from leaving their estates; and, as already mentioned, at the very beginning of the revolutionary struggle issued an order desiring the nobles in Warsaw to return to them, for its power was great over the nobles dwelling in isolated châteaux, or small towns adjoining their properties; and it could compel such men to pay any exaction they imposed, and obey any orders they issued.

In May, however, the National Government went further, for it endeavoured to prevent proprietors from leaving their estates without first procuring its passports; and issued another decree ordering all proprietors residing in foreign countries to return to Poland.

The most efficient weapon it wielded was its secret police. They were mainly recruited from the Schlachta and the artisans in the larger towns. It was the duty of this police to execute the sentences of their employers; and as those sentences were almost invariably death, this body was nothing else than a band of hired assassins.

These men were the blind tools of a sanguinary system. They knew not who were their employers; they knew not what crimes they might be instructed to commit; but they entered the service prompted by mercenary motives, or, at the best, by a most criminal patriotism.

The following statement shows the way in which the services of these men were secured:—

"On the 8th of July, at a late hour at night, there were arrested in one of the streets of Warsaw, Antoine Heine, fireman, aged 27 years; Ignace Stefanowski, care-taker of a house, aged 35 years; and Auguste Zawistowski, fireman, aged 37 years. All carried daggers, and on Heine was found a written order of the so-called chief of the rebel gendarmes to assassinate one Fritsche, *sergent de ville* of the fourth circle.

"On inquiry, it proved that all three formed part of the insurrectionary organization of Polish gendarmes, which had for its object political murders. Heine had been affiliated to the society by one François Nowicki, who in consequence of this information was likewise arrested.

"These four avowed that they had consented to charge themselves with the execution of political murders, and had taken the oath required of them; Heine and Zawistowski in the cloister of the Trinity before a priest whom they did not know; Stefanowski and Nowicki, in the house of the so-called chief of the gendarmes, before a priest of the same cloister, whom they could not, they said, recollect, as they had taken this oath in a dark garret. Fifty copecks (1*s.* 7*d.*) a day was paid them as members of this organization.

"The 7th July, Heine and Zawistowski had each received, in the town, from Stefanowski, a dagger, and Nowicki at the same time gave them the order for the assassination. These three men—Heine, Zawistowski, and Stefanowski—assembled in a cabaret, and were arrested at ten o'clock at night, as they were on the point of starting for the accomplishment of the murder."

When public opinion had recovered its tone, and loathing was excited by that sanguinary system which at first had only produced dismay, the great proprietors indignantly disavowed all participation in these deeds of blood. The National Government, they said, were mechanics and students, men without education, or youths in their teens; they did not recognize its jurisdiction, they disclaimed many of its acts, and they protested against being identified with its crimes.

The disclaimer came too late;* for weeks and months that Government had been obeyed, and the homage rendered to it was cited to Europe as the most convincing evidence of

---

* The best proof of this is the speech of Prince Czartoryski, as reported in the *Times*, May 11, 1863:—"Is it not a subject of consolation and of hope for our future prospects to see a nation so united in its efforts and so well disciplined in its struggles? A Polish Government has been established under the very eye of the enemy and in the midst of its spies and its executioners, which has no executive force at its disposal, and which dispenses with police and gendarmes (?); which has no name, and the commands of which, nevertheless, are not the less executed throughout Poland. The entire country is subject to it, and all we emigrants obey it. Our people, whom our enemies have always accused of disturbance and anarchy, have given a decisive proof of their obedience to Government—of their respect for authority, provided it be national."

Polish unanimity. Its first act, the free gift of land to the peasant, had been confirmed by the proprietors, who thus testified their approbation of its rule, although they could only do so by abandoning the principles they had championed for upwards of thirty years; and they qualified this act of unconditional obedience by no protest against murder, robbery, and arson, till those crimes had destroyed the popularity and undermined the power of the National Government.

It was indeed impossible that any political grievance should be held to excuse such a system. The murder of Minnislewski, a literary man who supported the policy of the Marquis Wielopolski, is an example of it. He was sentenced by the National Government to death as a traitor, for some unknown offence, and his murder is thus described:—" It is said that he was warned some days beforehand that he was to die, and after receiving the warning never went out without being accompanied by two police agents. The day, however, of the murder being committed, there happened to be a street fight near the door of his house, and one of the attendants took the chief of the brawlers into custody. Just then, a barrel-organ began to grind forth " No, Poland is not lost," and the remaining attendant, having a sharp ear for forbidden tunes, and being moreover a man of zeal, arrested the offender before he had got to the third bar. At that moment the long-meditated blow was struck. The appointed executioner (who by this time must be a practised hand) had followed Minnislewski into the house, and, seizing him from behind, and laying his hand over his mouth to silence his cries, stabbed him to the heart. The executioner, or murderer, or whatever he is, got into a carriage when he had done the deed, and calling to the police agent who had an ear for music, said to him, ' You amuse yourself by running after organ-players, and you don't see that in that house a man is being assassinated.' "*

At length the unpopularity which these murders brought upon the National Government was so great that, in a special circular addressed to its " Diplomatic Agents," it thus endeavoured to vindicate them:—

* Letter of correspondent in *Times* of 11th June.

"In various announcements of the national authorities, and more particularly in the decrees of the provost of Warsaw, the public have been informed that sentence of death has been passed on persons proved to have acted as Muscovite spies. The Muscovite journals, in viewing these executions in another light, endeavour to misrepresent their bearing and character. Above all, they have attempted to circulate the news that the National Government is relying upon murder as an incentive to patriotism, which would have died away without the application of this particular means. * * * *

"The National Government never entertained the idea of supporting by executions a cause whose entire force lies in the principles it represents, and in which it persists; in those principles on which all good Poles are agreed, on the principles, in fact, of culture and civilization, which are everywhere disregarded and trodden under foot by the Muscovites. These principles are our only object and incentive. By them incited, we seek, at the price of so many sacrifices, that liberty which alone can restore us the blessings of a civilized and well-ordered commonwealth. It is very evident,—and who can be more convinced of it than the National Government?—that executions would be utterly insufficient to create a spirit of patriotism among the people, even for a time, were it determined to abandon the country and surrender Poland to her foes. In our eyes, they are no more than an inevitable evil, to be employed in obviating still greater evils; no more than a means of protection, justified as the only efficient arms against a hostile power, which does not even shrink from calling to its aid the services of some miserable and corrupt individuals.

"The exceptional character of our judicial proceedings, which, however, is modified by the strictest regard to the correctness of the evidence, will be justified in the eyes of unprejudiced observers by our unexampled position. In all history it would be impossible to find a parallel to the system of injustice, robbery, murder, and incessant contempt of all rights of humanity so long imposed upon our country by the Muscovite Government, and now carried on with increased wickedness and barbarity. The daily aggravating character of Muscovite espionage and terrorism, whose savage deeds are denounced in so many reports of our patriotic police, alone induced the National Government to have recourse to exceptional measures, which in the history of our commonwealth, and under an ordinary state of things, would never have occurred. But it is existence itself which we have hourly to defend. If some abandoned ruffians have been visited, here and there, with execution, a glance at the real state of things will suffice to show that we should have failed to breathe the soul of patriotism into the people had it not been its own will to pass through the trials awaiting it. Nor is it at all doubtful that the lawless executions, whose heart-rending spectacle the Muscovite authorities are thrusting before our eyes, will be altogether powerless in quenching that spirit.

"A comparison between our official notifications and those of the Muscovites will serve to unveil the faults and unprincipled character of their reports at the side of our indisputable facts. Thus, for instance, the murders, whose private and criminal nature was announced and publicly exposed by the National Government, were converted into political executions by the enemy, who, at the same time, endeavoured to sully the memory of the slain by adding them to the number of their tyrannic allies. But what is revolting above all, persons altogether unconnected with the national police and the execution of our sentences, have been carried off to the gallows, only to protect the Muscovite courts against the reproach of inefficiency. Thus Kaminski was hung at Warsaw, and the two brothers Rewkowski, Lipowicz and Jablonski, at Wilna. But even here Muscovite effrontery and wickedness does not stop. While glossing over their atrocities, their papers have been made to slander their victims, and start a whole system of mendacious attacks from the very beginning of our revolt."

The vindication of the National Government, therefore, is, that in the cause of culture and civilization they committed murder, and that the espionage and terrorism of Muscovite agents rendered it necessary they should do so. They should show how culture and civilization can be injured by espionage, and how far the Russians attempted to repress them by terrorism.

The pretence that spies alone were murdered is completely false, and could only be advanced to deceive Europe; no one in Poland would be misled by it. The allegation that Lipowicz and Jablonski were unjustly executed is, I have reason to believe, equally so, for I was present at the time, and was assured by members of the court-martial that they had confessed the crimes with which they were charged.

But it was not murder only which disgraced the National Government. Their secret organization was often defective, and their agents committed excesses which added to the hatred with which the peasants regarded them.

In looking through some of the records of legal proceedings at Wilna, I found a document, of which the following is a literal translation :—

ACT.

Arrived at the property of Pomoossya, which belongs to the proprietor Rossohatsky, I found the peasants holding some land at a rent under a contract concluded two years ago. I read them the manifesto of the 2nd January, 1863, and, in the name of the National Government, gave them those lands as their own property by virtue of this Act. I commanded the proprietor Rossohatsky that he should never require any rent or service from them, which he solemnly promised with oath (under menace of death).

The present Act, written in three true copies, is given to the participating parties.

Attest the exactness of this Act. Pomoosya, the 3rd July, 1863.

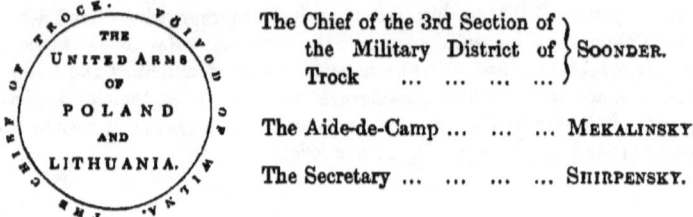

The Chief of the 3rd Section of the Military District of Trock	SOONDER.
The Aide-de-Camp	MEKALINSKY.
The Secretary	SHIRPENSKY.

Vöivodship of Wilna.
    The Chief of the District of Trock.

The history of this document was as follows. A band of insurgents arrived at the estate of the proprietor Rossohatsky; they summoned the tenants, and informed them that the National Government had given them their land free from all claim on the part of the proprietor. They then sent for the proprietor, and were equally explicit with him. Under menace of death, as they are careful to record, they made the unhappy man subscribe whatever document, and take whatever oath they pleased, and then they handed the formal instrument, sealed with the official seal, to the liberated peasants and the plundered proprietor. Before departing, however, they made a demand for money on the peasants, to which the latter entirely demurred: there seemed in their eyes to be an inconsistency in first giving them land, and then asking them for roubles, which they were very anxious their new friends should not be betrayed into; but the band became importunate; where they had asked roubles they gradually lessened their demand till it dwindled into copecks, and at length, under the pressure of requests they could, and menaces they could not, resist, the peasants surrendered their cash to the band, which forthwith departed.

The liberators gone, the next question was what was to be done with the document they left behind them. Proprietor and tenants alike regarded it as valueless, and, on the whole, they judged it best to take it to the nearest Russian authority, depose to the facts, and leave it in his custody.

The mischievous interference of the National Government did not stop even at acts like these; it meddled with public contracts, with private employment, with the management of estates.

Sir Morton Peto and his partners had contracted to construct some waterworks in Warsaw, and on the 11th of May the following decree on the subject was issued :—

"ART. 1.—The contract relating to waterworks for the city of Warsaw, concluded on the 20th day of April of the present year, between the President of the city of Warsaw and the foreign contractors, Sir Samuel Morton Peto, Member of Parliament, Edward Ladd Betts, and the house of John Aird & Co., is hereby dissolved, and must be regarded as null and void.

"ART. 2.—We entrust the carrying out of this decree to the civil and military functionaries."

A German or Frenchman was employed on the Warsaw and Petersburg Railway in a position of responsibility. He and his family were solely dependent on the salary he received from his situation. He was a man who did not mix in politics, and who, as far as he knew, had never done a thing to offend any political faction. He was warned to quit his situation, and leave Warsaw within two days. He hesitated; to him the change was ruin; he thought the warning might have been given him in error, or that at least he would be allowed to plead his cause before the invisible tribunal which condemned him; but no,—when the two days had passed, a second missive reached him, telling him that as a foreigner the National Government gave him twenty-four hours more in which to depart; if he did not leave within that period, his life would pay the forfeit. So in terror the miserable and ruined man shook the dust from off his feet and left the accursed city.

Pages could be filled with the recital of similar actions, but my only object is to show the general scope and tenour of the policy of the National Government, and then leave it to the reader to judge whether such a tyranny could be willingly endured by a high-spirited and patriotic race.

One mistake into which the National Government was betrayed bears on it the impress of such utter incompetence that it should be recorded. It forbade the payment of taxes to the established Government; so its officers naturally levied on the goods of the defaulters; thereupon a decree was published forbidding any one to buy the goods so taken in execution; and in consequence, goods and live stock were seized and sold at the most absurd prices; a cow or a horse might be bought for a few shillings, and other things in the same proportion. Of course the loss fell on the proprietors who obeyed the National Government.

In opposition to the secret organization, the Government resolved to bring a new and untried power into the field. The peasants had not been prompt to side with either party, but their sympathies were opposed to the insurgents. The cry in favour of Polish nationality seemed to their dull but very practical common sense to mean, if not the restoration of serfdom, at least the withholding of all those rights which they believed should have been granted to them more than half a century before. The Polish landowners never attempted to give the peasants land till they saw the Government would insist on it, and then the scheme they propounded was only proposed for the almost avowed purpose of embarrassing the authorities; the proclamation of the Central Committee was worthless, for it had no power to confer the land it pretended so generously to alienate; and supposing the committee were eventually to succeed in procuring the independence of their country, what guarantee was there that it would act up to its own proclamation?

On the other hand, the Russian Government had evinced a real desire for the amelioration of the condition of the peasants. In Russia it had emancipated them and secured them their land; in Poland, before the troubles broke out, it had shown similar intentions, and had it not been for the insurrection, would perhaps by this time have accomplished its wishes. Moreover, it was the stronger party, and would in the end be certain to prevail. Moved by these considerations, the peasants, as a class, early declared in favour of the Government, and assisted it both by the intelligence they procured for it, and by seizing and delivering up fugitive insurgents to the troops.

On the 6th of March the Grand Duke issued a proclamation,

by which, after recognizing the loyalty of the peasants and the assistance they at all times gave the troops, he directed the village authorities to employ watchmen for the purpose of examining all suspected persons, whether residents or travellers. The peasants, elders, and bailiffs were also desired to apprehend all armed individuals and persons belonging to insurgent bands, as well as marauders, and to convey them to the nearest military station. These instructions were to be carried out without committing excesses, and without doing any violent or arbitrary act.

On the following day General Nazimow issued a similar proclamation to apply to four of the governments under his charge.

The step which the Grand Duke had thus taken was viewed with the utmost displeasure by the great Polish nobles. Since the revolt had broken out, they complained that no overture had been made to them by the Government.

They had crowded into Warsaw the moment the safety of the State was imperilled; they had consulted anxiously how best to serve their country and their sovereign, and his representative had given them neither encouragement nor thanks. This they had silently endured, though it betokened suspicion and dislike. On the 3rd of March, the fête-day of their king, they had thronged to the levee of the Grand Duke, despite the threats of the revolutionary propaganda, and in so doing had incurred great peril; yet the Grand Duke did not notice them. And now, three days after that vain humiliation, the Government which had treated them so disdainfully gave the signal for a war of classes; it placed in the hands of a barbarous and ignorant peasantry the right to command and to tyrannize over their masters; it gave to men who were no better than the neighbouring serfs, authority to arrest the most powerful nobleman of Poland. Whose house was sacred from their intrusion? whose stable or farm-yard was secure from robbery? and what guarantee was there that duties ostensibly bestowed on them in the interests of the State, might not be converted to the vilest purposes that revenge could suggest or avarice indicate?

In haughty displeasure the great nobles withdrew from the

Council of State. Nothing less, they pronounced, was intended by this step than the plunder of the mansions and imprisonment of the persons of the proprietors, and subsequently the partition of their estates among those who were formerly their serfs. It was a socialist alliance between arbitrary power and the dregs of the people, and was levelled at all the education, all the intelligence, and all the patriotism of Poland.

To comprehend these incoherent utterances, it must be remembered that the land question was yet unsettled; the wildest notions upon that subject had been afloat, and the peasantry had doubtless entertained very utopian ideas as to the advantages they were to possess when their new position was ascertained.*

And these were the men, the proprietors urged, whom the Government were about to trust; these were the men who, temporarily at least, were to hold sway over their former masters; who were to be salaried for watching, and bribed for denouncing them; and who would see in every estate that was forfeited through their false witness, additional booty which a grateful Government would ere long divide among them. In truth, in many places, the peasants were neither courteous nor intelligent; they were uncouth, suspicious, and exacting; and if they were zealous guardians of the public peace, it cannot be denied that their mode of preserving it was open to grave complaint.

The peasant guard were a rough-looking police, and as they were drawn up at the railway stations armed, but dressed in their ordinary clothes, they appeared to be men who would not be very discriminating or very tender in their treatment of their captives. Nor indeed were they. At Mohileff, day

---

* An amusing illustration of their theories was given a few months previously in a remote district of Russia. The serfs on an estate waited on the proprietor, and told him they had been seriously considering how best to avail themselves of their new property when the land became their own; that they had settled most points, but that on one they could not agree, so they thought, as he was a man of education, they had better refer to him for advice. They knew how to cultivate the soil, but would he tell them into what species of manufactory they had better convert his castle, as soon as, by the Emperor's benevolence, it became their own?

after day, the proprietors were brought into the town in their carriages; on either side of a prisoner, whose hands were tied, would be a peasant armed with a musket or a sword, while another sat upon the box beside the driver, and others accompanied the equipage to preclude the possibility of rescue. Thus, one after another, most of the proprietors were brought into the town, and handed to the Russian authorities, that the charges against them might be investigated. One day the Governor was waited on by a body of peasants from a particular estate; they represented that, on all the properties round, the peasants had captured their masters and brought them into the town; *their* master, however, was, unluckily for them, staying at his town house, and all their neighbours mocked them as being alone unable to bring in their prisoner. Would the Governor, therefore, in order to save them from ridicule, permit them to seize the carriage of their master and his person, put him into it, and deliver him as a prisoner to the authorities?

Nevertheless a regular government cannot justly be blamed in revolutionary epochs for putting confidence in a class upon whose loyalty it can depend. Granting that the boors of Poland and the Western provinces are somewhat uncouth; granting that men who had received no education were not as fit for their offices as the members of the Metropolitan police; it must still be remembered that fidelity, not refinement, is required in civil war,—the honest and loyal performance of duty, not courtly insincerity and the traitor's smile. If, indeed, the Government had promised that the plunder of the wealthy should remunerate the services of the poor; if it had promised to partition among the faithful serfs the property of their late masters; if it had sought to create a servile insurrection against them, and a repetition of the Galician outrages of 1848; then, indeed, there would have been reason for an accusation which now falls to the ground as utterly causeless.

This complaint is, in truth, but the murmur of a defeated faction. The support of the peasants was essential to both parties, and the insurgents as well as the Government made every effort to secure it; had they succeeded, and had their ranks been filled by the people their oppression had alienated from them, nothing would have been heard of socialist theories, and a war of classes would not have been denounced.

The resignation of the independent members of the Municipal Council of Warsaw quickly followed, and a further evidence, beyond the limits of the kingdom, of the feeling among the higher class of the Poles, was conveyed by the resignation of the marshals of the nobility in Lithuania. Thus isolated by the retirement of the Poles who had taken part in public affairs, the Marquis Wielopolski became an object of suspicion both to his own countrymen and to the Russians. The feeling of the former is sufficiently evidenced by the proclamation already cited, by which the Central Committee authorizes any one to murder him, and by the infamous attempts upon his life, which have also been referred to. The feeling of the Russians was of a different character; slowly they began first to wonder at the errors so able a man had committed, then to question the sincerity of the advice he tendered, and at length to suspect some deep-laid and Machiavellian conspiracy to annihilate the Russian power and restore the supremacy of the Poles. Suspicion once awakened soon finds food for itself, and when a nation is determined to discover premeditated treachery, every insignificant and unimportant fact has a tendency to confirm the creed. In all grades of society the Marquis was spoken of as a traitor who was secretly plotting for the independence of Poland.

Yet, apparently, the opinions the Marquis professed were those that he really held; and, holding such opinions, his course of action was such as many men under similar circumstances would have adopted. It is impossible to forgive the conscription—that one black and damning act—which must ever remain a blot upon his scutcheon; yet, even here, we should be wrong in visiting him with the same condemnation an English statesman would under similar circumstances deserve. There is nothing in his conduct to throw doubt upon his really entertaining the views expressed in his letter to Prince Metternich; he despaired of a free Poland, he detested Austrian treachery, and he shrunk from the political system of Prussia. In Russia he recognized a nation sprung, like his own, from the Sclavonic race, having much in common with Poland and sharing in her deep-seated detestation of Germany; he saw in her a young, a powerful, and an ambitious people, under whose supremacy Poland might advance in physical and moral development; he believed the time would come when the superior ability and education of the higher orders of the Poles would secure for them a large share in the government of Russia; and he was anxious that no vain struggle for an independence they could never obtain should retard the era he anticipated. We cannot blame him for discountenancing a nobility who he felt were hostile to the cause for which he struggled; neither can we denounce him for arming the peasants with unaccustomed power, for the peasants were loyal, and in the death-grapple of nations it is impossible always to select the weapons to be used.

The progress of the insurrection had been watched with deep anxiety by all classes in Russia. So long as it was thought that the autonomy or even independence of the Congress kingdom was the utmost the insurgents desired to obtain, the struggle had been regarded with an equanimity approaching to indifference; but of late they had avowed that the Poland of 1772 was the object for which they strove; that autonomy they did not value, and that absolute severance from Russia was their only aim. Moreover, there were rumours that the Western powers had made representations to the court of St. Petersburg which unduly interfered with the internal policy of the empire.

These reports deeply moved public opinion; the Western provinces had long been regarded as wholly Russian, and her people would never consent to surrender them unless they were torn from her as the issue of a long and calamitous war.

As evidence of this change in the feeling of the nation, Lord Napier's letter to Lord Russell of 4th April is very conclusive.—

"The first signal," he writes, "of patriotic agitation against Poland has been given. The Assembly of Nobility of the government of St. Petersburg have adopted by acclamation the accompanying address to the Emperor, expressive of their determination to support the integrity of the empire. In case of intervention or menace from abroad, this spirit will run very high. In the Polish question all the national and religious passions of the Russian people are touched. The recruits in the Russian provinces are coming in with unusual alacrity, and go off under the impression of an impending 'holy war.' I was not present when the address of the Assembly was adopted, but I am informed that there was a scene of enthusiasm, in which the feeling of devotion to Russia was, no doubt, at least as strong as that of devotion to the sovereign. It is not so much the insurrection in the kingdom of Poland which arouses the indignation of the Russians, as the alleged views of the Poles on the frontier provinces, extending even to the sacred city of Kieff. The frontier provinces are the traditional battle-ground and debateable land between the Polish and Russian nations. They will never be relinquished by Russia without a mortal struggle."

The address was couched in the following terms :—

"The nobility of the government of St. Petersburg, being animated by an ancient devotion to the throne and to their native country, consider it their sacred duty solemnly to express to you, sire, the sentiments by which they are inspired. The pretensions of the Polish insurgents to the possessions of Russia fill us with grief and indignation. Our enemies conceive the era of the great reforms undertaken by you for the happiness and welfare of the State is a favourable one for their attacks upon the integrity of the Russian empire; but they are deceived. The nobility, tried in devotion and abnegation, and sparing neither exertion nor sacrifice, will, in connection with all the orders of the nation, know how to take its stand firmly and immovably in defence of the territory of the empire. Let the enemies of Russia know that the spirit of our ancestors lives in us,—the spirit which succeeded in establishing the unity of our beloved country."

But it was not alone from St. Petersburg that such addresses came; from all parts of the kingdom and from all classes they poured in; assemblies of nobles, municipal bodies, merchants, and peasants, all vied with each other in their professions of loyalty and of patriotism; the Government, which so long had struggled against the general apathy, was at length impelled onward by the violent blast of public opinion; its difficulty now was rather to restrain the passion of the people than to arouse their zeal.

The situation had greatly changed; no longer opposed by an army which, under the command of a competent general, defied their power; no longer having any open opponent save the guerilla bands, who might, indeed, annoy, but who could never seriously damage it; wielding an overpowering army, and supported by an unanimous people, the Government felt that the time had arrived when it could offer pardon to the rebels without the offer being construed into an evidence of weakness.

Accordingly, on the 31st March (12th April) a proclamation* signed by the Emperor appeared, in which, after exonerating the Polish nation from the responsibility of the revolt, and attributing it to external influences, he offered to consign the past to oblivion, and then continued: "Therefore, ardently desiring to put a stop to an effusion of blood as useless as it is regrettable, we grant a free pardon to all those of our subjects in the kingdom implicated in the late troubles who have not incurred responsibilities for other crimes, or for offences committed while serving in the ranks of our army, who may before the 1st (13th) of May lay down their arms and return to their allegiance;" and, after alluding to the liberal institutions recently conferred on Poland, he added, "While continuing for the present to maintain these institutions in their integrity, we reserve it to ourselves, when they shall have been tested by experience, to proceed to their further development, in accordance with the requirements of the times and of the country."

The insurgents, ever deceived as to their true position and prospects, and, perhaps, misled by a few ambitious partisans who were unwilling to return to their former insignificance, treated this amnesty with scorn. They regarded it as an evidence of want of power; they assumed it would never have been offered by the Russian Government unless it had felt convinced that in no other way could the insurrection be put down; and, instead of thinning the rebel bands, the effect of the amnesty was to urge hundreds into the field.

The Provisional Government issued a proclamation. "An amnesty," they said, "has been announced by the Russian Government, as also a promise to maintain the existing institutions. Poland is well aware what confidence she can place in this pretended amnesty and in the promises of the

---

* See Appendix C.

Russian Government. But, to avoid any mistake, we formally declare that we reject all these false concessions. It was not with the intention of obtaining more or less liberal institutions that we took up arms, but to get rid of the detested yoke of a foreign government, and to reconquer our ancient and complete independence. It is for this, and for this alone, that the nation makes great sacrifices, and does not spare its blood. No man who has the love of his country at heart can be indifferent to the blood which has been shed, to the destruction of property which has occurred, to the fact that towns have been burned down, and that the whole country is desolated. Every honest patriot will indignantly reject the so-called favours and concessions of the Czar. We have taken up arms; arms alone must decide the issue of the struggle."

The amnesty took the Russians by surprise; they had had their passions violently excited by what they regarded as the thankless and disloyal conduct of the Poles; they were making great sacrifices to subdue them, and they were not prepared for this sudden act of clemency. They thought that the excesses of which the insurgents had been guilty, the murders they had committed, and the devastation they had caused, demanded something more discriminate than a promiscuous pardon. The enthusiasm of the people was checked, and the press was dumb.

The English ambassador regarded it from a different point of view: it was, he said, conceived in a tone of humanity and clemency, which was congenial to the character of the Emperor, and was undoubtedly consistent with the interests of the Imperial cabinet and the wishes of the English Government.

Not so, however, thought Lord Russell. He addressed a despatch to Lord Napier,* in which he stated that an amnesty can lay the foundation of peace in only two cases; the first of these was where the insurgents had been thoroughly defeated, and only waited for a promise of pardon to enable them to return to their homes; and the second was, if the

---

* See Appendix, Lord Russell's letter of the 24th April, 1863.

amnesty were accompanied with such ample promises of the redress of the grievances which gave occasion to the insurrection, as to induce the insurgents to think that their object was attained.

The former of these events, he stated, had not happened, because the insurrection was more extensive than it had been a few weeks before.

The second of these proposed cases, he pronounced, did not arise; for after the evidence the conscription gave of the worthlessness of the existing laws, he said the insurgents would not be satisfied to recur to them.

The promise to develop existing institutions, he also declared to be unsatisfactory, because he said that promise was contingent on their working well; and as the Poles had refused to co-operate in carrying them out, it was impossible they should work at all. He followed up this observation by a quotation from Lord Durham's despatches, thirty-one years previously, in which he alleged that hatred existed between the Russians and the Poles; and remarked, " Her Majesty's Government observe that the feelings of hatred between the Russians and the Poles have not in the lapse of thirty years been softened or modified;" and concluded that the amnesty would give no solid security to the most moderate of Polish patriots.

Yet impartial observers will probably agree with the view taken by the Ambassador, rather than with that of the Foreign Secretary.

In his despatch of 2nd March, Lord Russell urged upon the Russian Government the propriety of proclaiming an immediate and unconditional amnesty, and of restoring the constitution granted in 1815. At that time the army of Langiewicz was in the field, and gave the revolution an apparent strength which precluded the Emperor from adopting a suggestion which would have been construed into an evidence of fear. The defeat of the Dictator changed the nature of the situation. It was to be assumed that no one would see in wandering bands, acting without concert or arrangement, an aggressive power dangerous to a military state. The Emperor, therefore, was free to follow the dictates of a humane disposition, and without compromise of dignity, to extend his pardon to those who would lay down their arms. Objections to this act of mercy came with no good grace from the Minister and Cabinet who five weeks before had recommended it.

Neither does the second objection of Lord Russell appear to rest upon a more satisfactory basis. If indeed the English Minister had shown that the institutions of 1815 had within them any self-maintaining power which those recently granted did not possess; if he could have proved, although an emperor or a government might break the Recruitment act of 1859, that the constitution of Alexander I., once restored, would have been beyond their reach; then his argument would have been intelligible, though perhaps it would have been open to dissent. But, in truth, there is nothing to prevent armed power setting law at defiance whenever it is so disposed; and the only guarantee a constitution can possess is to be found either in the physical power it vests in those who are interested in its preservation, or in the character and honour of the prince who gives it.

Did history lead Lord Russell to think that the constitution of 1815 could sustain itself? We look into her pages, and find that from the moment of its birth to that of its dissolution, it was never observed; to restore it would have been to invite a repetition of those sad and shameful scenes in which the revolt of 1831 had its origin; it would have been to place before the Russian Government the ever present example of how freedom can be repressed; and it would have been to substitute for institutions really fit for the requirements of the country, a paper constitution, which, as we shall hereafter see, contained little more than a mockery of national representation.

The argument, however, which of all others Lord Russell should have avoided, was that which was founded on the refusal of the Poles to assist in the development of liberal institutions. Lord Russell knew from the despatches of Colonel Stanton, that the resignation of the Polish members of the Council of State, and provincial and municipal assemblies, was due, not to the conscription or to any act that provoked the revolt, but to the employment of the peasants as a temporary rural police; that this delegation of power to them had irritated the higher orders, and so they resigned *en masse;* it was the result of the bad feeling which existed between different classes in Poland, and not of any hostility which the Government had provoked. Taking, however, Lord Russell's statement as correct, it was the most damning argument which could be adduced against granting the Poles any free institutions at all; for if " the co-operation of native Poles of property and character" could not be secured in favour of the institutions recently granted them, what chance was there that they would give their aid in working the revived institutions of 1815? The national party had never asked the restoration of that constitution; they regarded it with complete apathy; the insurgents had studiously disavowed all sympathy with it; and no one could indicate in what way it would advance the interests of the people, of progress, or of good government. The logical deduction from Lord Russell's letter would seem to be that the Poles would not aid in working free institutions, and therefore (not that the constitution of 1815 should be restored to them), that free institutions were not fitted to their present state of social or political development. But the fact is, the Poles would have gladly assisted in carrying out liberal institutions, and the letter of the English Minister appears to have been written hurriedly and without due thought. The way in which it wound up, also, was an outrage on all the forms of diplomatic courtesy. England recognized Russia as her friend and her ally, yet Lord Russell, for the sake of indulging in the infelicitous luxury of an apt quotation, cast at her one of those sneers which, even when they are not openly noticed, are seldom overlooked or forgiven.

CHAPTER XIV.

Moral Force.—Fabricated Intelligence.—Mouravieff.—Mourning Proclamation.—Debate in the House of Lords.—Property-tax.—Sequestrations.

GREAT reliance was expressed from time to time in England on the "moral force" exercised by public opinion. It was alleged that the Poles neither asked for nor desired armed interference; all they hoped was sympathy on the part of our people and Government in the struggle they had commenced; such aid was worth far more than money, arms, or men, and the Russians could not long ignore it or withstand its power. The theory may be correct, its application was certainly erroneous. Two parties were in arms. On one side were the insurgents—strong in their conviction of the justice of their cause, *they* certainly did not require the moral force which foreign sympathy could afford them; on the other side was the Government—the moral force which public opinion could bring to bear upon it was certainly great; but then it was the public opinion of Russia, and not that of England, which was thus effectual. For almost the first time in the modern history of Russia, its Government was surrounded by strong evidences of national support; and this was the moral force by which its acts were vindicated and its policy upheld. The public opinion of England might have swayed the Russian mind, if the subject had been one on which our superiority was admitted, in consequence of our deeper knowledge of liberal institutions; but here we had no knowledge which gave us any special opportunity of arriving at a just result. The Russians found, on this subject, that the most pernicious doctrines were promulgated in England, and learned that they were founded on fables more preposterous still. The most ridiculous assertions, the grossest calumnies, the most transparent falsehoods, were not too absurd to find credence among our people; and out of that huge pile of mendacity and folly they selected the materials from which their boasted public opinion was created. The Russians naturally disregarded a conclusion based on such premises, and declined to be guided by it in their present action or future policy.

If, indeed, those men who insisted on the moral force of English opinion, had endeavoured to diminish its value, they could not have taken a surer way to do so than that which they persistently adopted. Public declamation was poured forth, in which Russia was denounced as a semi-civilized state; her Asiatic barbarism was continually railed against; she was described as the violator of treaties, the perfidious instigator of troubles in friendly states, the insincere friend, and the relentless enemy. The press stimulated the illusions of the people; extraordinary stories of successes which the insurgents had never won, were balanced by equally extraordinary statements of wrongs they had never suffered; documents were forged and attributed to the Czar, so palpably and clumsily manipulated,* that even the most credu-

---

* As examples of these documents, the following may be mentioned :— Towards the end of May the Paris papers spread the report that in Livonia the sect of Old Believers (the Dissenters of Russia) had massacred all the Catholics, in consequence of an order from the Emperor. The translation of this pretended order having appeared in some papers, its authenticity was denied in the *Journal de St. Pétersbourg*, which challenged the authors of the statement to produce the original Russ. This they did, entitling it, " *Document trouvé sur les Raskolniki (vieux croyants) après les massacres de Livonie des 27, 28, et 29 avril,* 1863." This document was not only one which never did or could have emanated from a public department, or from any other well-informed source; but it was full of faults of syntax, of spelling, of grammar, and of construction, and was such a production as an individual knowing by ear a few Russian words might have drawn up with the aid of a dictionary, but without a grammar. Some of the words employed are used in their wrong sense, and could only have been arrived at in the manner suggested.

A few months subsequently a London journal stated that the Emperor had commanded the Russian language to be introduced into all official proceedings in Poland. The fact was at once denied, and then, in confirmation of it, a translation of an order appeared, in which Prince Dolgorouki commanded the change to be made. Unfortunately for him, the person inventing the intelligence forgot the difference between the New and the Old Style, or overlooked the fact that official documents emanating from St. Petersburg are

lous were astounded, and for a time withheld their belief. And thus was public opinion made the prey of designing always dated according to the latter. Allowing for this difference, the copy of the order was in the hands of the Paris correspondent of the journal in question within twenty-four hours from the time when the order was signed. The post would have taken about four days to deliver it!

In November a still more astounding revelation was made by the same correspondent:—

"I will now give you a document which, I tell you beforehand, will be contradicted by the Russian Government as soon as it appears. Indeed, I scarcely expect that your readers will credit it, and yet I can assure them I derive it from a source worthy of unlimited confidence. It is proposed by the Imperial Government of St. Petersburg, acting on a traditional idea of the Empress Catherine, to destroy Protestants and Poles in one great massacre something like that of St. Bartholomew. The Ruthenian provinces are destined to be the scene of the first act of this bloody tragedy, and these are the steps which the Imperial agents are taking to prepare it. The military commander of the district, having received an ukase from St. Petersburg, sends privately for each pope, and has an audience—*tête-à-tête*, of course—with him, during which he compels the pope to write from his dictation, and sign with his own name the following order, which being thus only left in the handwriting of the persons who are to execute it, can easily be disavowed by the Government. This copy has been received from an honest pope, who, regardless of consequences, carried it off to one of the provincial landowners to denounce the horrid plot, and ask advice what to do. Here is the text of the 'ukase,' which has been sent me by the hereditary chief of the Polish emigration :—

"'His Majesty the Emperor has ordered me to inform you that you will shortly receive a circular from his Majesty requiring you to organize in all the orthodox churches of Russia a solemn service, to pray the Omnipotent to save the Church and the Empire from another invasion of the French, and twenty other pagan nations, and that then you must also execute the imperial order which now follows:—His Majesty believes that the religious service will be more acceptable to God if you bring to him as a holocaust the life of all the Poles. Therefore you are commanded to prepare, as is your duty, the peasants of your parish to execute the imperial will the evening before the day named for the holy ceremony, so that no Pole or Roman Catholic shall escape. You must appreciate the serious importance of this charge, which his Majesty confides to your known loyalty, and you will keep *strictly* the secret confided to you. The violation of that secret on your part will be held to be a state crime of the gravest order, and punished with the extremest possible severity.'

"Such is the document, a copy of which is now before me, and which one hesitates to ask any Englishman to believe, and yet, when I spoke to a Polish men, who, to obtain a moment's sympathy, scrupled at no falsehood which they thought could blacken their enemies or improve the position of their own party.

The moral force of public opinion is doubtless very useful in correcting home abuses, but it does not aid in controlling the events of distant war. Public opinion in England was strongly excited by the war between the Northern and Southern States in America; but its moral force did not save one burning city or one wasted farm. Public opinion was equally excited by the Polish struggle, and in the result was equally inefficacious. The Russian army conquered while its Government negotiated, and the only result was to impress the stronger nation with the belief that it had been unduly interfered with, and to leave on the minds of the weaker the conviction that it had been encouraged and betrayed.

If the effect of the intervention of the Western powers was thus disastrous so far as Russian policy and public opinion were concerned, it was no less prejudicial to the Poles, owing to the false hopes in which it led them to indulge. They believed that the Western powers would not restrict themselves to a diplomatic negotiation, but that they would extort with the sword concessions the pen was powerless to win. Once entertaining anticipations so delusive, they persuaded themselves that the terms on which peace or war depended could be dictated by the National Government instead of by the Cabinets of the West; and they resolved to dispel all illusions as to the moderation of their views, and let Europe know in an authoritative manner what objects they intended to achieve.

In a manifesto, therefore, published by the Central Committee at the end of March, they declared that they abhorred the constitution of 1815, and the rights springing from it, for they were given by the Congress of Vienna, where their

gentleman yesterday, he said: 'Believe it! Of course I believe it; and the Government are further prepared, no doubt, to throw the blame of the massacre on the fanaticism of some of the lower clergy; and when the crime is over, punish them, and even some of the popes on whom they find the ukase, for the murders they have themselves commanded.'"

This effusion was translated into the *Journal de St. Pétersbourg* with some unflattering comments on the facile disposition of those who believed it.

national feelings were insulted, and where their nation had no representative. The treaty which confined the kingdom within its present frontier they repudiated, and they declared the principles of eternal justice required that Poland should be re-established in her former limits; that the Kingdom and Western provinces should be torn from Russia, and that Galicia and Posen should be voluntarily ceded by Austria and Prussia.

Popular feeling, roused by the conduct of the Poles, chilled somewhat by the amnesty, was now again excited to the utmost, and men of all parties and shades of opinion united in requiring that the ablest man who could be found should be appointed to rule over the disturbed provinces. In the kingdom it was believed that the Grand Duke would succeed in suppressing the revolt; in the south-west, General Annenkoff held the discontented factions in control; but in the North-western provinces it was felt by men of all ranks and opinions that the wavering policy of General Nazimoff must be altered, and that a sterner ruler must be found to govern at Wilna. The individual who was pointed out alike by the people and their rulers was General Mouravieff, and he was appointed by the Emperor the Governor of the North-western provinces, and reached Wilna on the 26th May.

General Mouravieff had the character of being one of the most resolute and determined officers in the Russian service. He had been thoroughly trained during a long life in the iron system of the late Emperor; he had taken part in the suppression of the rebellion of 1831; he had subsequently continued for some short time in the army, and then held high rank in the civil service. Men differed in their estimate of him; some pronounced him stern, harsh, and unfeeling; declared him to be a false friend and a cruel enemy; spoke disparagingly of his abilities as well as of his honesty; enumerated the offices he had held, and asked how it happened, out of their inadequate salaries, that he had heaped up wealth.

He had for some years been Minister of the Domains, and they pointed to the crown lands, and asked during his administration what useful reform had been introduced, what recognized abuse had been extirpated; was it not, they inquired, the fact that his own benefit and the advantage of his useful friends had ever been more considered than the public good? was it not the fact that *they* had made large fortunes, while the interests of the State were never consulted? General Mouravieff was unpopular also with the Liberals of Russia, for he had no sympathy with their doctrines or hopes. A man of the old school, he disliked innovation and dreaded change, and from the emancipation downwards he viewed with extreme disquietude all the reforms which were so greatly changing the political and social relations of his countrymen.

While he thus had his enemies, he had also a large number of adherents; they declared him to be a most able administrator, a true and kind friend, and a conscientious servant of the State. The fortune he had acquired, they said, was the gift of a grateful sovereign, who had appreciated his merits, and thus rewarded them.

But whatever might be the dispute as to some of his antecedents, all Russia was confident he was the only man who was fit to rule at Wilna. A turbulent nobility, who had conspired as they pleased, while the nerveless Nazimoff governed, required to be restrained by a strong and steadfast hand; the peasants, who were suffering persecution because they would not rebel, were entitled to be protected by the Government to which they were faithful; the Russian officials should have a chief to whom they could look up with confidence; and finally the army must be so handled that the rebellion might forthwith be crushed.

General Mouravieff was exactly suited to meet the difficulties of the moment with energy and success. He was not a man of great and far-reaching views, who looked with a statesman's glance through the mists and uncertainties of the future; nor could he take any very liberal or generous estimate of the policy suited to the present; but he was a man who, having a task to perform, would perform it thoroughly; who would concentrate his energies on it; who would bring to bear upon it all the resources of a strong common sense, guided by the experience collected in a long and varied official career. There was a singleness and intensity of purpose about all his acts which carried much weight with it; no one about him could doubt his intention to quell the revolt, or fail to see that he would deem no measure too severe which was calculated to effect that end.

His remarkable energy gave new life to the executive. Officers, whose official routine began a little before noon, shuddered when they heard that the general received the reports of his subordinates at from six to nine a.m.; but they were obliged to attend him. During the whole day to five or six o'clock, except for an hour devoted to exercise, he sat in his cabinet writing, dictating, and transacting the business of his office; at eight o'clock at night he recommenced his labours, and generally did not cease until two in the morning.

His knowledge of the character and capabilities of those who surrounded him was very great, and he used them accordingly; he was prompt to take a resolution and slow to vary it; if intelligence were suddenly brought to him of an unexpected difficulty, he would, without hesitation, give his orders, which were precise, appropriate, and generally successful. He possessed an extraordinary memory, which enabled him to recall at will the obscure occurrences of many bygone years; every paper he had signed, every interview he had held seemed graven imperishably on his mind. He was not a cruel man, but he appeared indifferent to the sufferings which were caused by the measures he adopted, and his enemies availed themselves of that fact to denounce him as the embodiment of harsh and malignant energy. The proclamations which he issued soon after his appointment clearly indicate the nature of his policy and the view he took of the exigences of the public service.

The act which of all others tended most to excite popular feeling against General Mouravieff was one which, had it been properly understood, would have attracted little or no notice. It has been already shown that one of the symbols of the revolutionary party was the constant use of mourning, and this badge was continued without intermission from "the Warsaw massacres" to the date of his appointment.

In grave and anxious periods, when rebellion devastates a country, and the ordinary machinery of civil government is displaced, every sign of insubordination or of opposition to the law must be repressed with decision and promptitude. The North-western provinces were in a state of siege, and the Polish women took every opportunity to mark their hostility to those who imposed it; feminine invention taxed itself to the utmost to mortify the authorities and cover them with contumely and scorn: in a thousand ingenious ways the Russians were taught to feel that the educated classes detested them, and gave at least their moral support to the revolutionary cause.

With some of these demonstrations it was obviously impossible to interfere. The Poles absented themselves from the theatres, and the actors performed to empty houses; the public walks were deserted by the animated crowd which formerly gave them life; and when a Polish lady met a Russian officer in the street, she would cross it in order to avoid him: all these annoyances it was necessary to bear, and they were borne in silence.

The wearing of mourning, however, stood in a very different category; it had become the emblem of disaffection to the Government, and of adherence to the insurgents; it was as purely a party badge as an orange ribbon is in Ireland, or a white cockade was formerly in France, and neither precedent nor public law, nor the usages common among civilized nations, prevented the Government from suppressing its use.

Believing it to be essential that these overt acts of insubordination should be stopped, General Mouravieff issued the following order:—

"Even before political troubles broke out in this country, the larger portion of the female population of the town of Wilna commenced wearing different kinds of mourning, in order to signify their sympathy with the revolutionary movements in the kingdom of Poland. The mourning consisted of black dresses with or without white borders, or black bonnets with white feathers, together with certain tokens previously agreed upon, such as metal bracelets with the arms of Lithuania and Poland combined, broken crosses with crowns of thorns, &c. These manifestations still continue in greater or less degree. As, however, all sympathy with the present insurrectionary movements, equally with rebellious acts, is forbidden by law, the general commanding in the country has ordered the governmental chief, upon the 31st May (12th June), to issue the following directions, in order to suppress these criminal manifestations:—

"1. Proclamation is to be made throughout the town of Wilna that mourning and the wearing of black dresses and other revolutionary symbols cannot at present be permitted.

"2. Officials are to be instantly dismissed from their posts in all cases where females belonging to their families have appeared publicly in black dresses or other mourning garb.

"3. Females, without distinction of position, calling, or nationality, who appear in public places in black dresses, or generally attired in mourning, or with revolutionary accessories to the toilette, are to be punished in the following way:—For the first offence a fine of 25 silver roubles; for the second offence a fine of 50 silver roubles. Upon repetition of the offence such women are to be arrested, in order that they may be treated as persons who participate in the insurrection.

"4. In case the guilty party do not pay the fines imposed, a sufficient portion of their property is to be immediately sold to defray the amount.

"5. The fines are to be paid over to the governmental chief, and will be devoted to the support of families in the rural districts whose houses have been plundered and devastated by the insurrectionary bands.

"6. Persons mourning for their nearest relatives must produce legal proofs to the police of the actual death of such relatives. They will only be allowed to wear mourning for the period recognized by ordinary custom upon compliance with this requisition.

"7. All that has been ordered in the above six paragraphs relates equally to individuals of the male sex found publicly wearing mourning symbols, as also to persons furnished with *czamarks*, *confederatkis*, long boots above their trousers, or other tokens of the insurrectionary party.

"The governmental tribunal has communicated this present order by special circular to all district police courts for their general guidance."

Such was in its integrity the celebrated "mourning proclamation" of General Mouravieff. It was subsequently represented in England and France to have been couched in very different terms, and the fabricated versions of it were used as a principal reason for urging intervention upon the Governments of Western Europe.

The addition of corporal punishment which the papers in the Polish interest introduced was, of course, one of those shameless inventions with which, throughout the whole struggle, they disgraced their cause: there was absolutely *no* foundation for it.

The administration of General Nazimoff had induced the Poles to trifle with the orders of Government, and there was an expectation that this decree would not be persevered in: it was an empty menace, and might be disregarded with impunity. On the day when the mourning was to be discarded, there was no sign of the proclamation being obeyed, and all parties anxiously anticipated the conduct of the governor.*

* I believe the following account to be an accurate narrative of this transaction :—" It is a grave misfortune, both to Russia and England, that the reports which are accepted in most of the London papers as true are almost uniformly penned by the emissaries of 'the National Government.' These statements are frequently devoid of any foundation, and generally they so represent facts as completely to falsify the truth. The reports which excited so great an outcry against Mouravieff are a good example of the way in which violent opinions are generated. There was a lull in political feeling; men suspected that the interests of liberty and good government were not exclusively on the side of the insurgents, and began to weary of a contest in which a thousand successful battles had failed to yield them an inch of territory, or secure them even a passing indication of popular support.

"Just, then, to raise the sinking hopes of the friends of Poland, the public were electrified by a report that the sanguinary Mouravieff had determined to administer the knout to every woman who wore mourning. Enthusiastic Radicals summoned other people to arms; they entreated the Poles, great and small, to sing the *Mourir pour la Patrie*,' and promised to wreathe chaplets of cypress and laurel, and hang them above their graves.

"The Liberal journals re-echo the startling cry; England is told that the widows and orphans of Poland must weep in silence, and wear gay colours at the tomb of the loved and lost; and then a picture is limned, by a cunning hand, of the Spartan heroism of the matron who will wear black, and who is handed over to the polluting custody of the Calcraft of the knout. The readers of the journals referred to are told how hideous a punishment this Polish lady is fated to undergo, how the flesh shrinks, though the mind is constant yet, until at length, surrounded by a crowd of unsympathizing butchers, the spirit emancipates itself from the bleeding and mangled corpse to wing its angry way to the throne of justice and retribution.

"These are effective themes when handled well; and if the shield had no other side, the chameleon no other hue, certainly the insurgents would have found in Mouravieff as able an ally as they had already secured in Wielopolski. Unluckily for them, however, history is in the main a castle of truth, and in this instance its voice will ere long penetrate through Europe. The facts are these: General Mouravieff had confided to him by his sovereign the supreme command of a district in the throes of insurrection; his predecessor had been a weak, uncertain administrator, whose orders of to-day were frequently revoked on the morrow, and the Poles, supposing the new governor to be a man of similar temperament, believed, though he might threaten, he would never dare to act.

* * * *

" In Wilna, on the Sunday after the proclamation, came the trial of strength. The Polish ladies all wore black, and paraded themselves before the Russians

General Mouravieff was, however, a man of very different character from his predecessor, and when he put his name to the proclamation he had fully resolved that it should be obeyed. With firmness but without acting in an offensive manner, the regulations he had imposed were carried out, a few fines were levied, and mourning was discontinued. The completeness of this easy triumph will readily be understood when it is mentioned that the whole amount of fines levied under this proclamation did not exceed 700 roubles.

In August, when I visited Wilna, there was nothing unusual in the dresses of the ladies, and they would have attracted no notice had it not been for the notoriety of the "mourning" regulations. Having obtained their victory, the authorities used it leniently, for a little piece of coloured ribbon, or a coloured flower in a bonnet, was deemed a sufficent compliance with the order, although they were worn over a dress which would otherwise have been considered an infringement of it.

The people of England were supplied with a very different version of this proclamation. They were persuaded that if any lady thrice offended against the regulation she would be subjected to the punishment of the knout, and popular feeling was

and the governor. He would not dare to punish them; were they not noble? The proclamation was only a threat, and they would 'put the governor down!'

"Alas for the ardent, unthinking confidence of feminine patriotism! An extremely civil, gentlemanlike individual approached the carriage of the principal offender. He raised his hat, and informed her that, as an *employé* of the Government, he was directed to inquire why the lady he addressed wore morning. Had she lost a relative, or for what cause was she in black? 'I am a Pole, sir,' was the haughty reply. The official regretted that such should be her only answer, for in that case he was bound to ask her for 25 roubles, for which he begged to hand her the receipt. If she had not the money with her, he begged she would not distress herself; he would send for it to her residence in the afternoon.

"The fines were duly paid, and from that day forth the ladies of Wilna have arrayed themselves in all the colours of the rainbow. Their patriotism could not sustain the practical test the governor applied to it, and since that hour all parties have felt assured that a decree signed by him will be enforced, and they have obeyed without attempting to evade it."

excited to the utmost on the strength of this most absurd and groundless charge. Yet we can hardly blame this credulity when we find that great names were not ashamed to pledge themselves to the truth of the calumny, and that a quondam Cabinet Minister, who had himself in former times been ambassador at St. Petersburg, repeated a yet more loathsome fabrication.

Lord Clanricarde is reported* to have said in his place in the House of Lords—" Since March, when our representations were first made, General Mouravieff had been appointed, whose proclamations could not be read without horror and indignation. Few people knew the full extent of these proclamations. Among other things, women wearing mourning in the streets, no matter what bereavement they might have undergone, were to be treated like common women of the town, registered, and subjected to all the examinations to which that class were liable." And he concluded by moving for reports of " atrocities " committed or threatened by Russians or Poles since 1st May, and by inquiring " whether her Majesty's Government had reason to hope that the civil war now raging in Poland would be henceforth conducted according to the rules of civilized warfare."

Lord Ellenborough the same night said—" There have been atrocities mentioned arising out of the proclamations with respect to the treatment of women, which it appears to me impossible that any one who lives in civilized Europe should at any time have sanctioned. The man who outrages a woman makes mankind his enemy, and exposes himself to all the loathing he excites. And yet it is impossible to doubt that under the orders of Mouravieff—and Mouravieff is at this time apparently the favourite agent of the Russian Government—these atrocities have been committed."

When these noblemen found it necessary thus to lay the lance in rest on behalf of the women of Poland, there is every excuse for those who had not their advantages, if they credited the fabrications which had thus deceived their superiors in rank.

The next step of political importance taken by General Mouravieff was the issue of a proclamation on the 13th (25th)

* *Times*, July 25, 1863.

of June, by which he imposed a temporary property tax of ten per cent. on the income of the landed proprietors. At the same time he required the chiefs of the various governments under his command to give him a return of the names of such individuals as had satisfactorily evidenced their loyalty to the Government, in order that he might lighten the imposition so far as they were concerned, or grant them such time for its payment as he might see fit. In other cases the tax he imposed was to be paid within seven days, and if default was made in so doing, the movable property of the defaulter was to be seized and sold to liquidate the claim.

This severe proclamation was issued for the purpose of depriving the Poles of the means of encouraging the revolt. It was known, although the Lithuanian proprietors had not in any great numbers personally joined the insurgents, that they had given them every encouragement they believed they could safely extend to them. In addition to affording them shelter when they required it, they supplied them with horses, provisions, and all other requisites that their estates afforded, and above all, placed at their disposal every rouble they could command.

The tax, therefore, which General Mouravieff imposed upon the proprietors he defended on the plea that it only deprived them of money which would otherwise have found its way into the military chest of the insurgents; and while he thus crippled the resources on which the leaders of the revolt depended, he prevented the proprietors from committing acts of treason which would have been fatal to themselves.

A few days later a circular was addressed by General Mouravieff to the chiefs of the various governments under his authority. He stated, information had reached him that many proprietors furnished the insurgent bands with provisions, under the pretext of being forced so to do, and that they gave no information to the authorities of the movements of the bands, which were composed mainly of their sons, parents, friends, and servants. In such cases the chiefs of the governments were instructed to place a sequestration on the goods of the offender; the corn and flour were to be given to the troops, and the horses and waggons appropriated for transport purposes. The proprietors and their stewards were to be arrested and tried by court-martial, and their families compelled to quit their properties.

This order vested in the hands of military officers summary powers of the most extensive kind. Execution preceded judgment, and the property of any landowner in the country was at the mercy of informers and spies. In a period when men's minds were exasperated in the highest degree by mutual wrongs, when a contest raged, in which race, religion, and national sentiments were all involved, it was too much to expect that the Russian official would preserve the calmness and equity of the judgment-seat.

The acts for which the Polish proprietors might lose their property were certainly acts of hostility to Russia, but in some cases at least they were so natural as hardly to rank as crimes. If, as stated in the circular, the immediate relatives, friends, and servants of a proprietor requested temporary assistance or shelter, his heart must have been very hard, or his loyalty to Russia very overwhelming, if he sent word of their movements to the nearest military station; and where a band forcibly extorted aid from the fears of a proprietor, it was scarcely just to sequestrate his property for the offence.

On the other hand it must be remembered that if terrorism had been deemed a valid excuse, there was not a Polish proprietor who would not loudly have alleged it. Under cover of such a pretext, the insurgents would have invariably been received; the horses, the arms, the money of the landowners would have been at their disposal; and even their servants and sons would have been enlisted, likewise without their consent, in the ranks of the rebels.

Even as it was, the story told by three-fourths of the Polish prisoners was that against their will they were forced into the bands, and they frequently elaborated ingenious stories to account for their presence there. I asked prisoner after prisoner in Warsaw and Wilna, how they came to join in the insurrection, and almost without exception (save where they had been tried and condemned), there was the same attempt to prove that they were forced into it. Similar attempts would have been made with greater success by the landed proprietors, and it was absolutely necessary for the authorities to refuse to recognize coercion as a valid plea.

While, therefore, it is impossible to defend on abstract grounds this decree of General Mouravieff, and while it is open to the charge of a recklessness of civil rights which must be pronounced unjust, it must yet be acknowledged to be a formidable instrument of war. The man who openly declares that he will sequester the property of any one who has afforded the least asylum to insurgents, and who shows by his subsequent acts that he is determined to act upon that declaration to the uttermost, is very likely to suppress all open sympathy with revolt; whether the measure is a wise or just one is a different question, and one upon which few individuals will give precisely the same reply.

Yet it would be unjust to omit from consideration the difficult and exceptional circumstances under which General Mouravieff assumed the government. He knew that "the nobility, clergy, citizens, and scattered gentry" were all opposed to the Russian supremacy; he knew, from his point of view, that they were all traitors, and that, whatever might be the difficulties attendant upon proving their guilt, they were all nevertheless equally culpable. If he had gone into the first six country houses he approached and arrested their owners, he might have found it difficult to justify the act, but none the less he would have been certain that most of the men he arrested were implicated in the revolt.

In well-ordered communities the right to life has ever been deemed more sacred than the right to property, and if one has to be sacrificed in order that the other may be preserved, it is the right to property which would everywhere be abandoned. The Russians urged this principle in justification of the acts of Mouravieff. He saw the predatory bands with which the country was infested not only waging open war, but indulging in wholesale assassination; he saw these bands encouraged and sheltered by men who as a class were hostile to the Government; and, if this system was allowed to continue unchecked, the whole country would become a scene of terrorism and murder. The authorities were not to be blamed for the wild chaos into which the acts of the rebels and the complicity of a hostile proprietary had hurried the country; and if, for the sake of preserving order and protecting life, some civil rights were for the moment endangered, such was the necessary and unavoidable penalty which attached to the lawless plots of a guilty faction.

The executions in his government were few in number, if the crimes for which they atoned are taken into account. Some Polish officers holding commissions in the Russian service who were found at the head of insurgent bands, were shot or hanged; but in any country such would have been their fate. They may be the objects of commiseration, for it is fair to assume that a mistaken sense of duty led them to forsake their colours; but in every army desertion to the enemy is punished with death. Some priests also perished; but they were either guilty of murder or had used their churches as revolutionary temples, where the creed of treason and assassination was preached. The remainder of those who suffered death were, almost without exception, men who had been guilty of cold-blooded murders or else members of that infamous corporation of hanging gendarmes who were hired by the National Government to commit political assassinations.

The whole number of these executions up to a recent date* was 128, of which about 40 were officers and men who had deserted from the army and joined the insurgents. Although it is to be regretted that so much blood was poured out upon the scaffold, it is not a large number of executions, considering the circumstances of the period and the nature of many of the acts by which the insurrection was debased.

* These numbers were given me by General Mouravieff personally, on 17th March, 1865.

CHAPTER XV.

Seriakoffski, his Capture and Execution.—Attempted Murder of the Marshal of Nobility at Wilna.—Death of Nullo.—Rising in Kieff.—Wysocki's Invasion.—Letter of a Patriot Pole.

AMONG the leaders of the insurgents in Lithuania, the most remarkable and most ill-fated was Seriakoffski, a captain in the Russian army. He was a Pole by birth, and while very young had for some trifling offence been appointed to serve in a regiment stationed in the distant government of Orenburg. He appears to have been a man of quick feeling and perception, but of little depth. Professedly devoted to the service of his superiors, his mind was secretly filled with schemes of vast and ill-regulated ambition, and while he held rank in the service of Russia and received its pay, he was pondering in secret how its power might be shaken and the independence of Poland achieved. He early acquired the confidence of the Minister of War, and distinguished himself by his efforts to procure the abolition of corporal punishment in the Russian army. He was sent by the Government to several countries in Europe to inquire and to report upon their systems of military discipline and the substitutes they adopted for the lash, and the report which he presented upon this subject was in a great measure acted upon by the Government. The road to rapid preferment seemed now to be open to him, but his mistaken patriotism and misplaced ambition destroyed his prospects.

The Russian Government in no instance compelled Polish officers to serve against their countrymen; on their intimating that they preferred to serve elsewhere, their desire was readily acquiesced in, for the Russians made every allowance for a national feeling, which they respected even while endeavouring to control it. Seriakoffski therefore had not the excuse of being driven to fight either for or against his countrymen. He was in the Russian service, and could not without dishonour be false to the colours under which he served, and the oaths of fidelity which he had taken. If he was determined to rebel, he should have resigned his grade, and then, though imprudent, he might have escaped shame. But the Russians charge him with more than ordinary treachery, for it is alleged that, under specious pretexts, he obtained money from the Government, which he subsequently applied in furtherance of the revolt; and it is said that he formed a plot to surprise the great fortress of Dünaburg, availing himself for that purpose of an official mission in connection with its inspection and government.*

He was appointed by the insurgents commander of their forces in Lithuania, and waged war with the success of an ordinary guerilla chief. At length, on the 7th May, intelligence was conveyed to the Russian forces at Medeika that the band of Dolengo (under which name Seriakoffski was known) was in the neighbourhood, and some Cossacks and infantry attacked it.

The insurgents hastily retreated into a forest which skirted the main road; but the Russian commanding officer did not think it prudent to follow them, as he believed it was their design, when his troops were disordered in the wood, to surround and cut them off.

Two days later, the Russians in the mean time having been reinforced, they marched against the insurgents. Seriakoffski's little army, amounting to 1,500 men, was posted on the border of a dense forest; the right flank rested on the village of Gondischki, and the left on a muddy brook. In front of this position were scattered about 300 skirmishers, and at some distance in the rear were compact masses of scythemen. The Russian skirmishers and Cossacks opened a murderous fire upon the enemy, on whom they inflicted heavy loss, and following up the attack, they endeavoured to surround

---

* I received this information from a source which I believe to be well informed, but a copy of the depositions taken at his trial which I was promised has not reached me, and I am therefore unable to speak with certainty as to the truth of these charges.

them on all sides. The scythe-men charged the left flank of the Russians and endeavoured to disperse them; but they were received by a steady fire from the Russian troops, to which, inefficiently armed as they were, they had no means of adequately replying. The conflict was too unequal, and their ranks were quickly broken; nearly 200 of them were killed, and the remainder fled.

The account of the capture of Seriakoffski, which occurred a few hours after the defeat of his band, is given in the following terms by a Russian officer who was engaged in the affair. It is so characteristic of the nature of the struggle, and gives so vivid an idea of the views of the men who mixed in it, that I introduce it without change or condensation.

"The day that followed the affair of the 27th, the peasants of the neighbourhood began bringing in prisoners, one or two at a time: after some hours they numbered, including those taken by our troops, about 100 men. They were all proprietors (pani) or Schlachta. The soldiers surrounded the prisoners and addressed speeches to them: 'Oh you, you Poles,' they said, 'why do you rebel against the Government? what can you want? you have land and money; it is far better for you to sit at home. Do you look like soldiers? No; it is a real shame!' Among the prisoners was one young man who looked silent and sullen. The Russians asked him, 'Who are you, where are you from, are you a Pole?' He simply answered, 'I know nothing.' Several such persons were met with; their silence is owing to the interference of the priests, who make them swear, if they meet a Russian, that they will be dumb. If they torture you, say the priests, you go direct to Paradise and are a martyr: thus all the Schlachta are perfectly convinced, if they get shot in a wood, that they will go straight to heaven.

"An officer of the Hulans, who was among the troops, approached one of the prisoners, saying 'Good morning, Stanichewski, are you, too, in the band? this is a pleasant way of renewing our acquaintance!' 'As you see,' answered the other; 'I beg your pardon for not having executed your commission; you gave me money to buy an opera-glass, but I could not.' This surprised us, and we surrounded him, and made inquiries. It appears he was a lieutenant-captain, who had left our service very recently to take an appointment in the excise in the district of Wilcomirsk. A month before he was captured, he was going to St. Petersburg, and then had received the commission from the officer, but he was stopped by persons who were strangers to him, and threatened with death if he did not obey. He entered the band of Seriakoffski, and on the 26th commanded the right wing: he was the leader of the scythe-men. I do not know whether one can believe him, but he was the only Pole worthy of compassion. Every insurgent had his history—one was innocent, another was in the band by compulsion. The commander of the band affirmed that he entered it at the instigation of the ladies. When his neighbours went into the woods the ladies sneered at him, and he went also, to avoid being an object of scorn. Some, however, of the insurgents acknowledged that they went of their own will.

"In the evening an officer of the Koperski regiment arrived with some soldiers at the house of a proprietor: it was situated in the middle of some swampy ground in a wood, and was completely closed; they surrounded it—a window then opened, and a voice said, 'Enter, I am here, Seriakoffski.' In addition to Seriakoffski they found Kolichko and part of Seriakoffski's staff, twenty-one in number, who, after the battle, had been conveyed to this house, which belonged to a count, who was himself in the band. This place was 18 wersts (12 miles) from our staff at Medeika. Having heard of this occurrence, our general sent me with forty riflemen to convey the prisoners to our staff.

"We arrived at the house at twelve o'clock at night. The first room was occupied by our soldiers; I then entered a room guarded by two sentinels, in which were twelve prisoners; they were all asleep on straw, except one, who had a handsome but displeasing countenance, and who introduced himself as Kolichko; he told me he had been at the military school at Genoa; he added, that the Government had tried for two years to arrest him for political offences, but that he had always contrived to escape. Even the linen of those who slept was black, as a sign of mourning.

"I entered the next room, and was struck by what I saw. In the middle of the room, on a large bed, lay the wounded Seriakoffski; two doctors, in Polish costume, sat near his pillow; in another part of the room six wounded men were lying on the straw. One very handsome young man approached me on tiptoe, bowed, and said, 'I am Count Kossachoffsky, adjutant to our general.' I could not restrain a smile, and answered, 'Do put an end to this comedy; wake Seriakoffski; I have orders to convey him and all of you to our staff at Medeika.' But Kossachoffsky answered in the same tone, 'Lieutenant, it is perfectly impossible, the wound of our general is dangerous; wait till seven o'clock in the morning, when the crisis will be over.' The doctors likewise approached, and made the same request in French, hoping I should relent; at the same time the Poles, endeavouring to frighten us, said the band of Mazkiewitch, the priest, was advancing to deliver Seriakoffski. This made me anxious; I woke up the self-styled general; he said, 'You are come to fetch me, but I cannot go at present; wait till seven o'clock; it will be better for you to bring me alive than dead; I can then be of more use.' I answered him that his requests were rather suspicious. At about two o'clock in the morning, faint rays of light entered the room; I told every one to get up and dress—it was done, but with very great ill-will. At last they were all placed in the conveyances prepared for them. Seriakoffski, as a wounded man, was to be placed in an open carriage found in the house of the proprietor; but he would not come out, requesting some tea, as it would give him new strength. I allowed it; but the preparations were unduly protracted; I therefore approached Seriakoffski, and said, 'Seriakoffski, report describes you as a man of iron will; prove it; what can a cup of tea matter to you?' He immediately went out and seated himself in the carriage with the doctor and his adjutant.

"Before reaching Wolkomir we saw a beautiful place, almost a palace, which belonged to the adjutant. This man—young, rich, and handsome—could easily have fled to his own house after the affair, as no one knew he had been in the battle. 'I could not leave my general in misfortune,' said he, pressing Seriakoffski's hand. I do not know whether Seriakoffski had moral influence over the persons about him, but his personal appearance was not attractive; he had a yellow, sickly face, and dull, strange eyes.

"We continued our journey. I began to ask Kolichko about the state of the band. 'I have been leader of this band,' he said, 'for three months; I acquired strategic knowledge in the school of Genoa; the Russians have been trying to take me for two months, but I always escaped, and often passed between two detachments without being caught; it is Seriakoffski's fault that I am taken; if I had not joined him, I should still be in the woods with my band.' 'Why, then, did you join him?' I asked. 'He is our commander; we must obey him.' On several papers Seriakoffski had signed, 'Commander (Woiwode) of Lithuania and Kovno.' Kolichko accused Seriakoffski of refusing him permission to attack Medeika when it was only garrisoned by one company of Russian soldiers. 'Seriakoffski,' he continued, 'is a clever man, but no military chief,—he is not energetic enough.' In general he spoke unfavourably of him; it was easily seen that Kolichko was very vain.

"We approached a wood and advanced very slowly. I was sitting near Seriakoffski, and began to talk to him. 'I left Kovno with three men,' he said, 'and soon had a band of 1,000. Our march through the provinces was a real triumph,—*c'était une protestation sanglante;*—we were everywhere received as if we belonged to one family; the peasant women brought their sons to us, but we would not take them.' I could stand this no longer, and told him it was all untrue. We had followed him step by step, and seen the ravages he had made on the property of the unfortunate peasants. He found an answer immediately. 'We ordered the peasants to complain of us, that you might not touch them.' At this moment, some insurgents emerged from a wood and waved their hats in token of surrender. Two Cossacks therefore arrested them. One of these men was seventeen years old, with a wounded hand. I asked him if he was in the band of his own will. 'No,' he replied, 'they threatened to hang my father if I did not join.' 'He lies,' said Seriakoffski. 'Well, Seriakoffski,' I said, 'you must have a great load on your conscience; what miseries you have caused.' He replied, 'It is nothing; these bloody seeds will give white flowers; Poland must do something to record her existence.' 'Why, then,' I inquired, 'were you going to the Baltic provinces, where the peasants would have met you with axes, and where you would have perished with hunger?' 'All the band together formed 5,000 men,' he said; 'in a week I might have had double that number, and with 10,000 men I could have roused the Baltic provinces.' I really do not know how much further the imagination of Seriakoffski might have carried him, but we had reached Medeika."

The wound of Seriakoffski was mortal, and he used every endeavour in his power to prolong the legal proceedings, that he might avoid the ignominy of a public execution. The attempt was vain; no doubt of his guilt could be entertained, and there were no circumstances in his case which, in the view of a military tribunal, could be alleged as the slightest extenuation of his crime; but Seriakoffski had been honoured and esteemed by men high in rank in the public service, and if any intercession could have availed him, it would have been forthcoming on his behalf. He had been only married a few months, and his young wife entreated ministers and men high in the confidence of her sovereign to supplicate for her husband's life. They listened to her with respect, they sympathized in her despair, but they held out no hopes that the boon she asked would be granted. She went to Prince Souwaroff,* the kindness of whose heart is only equalled by the charm of his manners, and entreated him to use his all-powerful influence to avert the desolation that hung over her. He knew that in such a case all entreaty was in vain; she had begged to learn the truth from him, and he told it to her kindly but firmly. "Madam," he said, "you desire to know the truth, and I dare not trifle with you; I will not say that your husband's life cannot be spared, for with God nothing is impossible; but unless He interposes His omnipotent arm to save him, his life will not be spared; the offence he has committed is one which the Government cannot pardon."

* The Governor-General of St. Petersburg.

The sentence of the court-martial was that Seriakoffski should be hanged, and it evoked a deep burst of indignation from his friends, which to this hour has not subsided. They contended that, as a Russian officer, he should have been shot, and that the mode of execution resorted to was a needless insult to a brave but most unfortunate enthusiast; and they ascribed it to the fiendish cruelty and malevolence of General Mouravieff that this last indignity was put upon him. Such a charge, however, is very unjust; for according to martial law in Russia, the court passes its judgment upon the criminal, and in that judgment the mode of execution is prescribed; the law further directs that the sentence shall be confirmed or disallowed by the governor of the province, and that it shall be carried into execution within twenty-four hours. The sentence passed was in strict conformity with martial law; the only course open to General Mouravieff was to confirm it, and the cruelty, if cruelty there were in the sentence, must be attributed to the court-martial, and not to the superior officer, who simply confirmed its doom.*

Towards the end of July the insurrection in Lithuania was practically at an end; a few bands of robbers rather than insurgents were sometimes met with, and the country was unsafe for peaceful travellers; for all military purposes, however, it was completely in the hands of the Russians, and the proprietors throughout the provinces under the charge of General Mouravieff signed addresses expressive of their contrition for what had occurred, and of their loyal resolution for the future.

The National Government viewed these addresses with the

---

* Many absurd statements were circulated upon the subject of his execution. It was said that the English ambassador had written to request General Mouravieff to spare Seriakoffski's life, and that General Mouravieff had declared that he would teach the English ambassador not to interfere with him, and forthwith ordered his prisoner, although it was about midnight, to be hanged, without giving him a moment to prepare for death.

Another story equally false represented that Seriakoffski was hanged immediately opposite the windows of his wife, and that the first intelligence she had of his doom was the spectacle of his dead body suspended before her eyes.

Both these stories, as will be gathered from the statements I have made in the text, are untrue.

greatest alarm. They disclaimed its authority; they held it up to public odium as an unjust and usurping power; they professed the devotion of the men who signed them to the Russian Emperor, and solicited the protection of the Russian army.

The Press which was in the pay of the Emigration described these addresses as having been extorted by menace and violence: the proprietors, it declared, were at the mercy of the Russians, and no man's life or property was secure if he refused to sign any document Mouravieff or his myrmidons might require him to subscribe. This argument, however, was a dangerous one to employ; for the more completely the proprietors were at the mercy of the authorities, the more evident did it become that the insurrection was finally extinguished.

It was therefore necessary to resort to violent means to repress these indications of returning loyalty, and the National Government resolved, by the murder of one of the offenders, to prevent any repetition of the fault. An address to the Emperor had been signed on behalf of the nobility of Wilna by M. Domeiko, their Marshal.

On the morning of the 11th of August, in broad daylight, and without a sign of concealment or fear, a stranger presented himself at the house of the Marshal and requested to see him. He gave no reason for his visit, but there was nothing in his appearance to create alarm, and he was admitted without hesitation into the house. After waiting some little time, he was shown into the room where M. Domeiko received his business visitors. The ordinary salutations over, the stranger presented to the Marshal a paper, having the appearance of a government despatch, and as he took it from his hand, stabbed him with one of those long double-bladed daggers upon which the National Government relied for the propagation of their principles. The wound was not mortal, and the cries of his master brought a servant into the room. This man grappled with the assassin, and endeavoured to arrest him; he too was stabbed severely, and the assassin then left the house. As he passed out of the *porte cochère* he said to the wife of the porter, whom he met there, "Hasten up stairs, your master is ill—I go for a doctor." Suspicion being thus disarmed, he for the moment escaped; but subsequently, owing to an informality in his passport, he was arrested, and was executed for the crime. The paper presented to the Marshal was subsequently found to be his death-warrant, issued by the National Government.

The deliberation and the general immunity from punishment with which this class of crime was committed are evidences of the extent to which the town populations sympathized with the revolt. In fact, in this particular, the assassinations committed by order of the National Government were as remarkable as the agrarian murders which were some years since so common in Ireland. In both cases there was a wide class-feeling in favour of the criminal, which prevented the magnitude of his crime from being appreciated, and gave him an unfortunate immunity from punishment. Among the town populations of Poland this feeling extensively prevailed during the earlier part of the insurrection; but it gradually wore away, owing to the frequency and causelessness of these murders, and was replaced by a feeling of fear, loathing, and disgust.

While such was the course of events in Poland and the Western provinces, the Emigration continued to distort facts, and the journals in their pay to circulate the most grotesque misrepresentations.

About this time the Polish Committee in Paris issued an address, in which they stated that, " In the middle of the 19th century the Muscovite despotism presents a spectacle of atrocities unknown even in the annals of barbarous times. The deceitful mask which covered Russia has fallen off, and the barbarous Mongul appears in his hideous nakedness. The cruelties of Tamerlane and Ivan the Terrible pale before the horrors of the Government of Alexander II.

" Exasperated by the moral support that the sympathies of the civilized world have given to the Polish insurrection, Russia has launched her most savage hordes against Poland, and the autocrat has delivered over the victim as a prey to his most ferocious proconsuls. The war is no longer a war, it is a horrible carnage. Pillage and burnings are the order of the day; the gibbets are kept standing; fusillades and grape-shot shed streams of blood. Neither age nor sex are spared, and priests, while clothed in their sacred robes, are delivered without trial to the hangman.

"To stir up the flame, and crown the work of destruction, in contempt of all social laws, the Muscovite Government appeals to passions the most odious; it endeavours to place the torch and the axe in the hands of the peasants, and excites them to assail the proprietors, whom it promises they may plunder.

"Europe shudders at the recital of these atrocities . . . . . but for Poland more is required than empty wishes.

"Poland defends her religious creed and her domestic hearths; she demands her liberty and independence, and she will not cease to combat until she has reconquered from the oppressor her frontiers of 1772. The National Government has declared that Poland repudiates every negotiation (*trans-action*) as suicide, as treason, and from the Vistula to the Dnieper, the whole nation has vowed to perish rather than to treat with the foreign tyranny.

"Between Poland and the Muscovite despotism there is, then, a deadly strife (*duel à mort*); between a Christian people which is associated with all the progress of modern civilization, and claims rights the most dear and the most sacred, and the barbarous Mongul, who represents brute force, and tramples divine and human laws under its feet, there is henceforward an abyss of blood.

"Will Europe suffer that humanity shall be thus insolently outraged? Will she permit this war of extermination to be prolonged to the eternal shame of the nineteenth century?

"People of the West, hear the cry of alarm which this martyred nation raises! it is over its body that despotism hopes to force its way to the heart of civilization. But God is with us, and his justice will make us triumph."

While the Emigration thus endeavoured to stir up Western Europe, the Roman Catholic clergy did their best by word and act to goad the ignorant peasantry and the sluggish masses to take part in the revolutionary movement.

A portion of the over-excited and feverish population of Warsaw having persuaded itself that it had seen a fiery cross in the air, the news spread through the city that the sign of victory had shown itself, and an immense crowd collected at a spot thought to be advantageously situated for viewing the phenomenon. The commissary of the fifth and sixth police quarters of Warsaw made a formal report on the subject of the supposed aërial cross, saying that it was to be seen "just above a pear-tree in front of the house No. 2487," and that it had caused a crowd to assemble, whereby the public peace was likely to be disturbed. The Russians, finding that some intimate connection existed in the popular mind between the pear-tree and the miraculous symbol, ordered the former to be destroyed, and the tree, which is said to have been in full bloom, was cut down. This appears to have had the effect of dispelling the apparition; at least, no more was heard of it, and the crowd broke up, lamenting only the fall of the pear-tree.

Another example of miraculous but vain interposition on behalf of the insurgents was witnessed and officially recorded in the government of Grodno. A shepherdess twelve years old saw four birds come down from Heaven, who, when they reached the earth, changed themselves into as many saints; a chariot descended at the same time from Heaven, to which four horses were yoked. These saints said to the girl, "Poland will assuredly live, and that which the Poles are unable to accomplish, God will accomplish with his thunderbolts. Go and make this known to holy Poland!" The shepherdess stated that one of these personages was an angel, the second a cardinal, but she did not know who the two others were. The saints then took their seats in the chariot, and returned to Heaven.

Here, also, the Russians failed to acknowledge the truth of the alleged revelation, and they deprived the over-officious commissary of police who recorded it of his place, and handed him over, together with the curé who had vouched it, to be tried for their excess of faith.

The insurgents sustained a severe loss about 5th May, in the death of Francisco Nullo, a general in their service. He had been a distinguished officer in Garibaldi's army, and he brought with him from Italy thirty or forty of his former comrades, by whom he was greatly beloved. He was associated in command with Miniewski, and their little force consisted of some gentlemen calling themselves the "Zouaves à la mort," and the Italian company. They assembled at Cracow, intending to invade Poland from that neighbourhood. Instead of acting stealthily, and in a manner calculated to prevent their proceedings being remarked, the "Zouaves" made their progress a pageant and a show; their friends accompanied them to the plains of Wola, outside the city, and then took an affecting farewell of them. The consequence was, that the Russians were perfectly informed of their movements, and prepared an overwhelming force with which to oppose them. The hostile bands met, and the insurgents taking shelter in a wood, kept up an ineffectual fire on the Russians, which the latter, owing to the superior weapons with which they were armed, replied to with success. Finding his men were being sacrificed unavailingly, Nullo determined to charge and endeavour, in a hand-to-hand encounter, to change the fortunes of the day; the "Zouaves à la mort," however, preferred remaining under cover, and Nullo received a fatal wound almost on the moment of leaving the wood. Then ensued a strange and unexampled scene. Maddened by the death of the leader whom they loved, the Italians called out his name in the accents of bitterest grief; they sobbed, they shrieked, and by a general impulse rushed upon the enemy, and found a glorious death on the field they could not win.

The "Zouaves à la mort" were not so indiscreet; they retreated in a manner somewhat hurried and disorderly, and few of the friends who paid them so sad an honour on the plain of Wola had the additional sorrow of counting their heroes among the slain.

The Russians knew how to respect a noble foe. The following day they buried Nullo with all the honours of war. The army was drawn up in line, and saluted his remains as they were carried past. A solemn mass was performed in the church of Olkusz for the repose of his soul, and Prince Schakoffskoy, the commander of the Russian forces, with his staff, and detachments from each regiment, and all the Polish population of the town, followed him to the grave.

The peasantry of the South-western were even more hostile to the insurgents than those of the North-western provinces. Whatever may be their race, their language and customs are Russian, their religion is almost exclusively that of the Greek Church, and no bond of common interest unites them to the proprietors of the soil. Their masters have never been their friends; they are not so easily trampled on as the natives of the north-west, and consequently have not submitted to the same ignominious thraldom; but the cruelty, the injustice, and the persecutions of many years have left a deeper scar behind, and they regarded the insurgents with undisguised enmity. Emancipation they considered to be the gift of the Emperor against the will of the nobles, and it was in him only that they trusted to grant them their land in fee. The proclamation of the revolutionary Government, by which it assumed to give them the land, and the adoption of it by such of the proprietors as failed to demand their quarter's rent when it became due, did not win them. They considered this as a cunning device practised simply to delude them, and believed that concessions accorded in the moment of danger would be withdrawn in the hour of success.

The peasants somewhat unnecessarily feared, if the insurgents were victorious, that they would again be reduced to servitude; but their alarm on the subject of their land does not appear so causeless, when we remember the tenets on that subject held by the Polish proprietors up to the very commencement of the revolt; their conversion was suspiciously sudden, and the peasants might well doubt its sincerity.

They soon satisfied themselves that the Russians were the stronger party, and being quite clear on this point, gave full play to their loyalty. They afforded them information, and supplied them willingly with food when they required it; they assisted them wherever it was in their power, captured suspected persons, and hunted down fugitive Poles.

The difference in religion created a wide gulf between the peasants and the insurgents, and the result of a close inquiry will be to show that religion has had far greater influence than race in this contest. The Greek has universally sided with the Russian Government; the Roman Catholic peasant has frequently done so also; but the superior classes who profess the Roman Catholic faith have invariably given more or less overt assistance to the revolt. In the provinces of Podolia, Volhynia, and Kieff, the Roman Catholics numbered only 476,236 out of a population of 4,713,486.

The peasantry having thus evidenced their feelings, it was evident that no inroad into their provinces had a chance of success; but the insurgents organized an ill-timed and ill-advised rising, which took place at Kieff towards the end of May. Numerous individuals, and among them many of the students of the university, daily quitted the town. They procured their passports without difficulty, and the only measure of precaution the Government adopted was to confiscate such depôts of arms as they were able to find. On the 27th of May the streets were thronged with Poles dressed in the national costume; they hurried up and down in an agitated manner; they crowded the doorways of shops, and purchased provisions of all kinds.

The students hired the horses of a dragoon regiment, and rode into the country, where many of the proprietors in the district and some of the artisans of the town joined them. An armed force followed them, and at Borodinski, a place a short distance from the town, encountered and completely defeated them. This victory was so easily won, that one soldier killed and ten or eleven wounded was the total loss the Russians sustained.

The reason for this easy triumph was apparent when the prisoners were seen. Among them were schoolboys of thirteen and fourteen years old; their armament was incomplete, their commander was a riding-master of the university, and the unlucky insurgents were suffering greatly from wounds caused by their new high-heeled boots, which they thought it patriotic to wear, but which sorely pinched them on their march.

The troops would have had more trouble in arresting the fugitives than in defeating the enemy, had it not been for the exertions of the peasants. The inhabitants of the adjoining villages, armed with any weapons they could procure, scoured the country in all directions and attacked and arrested the insurgents. Day after day for some weeks they brought them in as prisoners to Kieff, and delivered them over to the authorities.

This was the only attempt of any importance made by the insurgents in that neighbourhood.

Nevertheless the National Government desired to show that the South-western provinces sympathized with the revolt, and only waited a favourable opportunity to rise against the Russian Government. The extreme ignorance which existed in Western Europe of the social and political condition of the various parts of the Poland of 1772 facilitated the leaders of the insurrection in the attempt, and very trifling successes or a long continuance of guerilla warfare in those provinces, would have enabled them to effect it. It was therefore resolved, as far back as the end of March, that an expeditionary corps should rendezvous at or in the vicinity of Lemberg, and thence invade Volhynia on the first opportunity that offered itself.

It was not an easy task either to procure the men or the weapons required for this attempt, for the Austrian troops were on the alert, and were constantly intercepting suspicious travellers, and searching for and finding the arms which the insurgents had concealed. Moreover, the peasants of Galicia were bitterly hostile to the Poles, whom they not unnaturally recognized as akin in race, object, and feeling to their own landlords—men whom they had never had reason to sympathize with or respect.

The insurgents were received into the houses of the Galician Poles, and were concealed there in great numbers for various periods, until at last the expeditionary corps having collected on the frontier, all was prepared for the invasion of Volhynia.

It had been originally intended that the force should consist of about 4,000 men, and be divided into five bands, who were to cross the frontier at different points. The combined movement was to be directed by General Wysocki, formerly the leader of the Polish legion in Hungary, and the title conferred upon him by the National Government was "General commanding in the province of Lublin, and in the Ruthenian Provinces."

When the moment of march arrived, it was found that about 1,200 was the total number of men who could be equipped and sent into the field, and these men were divided into two detachments, one of 750 under Wysocki, the other of 450 under Major Horodycki, an officer who had also seen service in the Hungarian war.

In the *Times'* correspondent's letters we have a very interesting narrative of the expedition, and highly instructive sketches of the men who took a share in it.

"With all the admiration," he says, "which I sincerely feel for the Langiewiczs, Frankowskis, Narbutts, Padlewskis, Horodyckis, Gliszminskis, and so many other noble-minded soldiers who have given dignity to the Polish movement, and who are now, for the most part, in prison or in the grave, there is one class of the Polish insurgents which I confess I cannot stand at all. These are the men and boys who are to the true patriots of the insurrection what youths who enter regular armies for the sake of the uniform are to true soldiers. For six weeks you may see them strutting about the streets and talking loud in the coffee-houses of Cracow and Lemberg, proud of their martial bearing, very proud indeed of their boots, and boasting of all sorts of things they are going to do, but have not yet done. Houses are open to them which at other times and under other circumstances they would not be allowed to enter; they have only to say that they are going into the cavalry to have excellent horses placed at their disposal, and there is scarcely anything they may not get by asking for it or hinting that they are in need of it. Then they are allowed to pay, and even themselves receive, an undue amount of attention from women, for the Polish ladies look upon patriotism as the first virtue, and are too patriotic themselves to imagine that those insurgents who are the most ferocious when they are a hundred miles away from the frontier can be among the mildest when they find themselves in presence of the enemy; and that, while the bravest and most pure-minded men in Poland are literally sacrificing themselves beneath the Russian sword in the supposed interest of their country, '*ces messieurs bottés*' (as I have heard them called by their own sex) are sniffing the battle a very long way off, and gracefully lounging on the Austrian barrier at least a mile from the scene of action. On the morning of the invasion of Volhynia (it was all over by 2 p.m.) a Polish gentleman arrested in my presence more than twenty of these faint-hearted patriots as they were hurrying from the rear of Wysocki's detachment to the Galician frontier. They had not the slightest idea who this gentleman was; but he threatened to report them to the National Government, took their names down, caught new fugitives one by one as they came up, and did it all in such a tone and decision, and with such an air of authority, that when he ordered them to form, and marched them to a convenient little nook in the wood which lines the right side of the road to Radziwilow, the score of armed men obeyed their unarmed, self-appointed chief, and were forced to proceed like lambs to the ambuscade, from which, if the opportunity presented itself, they with some sixty who afterwards joined them, were to fire upon the Russians. Then, finding that the Russians were not coming, they were lions once more, and boasted how they had been the last men to leave the field of battle (the action, as could be seen, had just begun), and how the rest of the detachment had been cut to pieces, and they alone had lived to tell the story, which they certainly told in the nursery sense of the word.

"'*Ces messieurs bottés*' are, after all, not the worst members of the Polish insurrection. What is to be said of the gentlemen who are not *bottés*, because they have no boots, and who have also no shirts, and who come to the insurgent camp clothed with vermin and rags? And is there any excuse for making brave officers risk their lives and reputations in endeavouring to lead such miserable creatures—the refuse of the Polish towns—against Russian troops who are no more 'demoralized' in Volhynia than they were in the Crimea, and who can certainly make as good a stand against a horde of Polish ragamuffins as they did against the well-trained soldiers of France and England?

"'I thought,' said one of Wysocki's captains to me, when I went to see him in the hospital at Brody, where he is lying with a bullet in his leg, 'I thought I should have found the same sort of men fighting here that I found in Hungary when I was in the Polish legion. It was too bad to give me such *rubbish* to command.'

"'If you could have seen your men beforehand,' I inquired,

'would you have left England and your wife and family to take charge of such soldiers?'

"'Of course not,' he replied. 'It is no use trying to lead men who cannot be got to follow. I was not merely disappointed but disgusted, when I saw what material I had to deal with.'

"'What class of men had you in your company?' I continued; 'do you think I could call them vagabonds?'

"'Well, they were covered with lice, and were the sort of persons you might find in swarms for any sort of work in Whitechapel. I should think vagabonds just the word for them.'

"'And how long did they remain under fire?' I asked.

"'Only for a few minutes. I was hit about twenty minutes after the battle had begun, and already half my company had got away. I had only forty men left. I believe they all wandered into the woods, and dispersed as soon as I was carried to the rear. People will be abusing the general; but he did his best, and the officers did their best to support him. The first and fourth companies were the only ones that did any real fighting. The others had so many bad men among them that, taken altogether, they were quite worthless.'"

This was the force with which the National Government proposed to revolutionize Volhynia, a province where the people were opposed to them, and which was efficiently held by a large and well-appointed Russian army. Contrasting the greatness of the end intended with the poverty of the means employed for effecting it, the only conclusion at which it is possible to arrive is that the National Government knew the expedition was certain to meet with immediate and ignominious defeat, but that they organized and sent it forth in order that they might advertise the spread of the insurrection, and persuade the great powers of Europe that it was extending to all the provinces included in the Poland of 1772.

The first object of the invaders was the capture of Radziwilow, an unimportant town, about two miles from the Austrian frontier; and the two detachments, commanded by Horodycki and Wysocki, were to approach it from different quarters, and simultaneously attack it.

Horodycki's detachment advanced, and not meeting with that under the command of Wysocki, marched into Radziwilow, which they entered about three o'clock a.m. In the market-place, a small Russian force, variously estimated at from five hundred to nine hundred men, was drawn up, and a conflict immediately ensued. The engagement lasted for upwards of an hour, and ended in the entire defeat of the insurgents, who lost their commander, Horodycki, many other of their officers, and a very large proportion of their men. So utterly were they beaten, that when, at seven o'clock, Wysocki reached the neighbourhood of the town, he thought they could not have arrived, but that the sound of firearms would bring them to his aid.

While Horodycki's detachment was thus being cut to pieces, the men under the command of Wysocki had difficulties of their own to encounter. They were pursued by the Austrian troops, and were compelled to take a long circuitous route to the frontier, and when at length they arrived before Radziwilow, they had marched nearly thirty miles, and had had nothing to eat for twenty-four hours.

In front of the town, some eight hundred Russians had taken up a position, and Wysocki, unconscious of the misfortunes which had overwhelmed him, looked anxiously round for the promised aid of Horodycki. As the succour came not, the action commenced; but it was not of a character to test the steadiness or military capacity of the invading force. There were no charges, no hand-to-hand encounters, not even any steady firing, and the cavalry were not engaged. The opposing parties were hundreds of yards distant from each other, the Poles taking shelter in a forest, from which they fired on the Russians, while the latter concealed themselves in some standing corn, whence they returned the fire of their enemy. In this ignominious skirmishing hours wore away, and General Wysocki, finding he could make no impression on the Russian troops, and that he had already lost several of his best officers, was reluctantly obliged to retreat. He buried his arms, and recrossed the Austrian frontier.

Major Synkiewicz, the second in command of Horodycki's detachment, " had to take refuge in a large pond or lake, where he remained for eight hours, while the peasants who had been pursuing him stood on the banks, armed with scythes, and ready to murder him if he returned to dry land. The major had swum to a little island of mud, and there remained concealed among rushes and weeds, until he at last thought of taking his Italian hat off, and sending it floating along the water. Then the peasants thought their victim was drowned, and went home to dinner."

The ill success of this expedition excited great discontent in Galicia. The papers in the interest of the insurgents complained that blow after blow was striking them, while their own most carefully prepared attempts invariably failed. The false reports, too, which excited Western Europe were beginning to lose their value, and it was found, in some instances, that they disheartened those they were intended to encourage.

The following is an extract from a pamphlet entitled, "Letter of a Patriot Pole," addressed, in the autumn of 1863, to the National Government:—

"What pleasure I and my brave companions in arms experienced on finding, in those copies of foreign newspapers which occasionally reached our forest, the announcement of the rapid increase of the forces of the insurrection, the news of so many victories won from the enemy! Pursued by superior forces, driven as we were like fallow-deer, we breathed more freely on learning that on other points our brothers were victorious, and that from all parts of the east and of the west succours were hastening their arrival to join with us in the great work of the liberation of our country. Intoxicated with happiness, every one forgot his sufferings, some their wounds, others the enervating effect of continual privations, when one day, among the catalogue of victories of which the papers spoke, we found the recital of that which our legion had achieved over two companies of infantry and fifty Cossacks. Our amazement was indescribable. On the day mentioned in the despatch, there had been no encounter; we were not in all more than 186 men, instead of 1,500, as the telegraph alleged, and, alas! in place of being victorious, we had taken that very morning the resolution to disperse, and each of us to join other bands more fortunate and more numerous than our own. Four of us were in the tent of Count A. to read with eagerness the bundle of papers sent him from Cracow, and to communicate to each other what we found remarkable among them. It was B. who met with the passage in question; I observed that he grew pale as he turned over the paper which he held in his hands. As he was wounded in the leg, I thought his wound must have re-opened; but he handed me the journal, saying, in a voice trembling with rage, ' Read !' We read, all three of us, this ill-omened despatch, the count in a loud voice, the other two of us following him with our eyes; and never shall I forget the terrible effect those five lines of print made upon us.

" So, these recitals of victories, these narratives of successes won over the enemy, were nothing but lies! We had the incontrovertible proof that they had lied once, we were entitled to believe that the other ' *brilliant affairs,*' the other ' *complete defeats of the Muscovites* ' were equally false. But if all this was a lie, the sympathies of the people for the cause we defended might also exist only in the imagination of those who deceived us; and then what were we ? Adventurers, filibusters, a band of brigands, acting by the order of its chiefs, and pursuing an object altogether selfish; an object which the people repudiated.

" This idea upset us. We wished to know the truth of all these shams; we wished to ascertain for ourselves what was true and what was false in all that was said and published on the revolutionary movement; we wished to know if we were the dupes of an intriguing minority or the champions of a truly popular cause. Under the influence of the first burst of passion, we adopted the most extreme resolutions : to protest publicly against the falsehood of the would-be patriots; to write to the Central Committee at Warsaw, and require them to tell us what was true and what was invented in the statements which described the insurrection as gaining strength every day; and, finally, to call together all our companions in arms, to read to them the lying despatch, and send them into various districts in Lithuania, Podolia, &c., with the commission to personally satisfy themselves of the condition of things, and to return on a day fixed to advise together on that which we had to decide. Nothing of the kind was done. The night, a sleepless night to all four, brought reflection with it, and the very excess of our grief caused renewed courage and hope to fill our hearts. The news of the victory that they said we had gained, was false; but this might be explained by an unintentional error; the name of a place, written indistinctly, or a mistake in printing might have caused what we found there. This explanation was highly improbable, but it was possible; we finished then by admitting it, so easily do we believe what we desire, and so much pain would our patriotism have caused us, had we thought that the brilliant successes of our brothers in arms in other districts had not been more real than our own. We, who had braved death which the Muscovite carbines scattered amongst us; we, who had faced in our ranks the Cossack pikes, we were afraid to look the truth in the face, we were afraid to say that we were deceived, we were afraid of losing our courage if we admitted what we thought, and, not to discourage our comrades, we resolved to deceive them, or at least not to undeceive them as to the value of the favourable intelligence which stimulated their patriotic zeal.

"With one accord we burned the paper containing the false despatch, and gave the remaining numbers to our companions in arms, which they read in a loud voice, a reading which was more than once interrupted by the cry of ' *Vive la Pologne* ' caused by the recital of the ' *victories* ' gained over Muscovites."

CHAPTER XVI.

The Six Points.—Public Opinion in Russia.—Diplomatic Correspondence.—Analysis of the Six Points.—Proclamation of the National Government.—Cessation of Foreign Interference.

AFTER prolonged negotiation between England, France, and Austria, the three great powers agreed to urge on Russia six points, which, in their opinion, should be conceded by her to the insurgents; and in a letter addressed by Lord Russell to Lord Napier, on 17th June, these points were embodied.*

Lord Russell prefaces the more important portions of his despatch by accepting the offer of Prince Gortschakoff "to enter upon an exchange of ideas, upon the ground and within the limits of the treaties of 1815." Before, however, commencing this discussion, the Foreign Secretary states that, in the opinion of the English Cabinet, there were two leading principles upon which the future government of Poland ought to rest: the first of these was the establishment of confidence in the Government on the part of the governed; the second was the stability of law over arbitrary will. Doubtless, both these principles are very important, but neither is exactly attainable amid the convulsions of a civil war; and it will presently be seen that the six points submitted for acceptance to the Government of Russia were not so well calculated eventually to secure them, as were the liberal institutions recently granted by the Emperor, and so scornfully rejected by the Poles.

The six points demanded of Russia were:

1st. A complete and general amnesty.

2nd. National representation, with powers similar to those which are fixed by the charter of 15th (27th) November, 1815.

3rd. Poles to be named to public offices in such a manner

* See Appendix.

as to form a distinct national administration, having the confidence of the country.

4th. Full and entire liberty of conscience; repeal of the restrictions imposed on Catholic worship.

5th. The Polish language to be recognized in the kingdom as the official language, and used as such in the administration of the law, and in education.

6th. The establishing of a legal and regular system of recruiting.

These six points were in the English despatch supplemented by the additional stipulations: That there should be a provisional suspension of arms, to be proclaimed by the Emperor of Russia, and that there should be a conference of the eight Powers which had signed the treaty of Vienna.

The first difficulty which the consideration of these six points creates, is to know with what aim they were proposed for the acceptance of Russia. They were so framed that she could not accept them without compromising her own dignity; while, at the same time, their acceptance would have placed the Poles in a worse position than that which they occupied under the recent decrees of the Emperor; and it was quite clear that if the Russians accepted them, the Poles would not. For what purpose, then, were they proposed?

No doubt, in politics, where the feelings of the people are strongly excited, it is sometimes necessary to minister to their ignorant sympathies and pander to their national vanity. Public opinion in France had for many months been carefully misled by lying telegrams, long, circumstantial, and artful misrepresentations from "the seat of war," recitals of Muscovite atrocities, of Polish sufferings and Polish wrongs, and high-wrought appeals to the mighty and magnanimous race which alone among nations goes to war for an idea. Thus the Emigration had succeeded in creating a very strong war feeling among the excitable population of Paris. In England, these feelings were to some extent reciprocated; there was an uneasy throbbing of the popular pulse, which any accident might stimulate into a fever for war; public meetings (many of them certainly insignificant, but more than one of them respectable) had sympathized with the Polish cause; members of both Houses of Parliament had made strong speeches in its behalf; and there were signs that much was expected of the Government, and that something must be done. Moreover, the conduct of the Opposition was not reassuring: almost as numerous and powerful as the Government they desired to overthrow, their policy was an expectant one; they did not declare themselves; and if the Government took no steps to advocate the Polish cause, it was at least possible that the Opposition might step in, and by the adoption of a bold and advanced line of action, enlist popular sympathies entirely on their side.

It was necessary, therefore, that something should be done —what should that something be?

It has already been seen how little was really known in England of the merits of the Polish question; the false reports which the National Government spread through the medium of the press, had persuaded the people that the Poles under the Russian Government were the victims of a cruel and jealous despotism, and consequently the six points would be supposed to secure to them a great increase in their liberty and rights. The people who in England were clamouring in favour of the Poles would probably be satisfied, or at least silenced, if those points were conceded. Was there not reason to suppose that Russia would willingly grant them? If they in some slight degree modified the institutions she had already conferred on Poland, such modifications were not on the side of liberality; there was nothing in them which could by possibility interfere with her present intentions on the subject of liberalized institutions, or with her future views; and if there was some indignity in adopting a series of resolutions dictated to her by other powers, she would probably overlook it and think her acceptance of the prescribed points an easy way of avoiding a disastrous war.

But the ministers of England, and perhaps the autocrat of France, forgot that Russia of to-day is not the Russia which obeyed the Emperor Nicholas. They were ready enough to applaud the liberal institutions recently granted to the great Empire of the North; they overlooked the fact that those institutions, together with the expectation of others of a more advanced kind, had created a public opinion there. While they praised the Emperor Alexander for sowing the seed, they failed to recognize that the plant had already struggled to the surface; that day by day it acquired importance and increased power; and that no emperor and no council of ministers could longer ignore it. There was, at length, a public opinion in Russia,—patriotic in its character, and decided in its tone. The Russians who, in the earlier stages of the Polish agitation, were most disposed to regard it with favour, and to consider it as a struggle for reasonable constitutional freedom, had now taken the alarm, and beheld in it a conspiracy to dismember their venerated empire. Had the revolutionary parties a year previously aimed at the autonomy, or even complete independence, of the kingdom of 1815, they would have found a large party among the liberal Russians who would have encouraged, or at least would not have opposed, the attempt; but the revolutionary programme, when it was extended to the Western provinces, threatened to dismember the empire; and this attempt every true Russian was determined to resist to the utmost.

Moreover, the press and the people had been taken into the confidence of the Government, and they were flattered and influenced by so unusual a condescension. The policy of the Emperor had been avowed; it had been shown that he had conferred franchises and immunities on his rebel subjects, and only waited till the insurrection was ended to endow them with more; he had offered them, an amnesty which they had insolently spurned; he had done all that a wise and benevolent monarch could do to win their confidence, and his efforts had been in vain.

The tide which had flowed so high in favour of the Poles, now ebbed beyond its ordinary margin, and they were regarded as influenced by a morbid antipathy to Russia—an antipathy which no good intentions and no reasonable concessions would ever avail to remove.

These feelings of hostility were aggravated beyond measure by the interference of the allied powers. An intensely national feeling sprang up, which, reasonable or not, *would* be listened to and *would* be obeyed. It may well be doubted if the Government could have withstood this feeling had it been so minded; as it was, the national sentiment gave power and expression to the policy on which it had resolved. Had it compromised the honour of Russia by complying with the six points, such compliance with the dictates of foreign powers would have involved it in measureless difficulties with the very men whose co-operation it secured by taking a more open and manly course.

The English Cabinet addressed their despatch to a nation whose honour and self-esteem were deeply pledged to a steadfast line of action,—a nation which had roused itself to a full sense of its own power, and was determined to maintain its rights. At this moment its new-born sense of its duties and its destiny made it more than usually jealous of foreign dictation; and, well advised as Lord Russell was of the internal condition of the country, it is inexplicable that he should have chosen such a crisis for blending supercilious advice with menaces but half concealed.

The suggestion of the six points might almost be regarded as an insult to an independent state; but one at least of the preliminaries suggested by Lord Russell was yet more humiliating

What likelihood was there that a powerful sovereign would "proclaim a suspension of arms" between himself and his rebel subjects? It would be at once to acknowledge them as belligerents; to give them a status and a consideration to which no act of theirs had ever entitled them; and to invest them with an importance which would subsequently have given the great powers of Europe the most obvious excuse for interfering on their behalf. Insurgents may be recognized as belligerents by foreign powers when they keep large armies in the field, hold possession of fortified places, and have a regular and avowed Government which can be made to answer for its shortcomings and misdeeds; but to ask the Emperor of Russia to recognize the guerilla bands which infested Poland as a belligerent power, was certainly an unprecedented act of eccentric statesmanship. Doubtless it was in the power of Russia to accede to this request; but was it reasonable to demand it? If her armies retired to the frontier or contented themselves with crowding into camps or fortifications, where was her guarantee that the rebels would lay down their arms? There was no known authority which could bind them, no recognized power with which it was possible to negotiate. And if Russia, at the instance of three nations, retired from the struggle, those nations would have been bound in honour and equity to impose similar terms upon the rebels in arms. Suppose, however, the rebels did for the moment acquiesce, and at the end of a few weeks again broke out in insurrection, what would have been our remedy? To compel the Imperial Government to perform its treaties, England could blockade its ports, capture its shipping, and lay siege to its citadels; but what was her hold upon the invisible conclave calling itself the National Government? How could she treat with it, and how punish it for a breach of faith? Common prudence should have taught Lord Russell not to treat with a body which could not answer for those it professed to govern, and which it was impossible to punish or bring to a reckoning should it trifle with him. This proposal, too, was made when the illusions as to the power of the insurgents were dispelled; when their armies were broken, their leaders in prison or flying from the scene of the insurrection; and when day by day the Government was gathering strength, and the rebellion itself was dwindling down into the compass of guerilla war.

To make this unpalatable overture more galling still, Lord Russell proposed to cite the London newspapers as authorities to prove that the Russians had committed excesses in Poland! If he wanted to show that excesses had been committed (and when has there been a civil war unstained by them?) the Ambassador at St. Petersburg and the Consul-General at Warsaw were the sources from whence his information might justly have been drawn. But their despatches were too true—too matter of fact for any such use to be made of them; so, to point a paragraph, and give a sting to uncalled-for counsel, Lord Russell relied on the chance rumours which had found their way into foreign and hostile journals.

There is, again, a difficulty arising out of this despatch, which conveys the idea that Lord Russell was really ignorant of the subject matter of the treaty upon which he wrote. It is clear that the treaty of 1815, which relates to Poland, refers only to the duchy of Warsaw, or rather to what is now known as the Congress kingdom. Lord Russell, however, cites a conversation between Lord Castlereagh and Alexander I., which conversation relates to a scheme that was never carried out, and in citing it contrives so to introduce " the Polish provinces, formerly dismembered," as to make it appear that he referred as much to the Western provinces as to the Congress kingdom. Whatever may be the right of the powers who were parties to the treaty of Vienna to interfere with the government of the Congress kingdom, it is clear they have as little title to interfere with the Western provinces as they have to dictate to England how the Isle of Man or Jersey are to be ruled; and thus, if the " suspension of arms " had been granted at the instance of Lord Russell, half the insurgents would have been included in its operation, while the other half would have been unaffected by it. This objection, however, is not singular to the question of suspension of arms, it runs through all the proposals of the English Government.

The six points taken seriatim were liable, among others, to the following objections:—

An amnesty had already been offered by the Government to such of the insurgents as would lay down their arms; it had been conceived in a humane and liberal spirit, and the exceptions from its operation were only such as were necessarily made. That amnesty, however, had been rejected by the Poles; it had been regarded by them as an evidence of weakness; it had encouraged the malcontents; and it had damped the zeal of loyal men. Alive to the evil results of that measure, the Russian Government was indisposed to repeat an offer which had been thus misinterpreted; and it was most unlikely that it would yield to foreign pressure a concession which could only be politic if it were an act of voluntary clemency.

The second stipulation, that a national representation should be granted, with powers similar to those fixed by the charter of 15th (27th) November, 1815, deserves investigation. Bearing in mind what the present Emperor had granted in the way of constitutional freedom to the kingdom of Poland, and remembering that he was pledged to develop the new institutions so soon as they had fairly taken root there, let us see for what advantages the Western powers wished to barter them away.

The Diet of 1815 consisted of two chambers; the first composed of a nominated Senate, and the second of Deputies from the different communes. The legislative power resided in the person of the king and in the two chambers of the Diet.

In the sovereign was the sole power to summon, adjourn, prorogue, and dissolve the Diet. It was provided, however, that it was to sit once in two years, and that its session was to last for thirty days. It was to deliberate only upon such projects of law as were submitted to it on the part of the king by the Council of State, and those projects of law it had no power to alter, but could only submit representations for the consideration of the Council, of the amendments it desired to introduce.

The sole subjects submitted to it, and they, as has been shown, were only discussed after, and in obedience to directions from the sovereign, were the augmentation and reduction of duties, contributions, taxes, and such other matters as might be specially submitted to it by the Crown.

Thus the national representation for which the Western powers contended was a Diet composed of a king, a nominated and an elected chamber, meeting for thirty days once in two years, and restricted to the discussion of such laws and such questions as were directly referred to it by the Government.

The revival of this institution would not have benefitted Poland. It had never worked to its advantage, and its restricted powers and its occasional session were not calculated to advance her interests now. Free and unfettered parliamentary discussion has done much for England; but does any one suppose that a Parliament having no power to originate a discussion, to amend a bill, or to stray out of the narrow limits of a ministerial programme, would be of any value in preserving or enlarging popular freedom? The institutions recently granted to the Poles were not, it is true, founded on our model, but they were suited to the requirements of the country; they met the demand for local legislation; they confided to municipal government many important details of administration;

and above all they paved the way to extended liberties in the future. No friend of constitutional freedom would have suggested the exchange of these substantial advantages for the illusory benefits to be derived from the reconstitution of the abandoned Diet.

The third and fifth stipulations evidence the same want of knowledge of the existing circumstances, as the second does of the past history of the kingdom. It has already been seen that all the civil employés, from the Marquis Wielopolski to the lowest clerk in the public offices, were Poles; that the Russians had all been dismissed; and that, while the Polish language was universally employed, the Russian was everywhere exluded from public offices, and the transaction of public business.

The fourth stipulation, providing for full and entire liberty of conscience, and a repeal of the restrictions imposed on Catholic worship, is equally unintelligible. The Catholic Church was burdened by no restrictions; her services were performed in public, and with all the solemnity her clergy and people chose to invest them; the number of her temples was unlimited, as was also the number and dignity of her priests. The only restriction by which the Catholic Church was in any degree shackled was to be found in the law which prescribed, where a Catholic married a member of the Greek Church, that the issue of the marriage should be brought up in the orthodox faith; but this law, objectionable as it doubtless is, has no particular reference to the Roman Catholic Church; for in every case of a mixed marriage, where one of the parents is of the Greek persuasion, the children are educated in that faith. Moreover the Catholics would hardly do wisely in mooting this question, for, wherever a Catholic intermarries with a Protestant, the Church will only consent to the marriage on condition that the children shall be educated in the Catholic faith; and the number of disciples they thus gain exceeds their losses under the existing law.

The sixth stipulation was the establishment of a legal and regular system of recruiting. This legal and regular system of recruiting, our minister should have known, was provided for by a law of 3rd (15th) March, 1859. The real ground of complaint was, that instead of acting upon that law, as legally he was bound to do, the Marquis Wielopolski ignored it, and acted under the old system, instituted in 1816, and which that law abolished.

Regarded from another aspect, these proposals were equally strange. The insurgents were fighting not for their rights under the treaty of Vienna, but for complete independence of Russia. They cared nothing for the treaty; they asked for no amnesty; they would agree to no suspension of arms; they refused even to recognize the Treaty kingdom. They required the restitution of the Poland of 1772, freed from Russian influence and supremacy, and declared repeatedly that nothing else would satisfy them.

The following is an extract from one of the proclamations of the National Government issued when these proposals were under discussion :—" The National Government pronounces that Poland repudiates negotiation as suicide, as treason, and declares that the whole country from the Vistula to the Dnieper has vowed to perish rather than treat with the foreign oppressor." Yet in the presence of all these difficulties English statesmen propose impracticable expedients, and base them on inferences they deduce from treaties which extended only to the ancient duchy of Warsaw.

The reply of Prince Gortschakoff to these representations* of Lord Russell was felt to be conclusive; and although it appears to have excited the deep resentment of the Foreign Secretary, he saw the only choice before him was acquiescence or war. The Cabinet of St. James's was not willing to involve the country in hostilities on behalf of Poland, so another wordy and ill-written despatch † was closed with an assurance which was couched in the following language :—" If Russia does not perform all that depends upon her to further the moderate and conciliatory views of the three powers; if she does not enter upon the path which is opened to her by friendly counsels, she makes herself responsible for the serious consequences which the prolongation of the troubles in Poland may produce."

---

* See Appendix. Prince Gortschakoff's despatch of 1st July, 1863.
† See Appendix. Lord Russell's despatch of 11th August, 1863.

The language employed by the French press had been more violent than that of our own; its Government also had done much to stimulate the hopes of the insurgents. The Palais Royal, if not the Tuileries, was thrown ostentatiously open to the representatives of the national cause, and rumour alleged that French gold and French arms were unsparingly lavished in support of the insurrection. Poland had claims on the magnanimity of a Napoleon which it was hard for the head of that aspiring house to disavow; and when significant words were spoken which pointed to armed redress; when officers were sent to join the insurgents and report on their numbers, their prospects, and their plans; when the friends of Poland, whether English senators or the leaders of the Emigration, had ready access to the Emperor and his ministers; when, above all, the diplomatic correspondence of France grew more and more hostile and threatening in its tone, it was natural that the insurgents should count on the aid of France, and that his Polish clients should sustain the rebellion until their imperial patron had time to unsheathe his sword.

It would occupy too much space to dwell at length on the correspondence between France and Russia. It must suffice to say, that while the language of M. Drouyn de Lhuys was certainly more dignified than that employed by Lord Russell, it indicated graver displeasure and more determined opposition. It was well understood, when the despatches of June 17th were sent, that France had resolved to follow up her remonstrances by an appeal to arms; but France had reckoned on the support of the English administration, and that support failed her.

The despatches of Prince Gortschakoff humiliated the pride of the French Emperor; they questioned his statements; they denounced his motives; and they challenged his power. Yet their language, bitter in all the courteous refinement of diplomacy, gave no handle to those who were unprepared to throw their sword into the scale; and submission, if submission were decided on, must be silent unless it were prophetic.

The French Emperor retired from the contest, sullen, indignant, complaining of the conduct of his allies, looking back with vain and undignified regret at the past; he endeavoured to reassert his position, and become once more the arbiter of Europe, by inducing its nations to meet in council beneath the shadow of his throne. The dream was a vain one; a short uncourteous refusal from Lord Russell awoke him from his delusion; and he was compelled to accept in its integrity the humiliating truth, that his policy had been an error, and that his prestige had received a severe, if not a fatal blow.

CHAPTER XVII.

Dispute between the White and Red Parties.—Public Opinion in Russia.—Resignation of Wielopolski.—Embarrassing Position of the Grand Duke.—Excesses of the National Government.—Robbery of the Treasury.—Compulsory Loan.—Death of Lelewel.—Hopeless Character of the Revolt.—Resignation of the Grand Duke.—Appointment and Character of Count Berg.—His Policy.—Attempt upon his Life.—The sacking of the Zamoyski Houses.—Suppression of Mourning.—Close of the Insurrection.

By the beginning of the month of June the revolt had ceased to be formidable. A long train of disasters had been unrelieved by a single success, and on all sides the insurgents were losing ground, and their bands were being defeated and dispersed. The lofty aspirations which had animated men like Seriakoffski had died out, for it was seen that the peasantry had no sympathy with the insurrection; the hopes of the White party had been crushed when Langiewicz fled; and every day the prospects of foreign intervention, in which some among the insurgents trusted, were becoming more doubtful and remote.

The insincere alliance between the Red and White parties was rudely shaken by these continued failures. It is impossible to trace with precision the changes which from time to time took place in the National Government. That mysterious body was always nominally the same, but its policy varied from month to month, and these variations were believed to reflect successive changes in its *personnel*. In truth it was impossible for two parties whose opinions differed so greatly to continue to act for any considerable period harmoniously together; for a time they might unite, and, forgetful of the wide difference which existed between them, they might act in concert against the common foe; but it was certain that success or failure must alike be fatal to their union. The rupture which had thus been distinctly foreseen was precipitated by the overthrow of Langiewicz. That general was regarded as the representative and champion of the White party, and his defeat was accepted as an evidence that its policy was faulty or its patriotism insincere. His defeat also, as we have already seen, threw the conduct of the insurrection into the hands of the Red party, and they attempted by a sanguinary and relentless course of action to compensate for diminished numbers and waning reputation.

The views of the Red party* are expressed with great distinctness in a pamphlet which about this time was published by, it is stated, one of the members of the ancient revolutionary organization of Galicia.

In this pamphlet the failure of the revolt of 1830 is attributed to the weakness and folly of its leaders. On the present occasion, however, the author stated the insurrection was commenced under other auspices, and the unarmed agitation and the propaganda, which was working through all the Polish provinces and through all classes of society, had prepared the ground for revolution.

Two parties had, at the commencement of the national organization, formed themselves—the White party and the party of action.

The White party desired to accomplish "organic changes by reform, by government measures, by the development of national prosperity and material well-being—in a word, by all those half-measures which the revolution had long since repudiated. Their rallying-point was the Agricultural Society."

"The other party, from which the Central Committee sprung, resolved to organize all Poland, politically as militarily, both towns and villages, and to create for this purpose a national Junto. In order to give the people the stimulus necessary to induce them to pass from the influence of dreams to that of action, they were incited by the crimes committed at Warsaw—

---

* In Appendix B will be found a letter of Mieroslawski, dated as far back as March, 1861, in which the policy and aims of the Red party are stated unreservedly. This letter shows that the unarmed agitation and subsequent revolt were even then resolved on, and that no concessions on the part of the Russian Government would have prevented it.

crimes which had the advantage of satisfying the impatient and moderating their feverish excitement."

The author insisted that the party of action had given a signal proof of its ability by so adroitly profiting by the recruitment to precipitate a national rising. The White party, however, rejected the movement, deemed it infatuated, refused pecuniary contributions to it, and even quitted the country. The *Czas* compromised the success of the revolution by declaring that it did not exist, and that there was nothing save a desperate resistance to the recruitment. The result was, that when their share of the national contribution was demanded from the Cracow Jews, they replied they would not pay until the revolution had really broken out.

"Although the insurrection had lasted more than five weeks, and the importation of arms and warlike stores was not stopped along the Austrian frontier, not one of the bands was properly equipped.

"The Central Committee had not punished the White party as they deserved. It should have given them some token that the national organization was not alone called upon to strive with the Muscovites, but that it ought to exterminate all parties opposed to itself, and govern the people exclusively by means of its own adherents . . . But moral courage was wanting to the Central Committee. The opposition terrified it; it had not sufficient courage to act in a revolutionary spirit against the Whites; it had the weakness to treat with them, until, after numberless concessions, it admitted into its councils those who were altogether strangers to the insurrection.

. . . . "Composed of incapables, the Committee distinguished itself by the worthlessness of its acts and the inefficacy of the half-measures it adopted . . . If the insurrection has continued, it is owing to the enthusiasm of that section of the Poles which constitutes the heart of the nation. In the next place, it is because the White party are convinced that thus they can increase their power, and that this is the only means to destroy the influence of Mieroslawski, who is their bugbear, and whom they regard as a socialist vampire . . . After the preliminary agitation and the enfeeblement of the Central Committee, the revolution entered on the much to be regretted period of dictatorship. The White party, although almost absolute masters of the situation, were haunted by the phantom of a Mieroslawski dictatorship, and resolved to protect themselves by a dictator of their own. At the commencement of the movement they had cast their eyes on Langiewicz, whose pliability they had discovered.

"The *Czas* extolled his clumsy skirmishes, as though they were incomparable military exploits. After having magnified his name and increased his influence, they offered him money to disband his troops, hoping to terminate the insurrection. . . . . The nation, which discerned not this mass of intrigue, accepted with enthusiasm the puppet which they presented to it. The White party triumphed, and the Committee remained open-mouthed, asking itself how Langiewicz had dared to proclaim himself dictator. Instead of energetically opposing and punishing him, and proclaiming him and his assistants traitors and knaves, the Committee addressed him in a diplomatic note, and vociferated 'Long live the Dictator.'

"The country is organized neither politically nor in an administrative sense. There are a multitude of papers, official or semi-official, and all—even those that are not secret, white, red, yellow, and violet—without distinction of colour chant hymns of praise to the Central Committee. They lie deliberately, under the pretext of patriotism and unity."

"Faithful to this system of invention, the *Czas* and other journals conceal our losses, the terrible state of our affairs, and thus plunge the people in apathy. . . Thus it has often happened that it has not been weapons that were required for combatants, but combatants for weapons.

"Organs of public information have a right to mislead popular opinion, so long as there are diplomatic negotiations pending, and if the Junto had not wished to crush the head of this diplomatic hydra, it is that it deceived itself into the belief that it would find safety from its efforts. It is with this view alone that the Central Committee have furnished Ladislaus Czartoryski with powers enabling him to cringe in imperial and princely ante-chambers, unmindful that this family of Czartoryski never worked save for its own aggrandizement" (*pro domo sua*).

The programme traced by this pamphlet for the future was as follows:—" Firstly, it is necessary to retrace our steps, and replace the revolution on the base originally intended for it. It is indispensable to unite to the national territory the provinces usurped by the Germans, not by the bonds of a feeble union, but by those of an intimate, organic, and irrevocable fusion. Secondly, it is necessary to create a revolutionary tribunal to which the Junto shall itself be subject. This tribunal will be the representative of the popular conscience, and will exercise the executive power with a firm and resolute hand; it will punish with inexorable justice, and its sentences must be executed by a well-organized body of executioners. Thirdly, it is necessary to act vigorously beyond the country, in order to terminate the isolated action of parties, and to sever the last links that unite us to Czarism. To this end it is necessary to get rid of the Czar, his brother, and the Marquis Wielopolski. It is necessary to get rid of, or at least to remove, Mouravieff, Annenkoff, Nazimoff, Schakoffskoy, Dlatowski, Droutzki, Gavidoff, etc., etc.; and it is necessary to do it, even should it cost thousands of lives and hundreds of thousands of roubles."

This pamphlet is a curious proof of the disunion which existed among the revolutionary parties. It was apparent from the first moment of their ill-starred coalition that the objects for which they strove were dissimilar, and that they sought to attain them by means which greatly varied. Both, it is true, desired to win the independence of their country; but in the way in which that independence was to be achieved they widely differed. One party would have secured it by peaceful progress, the other depended on revolutionary war-cries and the assassin's knife. During the unarmed agitation they worked together, and perhaps the difference in their ulterior views was forgotten amid the excitement of that strange period; and after the revolution broke out, they for a short time acted together, for they felt it absolutely necessary to forget their mutual distrust in face of the common foe.

Soon, however, the feuds, temporarily stifled, broke out again with redoubled violence, and the pamphlet from which the foregoing extracts are taken shows how irreconcilable they were.

The condition of affairs in the Congress kingdom did not satisfy public opinion in Russia; there was no system laid down by the authorities, and persevered in without deviation. Everything appeared to be done as chance or caprice dictated. The intentions of the Grand Duke were kind, his character was humane, and the desire of the Marquis Wielopolski was apparently to be merciful and conciliatory; yet the administration occasionally acted with great harshness, sometimes with unwise haughtiness, and constantly with misplaced clemency. The Russians contrasted the condition of affairs in Warsaw with that which they witnessed at Wilna. General Mouravieff they admitted was perhaps too severe a governor, but he had pacified the country over which he ruled; the insurrection was crushed; property was secure, and life was only imperilled when assassins were sent thither by the revolutionary Government which sat at Warsaw. In the kingdom, however, all was different; bands of insurgents traversed the country with impunity, terrorism everywhere prevailed, and under the very shadow of the Russian court and army murder was daily committed with impunity. Surely it was not difficult to detect a conspiracy whose ramifications were so widely spread, whose staff was evidently so numerous, and whose printing-presses were so busy. Among all the hundreds who were employed in the manufactory of treason, surely an able government could at least detect some of the subordinates; and if they failed to do so, it must be because at heart they sympathized with the insurgents. The Russian mind is prone to theorize; and from the facts before them, which simply showed that there was a lack of vigour in the administration of the affairs of the Congress kingdom, many wild ideas were broached and clung to with great pertinacity.

The Marquis Wielopolski was held up to universal execration. The Poles denounced him as a traitor who had sold his country to the Russians; the Russians regarded him as a traitor who had taken office only to betray them; so that at the same moment he was an object of hatred and suspicion to two parties who agreed upon no other point. He still had faith in his policy; his proud and self-reliant spirit was unbroken by difficulties, and he presented an assured front to the enemies by whom he was assailed; but all confidence in him was lost, no one credited his sincerity or was disposed to trust in his judgment; and it was felt on all sides that his retirement was inevitable. He resigned, and left the country.

The position of the Grand Duke, if less ambiguous, was equally embarrassing. He had come to Poland anxious to conciliate an alienated race; he had endeavoured to deserve their confidence and win their esteem. His first efforts had been answered by an attempt upon his life; later on, the country had plunged into anarchy and revolt. The attempt upon his life had not induced him to relax in his endeavours to benefit the people subjected to his care, and he had essayed to suppress the revolt by mild and moderate measures: he had failed, and nothing now remained save a stern system of repression, which was alien to his character and repugnant to his inclinations. Moreover, it did not become a prince of the Imperial house to be the administrator of such a system, and he foresaw the necessity of retiring from his high office, in order that a substitute might be appointed who, without inconsistency or dishonour, could adopt a severer policy.

The atrocities committed by the "hanging gendarmes" were calculated to excite the attention of the Russians, for they have been rarely equalled in cruelty or in number. Detailed lists of them from time to time appeared in the public journals, and the victims, by the beginning of July, amounted to five hundred. To such a condition was Poland reduced, that months after the Grand Duke had resigned, it was currently stated in Warsaw that a murderer could be hired who would take the life of any individual if he received a few roubles for the deed.

In addition to the murders committed by the agents of the National Government, its other acts were calculated to excite very angry feelings in the minds of its enemies. The system of terrorism introduced by it was brought to bear upon every rank, and upon occasions the most trifling. For example, two orders of their agents were found on the person of a proprietor in the province of Kowno. By the first of these orders he was directed, on pain of death, to present himself in the insurgent camp immediately, to receive instructions from the commander; by the second he was directed, at his own cost, to feed and attend to four horses which were sent him from the camp, and warned, in case he did not look after them properly, that he would be put to death, and that his property would be utterly destroyed.

On the 9th of June a daring robbery of the public treasury was discovered at Warsaw. The cash it contained was counted every week, and the money in question had been reckoned six days previously.

The office in which the money was lodged was locked and sealed every evening, in the presence of an inspector, and a guard was stationed at the door day and night. The chief cashier was assisted in the receipt and payment of money by an inspector and three clerks. Each cash-box had two keys—one remained with the inspector and the other with the cashier. Some days previous to June 9th the cashier was absent without leave, and his assistant having inquired for him, found him ill in bed. A messenger from the War-office having brought an order for 170,000 roubles, a soldier was sent to the sick man for the key; but it was found impossible to open the cash-box, the lock having been damaged. A locksmith was sent for, and when the cash-box was forced open, a deficiency was discovered of 3,000,000 roubles in bonds of the Credit Foncier of the kingdom of Poland, of 300,000 roubles in gold, and of 400,000 roubles in bank-notes. The same day the inspector and clerks disappeared. A decree of the National Government shortly afterwards acknowledged the receipt of the stolen securities, and pronounced that the thieves had deserved well of their country for what they had done.

On the 5th of July the National Government decreed that a compulsory loan should be raised for carrying on the struggle in Poland. The amount was to be 21,000,000 florins (or £575,000), and it was to be raised in three issues of 7,000,000 florins each. The management of this loan was intrusted to Prince Ladislaus Czartoryski and two coadjutors, and in their decree the National Government stated that the existence of the insurrection sufficiently guaranteed the return of the money, and arrangements would, it was stated, be made for the half-yearly payment of interest.

The assessment and negotiation of this loan " on the most opulent capitalists of the country " was left to the department of Finance of the National Government.

The decree was met by a proclamation from the Russian authorities, warning the inhabitants against contributing to this loan, and stating that doing so was an offence punishable with all the rigour of martial law, and that neither terror of the revolutionary emissaries, or ignorance of the law or proclamation, would be accepted by the authorities as an extenuation of the offence.

On the 6th September the cause of the insurgents received a severe blow in the defeat and death of the partisan leader who had taken the name of Lelewel.

This individual during his short career had shown courage and capacity. He had had some military experience, having served in the Engineers during the Hungarian campaign of 1848-9, and he brought it to bear with great effect in Poland. He was remarkable for the celerity and daring of his movements, his self-reliance, the confidence with which he inspired his men, and the promptitude with which he seized any advantage the errors or incapacity of his opponents placed within his reach.

He had made two inroads into the kingdom from Galicia, and on each occasion, after gaining some successes over his enemy, had been compelled by the pressure of superior numbers to disband his troop and make them separately seek for security in flight.

Once again in Galicia, he occupied himself in preparing the materials for a third expedition, and he collected together many of those who had formerly been under his command, and, combining them with fresh levies, formed a band of from 700 to 800 strong. Towards the end of August these men crossed the Austrian frontier in little detachments of some fifty men each, so as to escape the observation of the Austrian and Russian troops. They crossed in perfect safety without even meeting with an enemy.

For about a fortnight Lelewel occupied himself in exercising his band and in drilling the new recruits who joined him. He had penetrated some forty miles into the kingdom, when, on the 3rd of September, he was attacked by the Russians, with whom he had a severe engagement. The Poles lost upwards of 100 men, and a very large number of their officers. "The most remarkable event of the day was a charge of the insurgent cavalry,* in which ninety-seven men started, and only twenty-two returned. The charge was directed against the Russian artillery, and was so far successful that the artillerymen were driven from their guns, and the guns (four in number) spiked. The Poles, however, had to pass an ambuscade of sharpshooters before reaching their destination; they had to meet Cossacks on the other side, and they were charged by Cossacks as they were returning. It may be said that the insurgent cavalry was entirely destroyed in this heroic attack, for of the twenty-two men who rejoined the detachment, some were wounded, some unhorsed, and scarcely a dozen were in a fit state to continue their service. On the other hand, the enemy's artillery was completely silenced. It appears that the precise preconceived aim of the charge, undertaken at such terrible risk, was not merely to spike, but to capture the guns. Lelewel had fourteen experienced gunners with him, and not being able to reach a spot where artillery of his own awaited him, resolved to try whether he could not furnish himself with a battery at the expense of the enemy."

The insurgents laid claim to the victory, alleging that they had pursued the Russian troops for some miles; but on the following day their enemy was seen hovering near. On the 5th, skirmishes took place between them, and on the 6th Lelewel found his little army was surrounded by the enemy. All that remained for him was to endeavour to fight his way through them, and so regain the Austrian frontier; but to cut his way through superior numbers, and then retreat in safety for forty miles, was indeed a forlorn attempt. The

---

* This account is principally taken from the *Times* of September 22nd, and is a summary of the narratives of insurgents.

result may readily be anticipated : at the very commencement of the battle, Lelewel received a wound in the left arm, and shortly after, as he was leading his infantry to the charge, was mortally wounded by two shots in the body. Their leader fallen, the insurgents were repulsed on all sides, and those who did not fall in the fight, or were not captured by the Russians, were arrested by the Austrians on crossing the frontier.

It is difficult to understand why these continued expeditions left Galicia. The Russians were in such force in the kingdom, that the utmost the insurgents could accomplish was to maintain themselves there for a few weeks, and then retreat across the frontier. They gained no successes of the smallest importance; their constant study was how best to escape the forces by which they were surrounded; and the first important conflict was sure to terminate in their defeat. So long as it was possible to deceive the nations of Europe by fabricated intelligence and lying telegrams, there might have been a political reason for throwing the lives of brave men away. But in September the bubble had burst; men were no longer deceived by victories existing only on paper, and terminating in a hurried flight across the Galician frontier. Yet one band after another marched into Poland, only to be annihilated, their leaders hurried into the tomb, their rank and file into an Austrian or Russian dungeon.

Most mournful indeed became the strife. No glory was to be gained by death in some ignoble skirmish; no crown of martyrdom was to be won beneath the shadow of a Russian scaffold; but brave and generous and devoted men still sacrificed their lives in paltry enterprises; still thought they rendered their country an acceptable offering by pouring forth their blood in desperate and fruitless services.

The leaders of many of these bands could ill be spared by their sorrowing countrymen. Brave and chivalrous, their minds impressed with those vague and beautiful ideas of freedom which alone are given to the young, they were spurred into action by chimeras of which most men only dream. Boys who should have been at school, carried their impetuous daring into the foremost ranks of war; they inspired unimpassioned men with much of their own valour, and with something of their own enthusiasm. The portrait of one of them, a lad of nineteen years of age, lies before me now. The bearer of an ancient name, nobility and energy are written on his brow; he was the leader of a band of men, who, many of them his equals in station, and most of them his superiors in age, " were proud to follow one who was so proud to lead them." And now he lies in his early grave, one of the costly sacrifices of an utterly unavailing strife; his house is desolate; the patrimony of his race a forfeit; and in an obscure garret of a foreign capital, his father lingers out his broken-hearted years.

These men must not be confused with the unprincipled leaders of a sanguinary faction. They had nothing in common with the National Government or the executioners and hangmen in their pay. They were the worthy representatives of a gallant race, inheriting all its traditions, and unfortunately many of its errors.

At the end of August the Grand Duke Constantine resigned. He had not governed Poland long, but during his brief supremacy events had crowded rapidly upon each other; the moderate views which had animated him had resulted in the outbreak of revolt; the reforms to which he and his minister had trusted, had indignantly been rejected by the men he had striven to benefit; Poland had appealed to the sword, and the time for conciliation was gone by. The policy which, twelve months before, he had endeavoured to institute, was utterly out of date; and martial law, and not constitutional rule, was now supreme in Warsaw.

It needed no distant commentator to remind him of the change. The nobles and proprietors of Poland no longer thronged his palace; some of them had fled to Germany, to England, and to France, that they might not witness the desolation of their country, or be suspected of treachery by either of the contending parties; others had sought refuge on their estates, and were there breathlessly watching the progress of a revolt which had all their sympathies, but none of their active aid; while others again had immured themselves in their Warsaw mansions, where, in gloomy solitude, they held aloof from their Russian masters.

The lower orders were infected with the virus of the National Government. The assassinations which daily disgraced the city, the immunity of the murderers, the impossibility of detecting the men who composed, printed, and published the proclamations of the insurrection, proved that among the town population moderation had been tried in vain.

The measures which failed to win the Poles excited the deepest indignation in Russia. The long-suffering which strove to reclaim the insurgents without having recourse to extreme severity was misconstrued, and the humanity which dictated the policy of the Grand Duke was ascribed to indifference, incapacity, or disaffection. He could no longer govern with advantage to the kingdom or honour to himself. His was not the hand which could suitably preside over a system of punishment and repression; and if, despite all his efforts, such a system was inevitable, it must be administered by other hands. He had done his best to reconcile Poland to Russia, but his efforts had failed; and he therefore resigned his office, and retired from the country he had vainly striven to serve.

His successor in his high office was Count Berg, a nobleman who had for some months held an important place under him, and who was well acquainted with the condition of affairs in Poland.

Count Berg was well qualified for the post he was selected to fill. A man of mature years and great experience, he had spent his long life in the public service. His courtly and polished manners, it has been well remarked, carried the memory back to distant times, and reminded those who met him of the noblesse who thronged the halls of Versailles in the great days of Richelieu and of Louis XIV. He was well qualified in tranquil times to preside over the stately hospitalities of a court, for the only trace of age about him was to be found in an intimate knowledge of men and of events which have already become subjects of curious inquiry on the part of the present generation. From the close of the great European struggle to the present time, there were few men eminent in politics or literature to whom he was personally unknown, and while to the Continental he could converse of

Metternich, Polignac, or the first Alexander, to the Englishman he could speak of his personal recollections of Castlereagh, Wellington, and Byron.*

In addition to this knowledge of men, the new Viceroy had travelled extensively, and scanned all he had seen with an observant eye. His various duties had led him to an intimate acquaintance with Asiatic as well as European Russia. The Caucasus, with its warlike tribes, the distant Altai range, Siberia, with its winter snows and its summer garb of flowers, had all been traversed by him, and from each he apparently had brought home something of interest which he had stored up in the garner-house of his memory. Most of the countries of Europe and their capitals were also familiar to him, and from each of them he had collected some information which guided him in his views of foreign and domestic politics.

In addition to these varied experiences, he was not unaccustomed to rule in his sovereign's name. The appointment he held immediately before his departure for Poland was that of Governor of Finland, a post scarcely second in difficulty or responsibility to that of the kingdom itself.

The new lieutenant had little sympathy with modern liberalism; his opinions had been formed in an age and under auspices which showed it no favour, and he saw in the revolt one of its strange and portentous developments. As a patriot, he was constrained to oppose to the utmost a conspiracy which sought to dismember his country, and as a religious man, he resolved to quell an unexampled outburst of violence and crime.

The policy he adopted was energetic, effective, and severe. The immunity with which murders were committed was attributed by him, in a great measure, to the large number of Poles employed in the police: these men were known to be disaffected, and they were yet employed for the repression of crimes with which they sympathized. Every effort was now made to recast the entire force; Poles were gradually weeded out of it, and Russians were appointed in their room; the result was, that life and property became more secure, and

* Count Berg met Lord Byron in Greece, and told me several anecdotes of their acquaintance.

that the assassins of the National Government no longer pursued with ease and immunity an unchecked career of crime.

A vigilant watch was maintained upon the officials connected with the railways, and it was discovered that in numerous instances they were in league with the insurgents. The information they possessed of the contemplated movements of troops, the ease with which they could retard them, and the command they had over the telegraph, made these men valuable members of the revolutionary organization, and their dismissal greatly crippled its activity.

The monasteries and convents, which had hitherto been free from interference, were now subjected to the most searching scrutiny. Their immunity from surveillance had led to their being the repositories of many of the secret printing-presses; the proclamations which had been so mysteriously issued had frequently been struck off by their inmates or by conspirators in their confidence; and the current of the literature of the insurrection was dammed up and choked by the system Count Berg adopted. Occasionally, indeed, a proclamation or a gazette struggled into existence; but it was at rare intervals, and usually bore about it traces of haste and fear. The revolutionary press was paralyzed, and the unanimity in action of the various sections of the revolution was thereby destroyed.

The monasteries had afforded shelter for more than printing-presses. They had been converted into sanctuaries by the gendarmerie of the National Government, and under the shadow of their walls the assassin had escaped red-handed from his pursuers. In many of the monastic buildings poisoned daggers were discovered, which, together with uniforms, weapons, and ammunition, could not have been secreted there without the cognizance and consent of the fraternity. These discoveries led the authorities to take possession of the buildings which had thus been used; and in many of the monasteries of Warsaw, as for example that of the Bernardines, a portion was set apart for the reception of the Russian troops.*

* When, at a later date, I visited that monastery, its military and ecclesiastical occupants were apparently living in harmony together. The

In addition to these alterations introduced by Count Berg, an altered system gave increased efficiency to the army; at length all the troops at the disposal of the Government were regulated by one mind, and formed, as it were, parts of one machine, whose province it was to crush the revolt; and gradually, but certainly, the insurgent bands were defeated, and order restored to the districts their agitation had convulsed.

There are no stirring events to record in connection with these operations. Slowly, silently, and surely the revolt was crushed, and in dying made no sign; a few ignoble skirmishes, some isolated acts of gallantry, or an occasional murder, leave nothing for the historian to comment upon or to record. Measures of repression, skilfully conceived and inflexibly carried out, were followed by their natural result—the suppression of the insurrection.

Before the curtain fell upon the struggle, the National Government made one effort to divert the current of misfortune which was setting in against it. The measures which Count Berg had organized (for even before the resignation of the Grand Duke he had for some time been virtually the ruler of the country) were gradually depriving the insurrection of its power and vitality; but if Count Berg could be removed, the insurrection might perhaps be revived; it was determined, therefore, that he should be assassinated in the streets of Warsaw.

In one of the principal streets of the town are two large houses adjoining each other, and known as the Zamoyski House and the Zamoyski Palace. They belong to Count Andrew Zamoyski. These houses are built in the form of a quadrangle round a square plot of garden, and the only communication existing between them is through a door in one of the wings, which opens into a short passage communicating

monks, as a body, seemed to have reconciled themselves to their schismatic visitors; they allotted to them certain corridors, with the cells they contained, and gave them some rooms on the ground floor, where their cooking was carried on. The services of the Church were not interrupted, and no inconvenience of any consequence, except to the insurgents, resulted from the interference of the Government.

from one quadrangle to the other. The rooms in that portion of the two houses facing the street were, in September, 1863, let out in separate apartments to numerous tenants.

A few weeks after his appointment to the office of lieutenant, Count Berg returned from one of the hospitals he had been inspecting, and his road lay through the street in which the Zamoyski houses stood. He was seated with an aide-de-camp in an open caleche, and an escort of five Cossacks followed immediately behind his carriage, while an officer rode on either side. As he passed the Zamoyski House, a gun was fired at him from a window on the second or third floor; the ball entered the back of his great coat, and passed out without injuring him;* a second time the gun was ineffectually fired, and immediately afterwards several Orsini bombs were flung from the same window, which exploded beneath the carriage, and under the feet of the horses. Out of the nine horses belonging to Count Berg and his attendants, eight were wounded, six so severely that it was necessary to kill them; the aide-de-camp received a severe contusion, and the carriage was struck in seventeen different places.†

The Zamoyski House and Palace were immediately taken possession of by the troops, their inmates were placed under temporary arrest, and instructions were issued that the contents of both mansions should be destroyed. When the soldiers first entered, they made some attempts at plundering; but orders were quickly circulated prohibiting it; and from the time they reached the troops they were implicitly obeyed. The furniture,

* These facts were stated to me by Count Berg, and the great coat he wore was shown to me: it contained the two holes made by the musket-ball, and was a good voucher for the accuracy of the narrative, if any confirmation were needed.

† The statements made by the Russian press that a subterranean passage existed between the two houses were untrue. I made particular inquiries of the officer in command there, and ascertained not only that no such communication exists, but that there are not even vaults to either house. The only access is that which has already been described.

On the other hand, the statement made by the organs of the insurgents that a street or lane divides the palace from the house is equally false; they bear about them evident marks of belonging to the same owner, and the facilities for communication existing between them gave the authorities some excuse for treating them as the same property.

books, works of art, and other valuables, were taken or hurled into the courtyard; they were deliberately fired, and, without exception, destroyed.

The most exaggerated reports were circulated by the revolutionary party, of excesses they alleged had been committed during the "sacking of the Zamoyski Palaces." Prisoners were robbed and insulted; children were thrown out of the windows by the infuriated soldiery; and, in short, these writers tasked their well-trained powers of invention to the utmost, in multiplying charges of cruelty and wrong.

All these representations were, however, utterly false. Opinions may well differ as to the expediency or the justice of the act of confiscation; but it was carried out in strict pursuance of the directions given, in perfect order, and with no unnecessary harshness. Some acts of plunder were at first committed by the soldiery, but, in obedience to the officer in command, they at once desisted.

Subsequent inquiries brought to light some curious incidents. The time of Count Berg's passing through the street was known, and a few minutes previously, in front of the Zamoyski House, an individual, passing along the street at a gallop, gave a signal with his whip, and the moment the caleche arrived opposite the house, a white handkerchief was waived from one of the windows, apparently as a signal for the discharge of the Orsini bombs.

For some hours previously to this attempt, scarcely any carriages had passed through the street; and although it cannot be supposed that the intended assassination was communicated to any large number of individuals, the authorities inferred from these and other circumstances that the revolutionary agents must have cautioned their friends not to pass that way.

The measures adopted by Count Berg for the repression of the revolt were very severe, and some of them cannot be defended on the ground of justice; their only vindication must be the plea of necessity, and the excuse that they were adapted to the strange and wayward people they were intended to curb. In the abstract, nothing could be more unjust than this forfeiture of the Zamoyski property. Its owner was in France, the dwellings were let out to numerous lodgers, over whom he had no control, and the attempted murder was an act which he was too wise to have sanctioned; yet his property was sacrificed because some assassin temporarily resided there, and made his landlord's house a manufactory for hand-grenades. Nevertheless, however unjust the confiscation may be deemed, it is certain that no act of the Russian administration had so beneficial an effect in Warsaw; it impressed the Poles with the conviction that the Government was thoroughly in earnest, and that, no longer a thing to be cheaply indulged in, rebellion was a costly and a dangerous game. From the hour when the forfeiture was proclaimed, and the Poles found that no station was a shelter from the severities of the Russians, the revolution in Warsaw was paralyzed, and order restored.

The National Government lost its prestige in Poland, and many circumstances made its discomfiture apparent. It had ordered that every one connected with the *Official Journal* should abandon his employment by the 1st of October; but the 1st of October came and passed, and none of them obeyed the decree. In Warsaw, with the apparent intention of provoking a trial of strength and of proving that the National Government was no longer obeyed, Count Berg, on the 2nd of October issued the following proclamation:—

"For the last two years the city of Warsaw has been a den of crime, and the principal source of all the misfortunes which overwhelm the country. For this reason the Government is obliged considerably to increase the expenses of the state, which expenses have been caused by the present deplorable state of things. The Government is also bound to assist the numerous cases of distress originating from the same cause. Justice demands, therefore, that this increased expenditure should not be borne by the treasury of the kingdom alone, but that the city which tolerates and protects so large a number of perjurers and murderers should also bear part of the expenses arising from the present condition of the city. Taking these matters into consideration, I am compelled to impose an extraordinary contribution on the city of Warsaw, and order as follows:—

"1. An extraordinary contribution will be levied from all house proprietors and owners of plots of ground in Warsaw, and the suburb of Praga, at the rate of 8 per cent. of their net income, which shall be calculated from the returns of 1861.

"2. This contribution is to be collected by the 1st of November of this year.

"3. Whoever has not paid his contribution by the above date, will be compelled to do so by a military execution, and in the increased proportion of 12 per cent. upon his property.

"4. House and other proprietors have a right, if their property is mortgaged or otherwise burdened, to deduct 8 per cent. from the legal interest they are paying.

"5. The Committee of the Interior will convey to the magistrate of the city of Warsaw that it shall be his duty to issue such regulations as are indispensable for the carrying out of this decree.

"In communicating the above to the Administrative Council, I call upon them to issue the necessary orders."

The National Government issued a proclamation threatening all who paid this tax with death; and subsequently published in the revolutionary papers the names of those citizens who first paid the tax, and summoned them before the secret tribunals to answer for their crimes. Nevertheless the tax was paid and the menace disregarded.

On the 27th of October an order, to take effect from 10th November, prohibiting mourning except for the loss of a relation, was published in Warsaw. Offenders were to be subjected to fines estimated on the following scale: a woman on foot was to pay 10, in a hired carriage 15, and in a private carriage 100 roubles. If the offender was the wife or child of an official, that official lost one month's pay. The ladies of Warsaw discussed this proclamation (as the terms were known some time before it was to be carried into effect) anxiously. In a spirit of fervent patriotism, one lady determined to be fined five times, another ten, and a third twelve; but their resolution failed them in the hour of trial; mourning was entirely discontinued, and not a single fine had to be demanded.

On this occasion the National Government gave a striking evidence of its waning power; it had to the present time forbidden all compliance with the orders of the Russian police; it now changed its tactics, and published a proclamation directing that the authorities should be obeyed; and the reason it assigned was the desire that the ladies of Warsaw should be protected from insults at the hands of the Russian soldiers; but it was felt universally that the true cause of its altered tone was its conviction, in any case, that the police order would be obeyed.

From this date the insurrection may be considered to have ended. The revolutionary agitation which had for years been gaining over converts to the national party, and which had ever been increasing and consolidating its strength, had utterly collapsed when arrayed in arms against the might of an established government. The resources of men and money which had long been anxiously hoarded up, were vainly lavished in one brief and inglorious struggle. The improvements which had been creating wealth and paving the way to power, were paralyzed and arrested by the presence of intestine strife. The national character, which Europe had hitherto regarded as chivalrous, high-souled, and impassioned, had been sullied by the homage it rendered to the occult Government. The propagandism which had for years been converting Letts, Ruthenians, and Russians into Poles, had been detected, and its practice rendered impossible for the future; while the cup from which Poland might have drunk in the invigorating draughts of constitutional freedom had been dashed to earth in the fevered paroxysm of civil war.

It was, indeed, full time that the contest should end. The deeds which daily stained the streets of the capital with the blood of murdered men, and the executions which sternly avenged the slain, had induced a carelessness of the lives and an indifference to the sufferings of others, which roused the apprehensions of every wise and patriotic Pole. Commerce was extinct, ordinary employment there was little or none; but assassination had grown into a trade, and this loathsome trade flourished. Throughout the kingdom, also, other classes of crime and demoralization were rapidly extending their baneful influence, and even the men who longed for national independence were anxious that tranquillity should be on any terms restored. It was acknowledged that the insurrection had failed; it was foreseen that years must elapse, and the politics of Europe be again disturbed, before there was any prospect of a successful rising, and it was felt that the continuance of an abortive revolt would only lead to the sacrifice of many lives and the further embittering of national hatreds.

The occult Government could no longer control the expression of these feelings or the conduct to which they naturally led. The active aid it extorted from the proprietors when its power and organization were unbroken, it was unable at this crisis to exact; and thus while the Russian resources were for the first time guided by a skilful and accustomed hand, the cause of the insurrection was deprived of the material assistance and the prestige of secret power by which it had hitherto been upheld.

Such were the conditions under which the contest was now waged, and day by day the bands of desperate men who continued it were slain, defeated in battle, or driven across the frontier. At length, the long cold winter of the North set in; the hardiest were unable to keep the field; and, conquered partly by their enemy and partly by a climate that no one could resist, the last of the revolutionary bands dispersed, and the Polish insurrection was at an end.

CHAPTER XVIII.

Résumé of the Narrative.

My narrative is ended. I have traced, to the best of my judgment, the progress of events, the cabals of diplomatists, and the motives of the party of action; and endeavoured, without favour or partiality, to present them dispassionately to my readers. My work is necessarily imperfect; for materials, doubtless, exist which would explain some facts at present ill understood, and alter the lights and shades in which the historical painter would pourtray the men he endeavoured to describe. Many details might also be filled in which would interest the general reader, and invest the story with a degree of personal interest to which it now has little claim.

Such incidents would render the narrative more attractive, but would scarcely add to its historical value. The great danger in treating of the Polish insurrection is that leading principles may be lost sight of in a mass of individual experiences. Writers of unquestionable veracity have in Galicia and Posen mingled with the insurgents and with those who sympathized in their aims; they have listened with unfortunate credulity to their statements, and given them a wide and instant publicity. A knowledge so acquired has its value in so far as it enables an author to master details that a stranger will not understand, and may furnish materials for some spirited sketches and the introduction of some interesting descriptions; on the other hand, such an acquaintance with details often prevents their possessor from rightly appreciating principles; dwarfs his view of the subject which he treats to the level of the petty chiefs who surround him; and degrades the history of a national crisis into the chronicle of a local *émeute*. Let us endeavour to form a more impartial estimate, and base it on facts which admit of no cavil or dispute.

In the earlier pages of this work I have traced the history of Poland and the Western provinces during the reign of the Emperor Nicholas, and shown that it was one long conspiracy on the part of a monarch to denationalize a people. It was the supremacy of an unbending military despot, who ruled his subjects on the same principle on which he ruled his army, and who considered that in this instance his subjects were mutinous, and must be treated with more than ordinary severity. Such a tyranny justified resistance, and almost demanded it. When Hungary was in arms, or when the war in the Crimea was draining away the Russian army, every true friend of liberty, careless of the European complications it would have eventually involved, would have hailed with enthusiasm Poland's efforts to be free. In face of that cruel persecution, the whispers of expediency would have been forgotten; and, despite the stipulations of world-famed congresses and the traditionary wisdom of ancient statecraft, the kingdom of Poland might have been constituted anew. But then the hapless land made no struggle for freedom, and gave no signs of national life. Perhaps the iron had entered so deeply into her soul that she was conscious only that she was a slave; perhaps she thought herself unable to compete successfully with the master of a million bayonets, and gazed with fear upon the citadel which frowned beside her ancient capital; perhaps she thought that the tyranny, whose blighting influence was everywhere felt, had organized its secret agencies with so much skill that an informer was present in every company, and a spy was lurking by every hearth.

Whatever the reason, Poland, from the suppression of the revolt in 1831 to the death of Nicholas, stirred not; and when her oppressor died, the sympathy which would have overborne all ordinary prudential considerations died out also. Europe could not recognize in the Poland of 1857 the same conditions which had won for her so mournful an interest twenty-five years before; and as political and social improvement were seen moving on with a steady and measured step, it was felt that time, patience, and mutual forbearance would yet weld two hostile races into one united people.

In her captivity, however, opinion had been silently forming, though it was not evidenced by any outward signs which other nations recognized, and a fierce and deadly hatred of Russia had sprung up among the educated classes, which was the more dangerous because it was unavowed. Opinions nurtured in secret are always extreme, for they are unchecked by discussion, inquiry, and minute investigation; and we accordingly find that the views of the disaffected in Poland were remarkable for their violent and uncompromising character. That among the great proprietors were to be found many men of moderate opinion is unquestionable; but in political and revolutionary contests, moderate men lose their weight, and although they may guide the State through peaceful waters, when the storms are raging and the vessel is drifting on the rocks, it is the determined partisan who invariably springs to the helm.

In the absence of deep-seated disaffection, the reforms of the Emperor would have won the confidence of his people; and as it was, two parties, who were respectively represented by the Marquis Wielopolski and Count Andrew Zamoyski, were opposed to any revolutionary action; but the sentiments of loyalty or prudence which restrained them had no weight with less cautious politicians, and violent men refused to recognize that any change in their position should make a corresponding alteration in their policy. The heavy hand of tyranny no longer oppressed them; their Church was free from persecution; their universities were restored; the foundation of representative institutions was laid; and a practical autonomy was granted to them. All these concessions they would gladly have accepted thirty years before; but the day for such compromises was gone. Complete independence they now required, and nothing else would they accept, and that independence was to extend to the whole of ancient Poland, from Dantzic to Odessa, and was to be obtained by the reconquest from three of the great powers of Europe of territories which had been theirs for the greater part of a century. This visionary scheme was avowed with greater or less distinctness throughout the period of the insurrection and the agitation which preceded it. It was not convenient to give it reality by stirring up revolt in Galicia or Posen, but it was understood that these possessions were to be revolutionized after Poland and the Western provinces had been torn from Russia.

Reviewing this programme dispassionately, it is difficult to understand how any statesman could be so rash as to encourage it: it threatened to kindle a strife in Europe which might last for thirty years, and then leave behind it hatred and jealousies, the memory of injuries unatoned, and of humiliations yet to be obliterated, which would be the fertile source of many a future war.

The Poland springing into existence after such a preliminary struggle, would probably, if any success had been achieved, have included the Congress kingdom and some few of the adjoining governments. It was perfectly clear, however, that a state so constituted would be regarded as only a portion of that which was eventually to be formed; and it would have been the centre of a religious and political propaganda, having for its object the spread of the Roman Catholic religion and the re-establishment of the Polish supremacy over all the provinces of the kingdom of 1772.

Apart from the danger of encouraging such revolutionary ideas and efforts, the injustice of the scheme should have been patent to the statesmen of Europe; for why should the Western provinces of Russia, with their population of 9,868,771, be remitted to the domination of the 1,046,947 Poles those provinces contain? and why should the religious education of the country be confided to the Roman Catholic clergy, although their Church scarcely numbers within her pale one-fourth of that same population? Again, it would have been very unjust towards the German settlers who have done so much to cultivate and reclaim various parts of Poland, more especially of Posen, to have subjected them to the rule of an arrogant and hostile race; and it would have perilled the advancing rights and civilization of the peasants, over which every philanthropist and statesman desires to keep anxious guard.

Neither is there any reason to suppose that the Poles are more fit for self-government now than they were a century ago. The unarmed agitation did indeed evidence that under the pressure of strong excitement they could act in concert; that they could make considerable sacrifices in the supposed interests of their country; and that the Russian supremacy was unpopular among a large proportion of the city and privileged classes. Yet this very combination seems to evidence, with almost as great distinctness, that the educated classes were misled by sentiment, vanity, and vague historical theories, and that in action they altogether lacked the inspiration of a sound and vigorous policy. From the inferior orders, the mechanics of the towns, and the petty Schlachta, no enlightened resolve was to be looked for, and they joined with ignorant enthusiasm the unarmed agitation in the earlier stages of the struggle, and with ferocious brutality the insurrection which subsequently occurred.

The changes which the moderate party among the Polish nobility silently worked by the introduction of schools, the teaching of their national traditions and language among the peasantry, and the gradual amelioration of the condition of the poor, were doubtless calculated to serve their cause; but the unarmed agitation itself was a foolish and mischievous device, which only drew down on them the suspicion of their rulers, and induced them to take unusual measures for the preservation of the Russian supremacy.

When the insurrection actually broke out, nothing but the overwhelming necessities of the hour served to give even the semblance of unity to the efforts of the disaffected; and in a very few weeks the contentions of the Red party and the White, of the nobles and the democrats, of Langiewicz and Mieroslawski, betrayed to all who studied the question the utter hopelessness of the revolt. But, even supposing it possible for the effort to have been successful, the moment independence was won, fresh difficulties must have arisen; for the democrats would never have allowed their exertions and their sacrifices to result in the coronation of a Czartoryski in the cathedral of Warsaw; and the leaders of the emigration and great proprietors and magnates of Poland would never have permitted the Red party to have dictated to them the future constitution of their country. The immediate result of a successful insurrection would probably have been anarchy; and that anarchy, if terminated without the overthrow of the newly-constituted state, would have been followed by a condition of things still more to be deprecated, and yet more threatening to the peace of Europe—a state of things in which a policy of aggression and conquest must have been adopted by the Poles with the avowed object of re-conquering in its integrity an ancient kingdom according to its limits at a date capriciously selected by themselves. Who could foresee the complications such a policy would engender, or any termination of the dissensions it would immediately induce?

Despite these considerations, which rendered it madness to afford the insurgents encouragement or aid, it is impossible to have witnessed without compassion the headlong valour and the fervent patriotism which gave life and reality to their cause. They were mistaken in their highly-coloured visions of the past; but, in the midst of a miserable present, was it not natural that they should thus deceive themselves? Does not the Jew look fondly back to the mythical tales with which tradition has surrounded the history of his race? Does not the Irish peasant, as he sits at night by the dim peat fire, chant in a voice of low and monotonous dreaminess the deeds of mighty chiefs and sages who only find existence in that traditionary lay? Who, indeed, would not allow for national prejudices and the pride of race? What statesman or what historian can fail to recognize in them the most unfailing stimulants to future exertion? Prostrate a race may be, miserable in outward appearance, without the rights of free men, trodden in the dust, outcasts and slaves; yet, if they still cling to the memory of a prouder and a happier era, if in their humiliation they yet resolve that the day of their resurrection shall dawn, we may be sure that there exists among them the spirit to do and to suffer nobly, and that in some future exigency they will vindicate their ancient fame.

The struggle between Russia and Poland was necessarily short, for the resources at the disposal of the National Government were utterly inadequate to the end it had in view. When the forces of Langiewicz were scattered, there remained no army in the field; and although the wandering bands which haunted the forests and marshes of the Congress kingdom retained a show of organization, their efforts were as futile for all military purposes as are those of the brigands in Southern Italy. The annihilation of the only army that made a stand against the Russians served to bring out in clearer relief the acts and the principles of the National Government, and men witnessed with amazement the establishment of a secret tribunal, in face of which rank had no immunities, and before which innocence was no protection. Its decrees sentenced men to death, and the dagger of the murderer carried out the doom. Everywhere was terror. The police professed to be paralyzed; but they, it was alleged, were leagued with the guilty. Men high in rank and office declared themselves unable to combat this unseen power, to protect the victim, or to avenge the crime. Great names were muttered as though they sat on this secret committee, and it was whispered that the proudest nobility of Poland were not too proud to mingle in this conclave of assassins. Meanwhile the avowed emissaries of the National Government counted among them the historic names of Czartoryski and Sapieha. It was all but recognized by the French Government, and was spoken of considerately by English Ministers of State. It declared itself to be the only exponent of the will of the people; it issued its proclamations, appointed its officers, levied its taxes, published its gazettes, and travestied in every practicable form the operations of a regular government. It identified itself with the Polish cause, and in an evil hour for themselves the insurgents permitted the assumption. Perhaps this ready submission to the occult Government was a necessity. The Poles saw they were completely overmatched, and felt that internal dissension would accelerate the ruin of their cause; they clung, therefore, to the only body which had about it even the semblance of authority or action. Nevertheless, however necessary this acquiescence may have been, it greatly injured their cause among educated and thinking men. What is the principle, such men demanded, upon which this Government is conducted? And the inevitable reply was, that it was terrorism carried to a pitch that had never been surpassed; that it was power derived from, and solely reliant upon the dagger. Its malignant influence was not restricted to important enemies;

it extended its proscriptions to every class, and murdered for every fault. Orsini bombs were devoted to governors of provinces; the poniard was prepared for travellers who failed in the devotion this new sovereignty demanded; while for the peasant and the soldier there were tortures and mutilations, the hangman's rope, and the grave, into which, yet living, they were flung.

These outrages contrasted painfully with the previous conduct of the Poles, and the Russians asked what had become of that high and holy patience which this nation of martyrs claimed as their inheritance? For three years they said the Poles had held their national fasts, had observed their national anniversaries, and proclaimed that by meekness and long-suffering they would put to shame the counsels of the violent and the power of the mighty. During that period Russia had looked on with a troubled consciousness that she had no weapons wherewith to oppose an unarmed movement; her policy had been wavering, weak, and ineffective; and the public opinion of Europe had pronounced against her. Now, without any adequate reason, the Poles had quitted their vantage-ground, and descended into the arena; they had staked their cause on the vulgar arbitrament of war, and discarded the enormous advantages their former attitude had secured them. Nor was this all; for their false and treacherous nature was fully displaying itself in the acts of men who reduced murder into a system, who robbed for the sake of their country, and forged in the interests of truth!

It was under the influence of passions thus excited and expressed, that the struggle was subsequently carried on; assassination on one side seemed to call for a stern system of repression on the other; and the dictates of the supposed necessity were acquiesced in. Repudiating the calumnies which found too ready a credence in France and England, it will yet be admitted that some of the measures adopted by the Russian authorities tended to shake the rights, and therefore to destroy the value of property; and that there was somewhat too great a disposition to assume that every Polish proprietor was a traitor, and to punish him as such, unless his innocence was proved to the satisfaction of a government official. Some of the orders of General Mouravieff are certainly open to the former of these charges, and although the latter be not susceptible of such direct proof, it is believed by a considerable body of his countrymen to be equally true.

The feature in the Russian policy which excited the greatest indignation among the Poles, is one for which an impartial observer will not blame it. The great proprietors, the officials of Polish descent, the Catholic clergy, the professors of schools, and the educated classes generally, had plainly evinced their disaffection; it was only natural, therefore, that the Government should appeal to the masses. An arrogant and high-spirited aristocracy beheld with speechless anger the representative of the Emperor place weapons in the hands of peasants, who had never been so trusted before; permit them to arrest suspicious persons, even when those persons had recently been their masters; and reward them for their zeal in the public service, even when that zeal had been misplaced, and the license given to them had been exceeded. In civil convulsions, however, distinctions of rank are frequently obliterated, and a Government assailed by conspirators may well prefer a loyal peasant to a malcontent noble.

The harshness with which the peasants had formerly been treated, made the change more marked and unpalatable, and the Polish proprietor, under the surveillance of his former serfs, bore the infliction as impatiently as would a South Carolinian if he were imprisoned and watched by his own slaves.

Prompt to take advantage of every opportunity, the disaffected party denounced the Government for socialist tendencies, and described emancipation and the subsequent arming of the peasants as the two first acts in a drama of which confiscation was to be the catastrophe. By this artifice they enlisted on their side much of the sober and temperate opinion which had not hitherto pronounced itself, and identified themselves in the minds of those whom they misled with the cause of order, property, and enlightenment.

The action of diplomacy reflected little credit on the wisdom or steadfastness of Western Europe. The despatches of Lord Russell were speeches in disguise, and speeches more worthy of the hustings than of a parliamentary assembly. As bids for popularity they might have succeeded, if Russia had been terrified by them; but as they were fruitless, they covered their author with ridicule and odium. To interpose and not to be regarded, to threaten and not to strike, to parade the name and power of England before the world, while he inwardly was convinced that he could never guide her into war—these were not acts of wisdom or high policy, and were unworthy the traditions of his office or the antecedents of his country.

Moreover it is evident that the Foreign Secretary had no accurate knowledge of the subject upon which he treated; for he allowed alleged cruelties at Wilna to be urged in both Houses of Parliament as reasons for interposing on behalf of the Poland of 1815: he pressed on the acceptance of the Russian Government six supposed reforms, some of which were already in existence, and others were absolutely inadmissible; and he made statements which were utterly at variance with the information furnished to him by the Ambassador at St. Petersburg and the Consul-General at Warsaw. The most favourable construction that can be placed upon his acts is to suppose that he really desired to embark in a war of liberation, and that he was only restrained by prudential considerations, and the remonstrances of less ardent colleagues. Be this, however, as it may, there is no doubt that the attitude taken by him helped to induce the insurgents to prolong a hopeless contest; that it encouraged the Emperor of the French in his schemes of ambition and of conquest; and that it shook the confidence of Russian statesmen and the Russian people in the honour and good faith of England.

The tortuous policy of France gradually inclined to war. After watching carefully the currents of popular opinion, and after meditations, lengthy if not profound, on the chances of the struggle in which he might possibly be involved, the Imperial Sphinx determined to try the arbitrament of arms. To pave the way to such a consummation, French gold and French blood were lavished in maintaining a guerilla war; a servile press adroitly imitated the utterances of a free people, and preached the doctrines of a fantastic liberalism to a nation which was itself enslaved. History was invoked in order to revive dormant animosities; treaties were misconstrued to justify interference in the internal affairs of another state; and diplomacy did its utmost to pave the way to a war for which armies were silently collecting, and campaigns had secretly been planned.

The passions of the French people were thoroughly roused, and the language of their statesmen became more stern and menacing. The Emperor perhaps relied on English aid and Austrian endurance, on the willing help of the Polish nationality, and the unpatriotic indifference of the Russian people—on the prestige of past triumphs and the confidence of Europe in his own far-seeing wisdom. Probably too he felt that some device was needed to divert the attention of his people from Mexico and Rome, and that a scrutiny of his home administration offered nothing in palliation of foreign and ignominious embarrassments.

The cast was dangerous, but it possessed attractions for one who gambled with empires for his stake, and apparently the risk was slighter than it eventually proved to be, while there seemed to be spoil obtainable which it was subsequently impossible to grasp. The calculation, however, was erroneous in every particular.

It is not surprising that foreigners often mistake us. The empty clamour, which sounds so loudly and is so little worth, seems to them the voice of the governors as well as of the governed; and they cannot understand debates arranged for the purpose of winning notoriety for a partisan. When they wade through the columns of monotonous dulness with which obscure members weary their hearers, they construe their unrefuted accusations into the scarcely veiled menaces of parties and cabinets; when they read of meetings which members of both Houses attended, and over which Lord Mayors presided, they imagine they peruse the semi-official announcements which precede an open rupture. It was, however, strange that the Emperor of the French should have fallen into this error; he must have known that the Polish cause had at most only a sentimental hold on the sympathies of

England, and that, in deference to her sentiments, England never goes to war; that the prominent leaders of the friends of Poland were men who, however respectable, had no political weight; and that the liberal policy of the Emperor Alexander had disarmed much of the anti-Russian feeling which the despotic rule of his father had provoked. If in the person of Lord Russell he found a confederate or an instrument, it was evident that the sway of the Foreign Secretary over the external policy of his country did not extend beyond the penning of voluminous despatches.

The chances of assistance from Austria were even less encouraging. Embarked in a career of constitutional development, her statesmen found it prudent to adopt a tone of enlightened liberality, and they united with France and England in diplomatic representations which bound them to no ulterior policy. One fatal inheritance, however, was always present to their thoughts; and although they might not have regretted any humiliation to which Russia might have been subjected, their liberal dreams of a restored Poland were scared by the fear of Galicia in revolt. In the cause of Polish independence it was impossible for Austria to unsheath her sword.

There remained the Polish nationality, and we have seen what that term includes. If a French army had ever reached the frontier of the Congress kingdom, there is no doubt a considerable number of recruits would have gathered to its camp. Prudential considerations would no longer have restrained many who had estates to lose and rank to forfeit, if they joined in a fruitless insurrection. Yet the success of such a crusade would have been very doubtful, the penalty of failure would have been hard to bear, and the guerdon of a successful war, unless Prussia were involved in it, would faintly recompense the risks and the peril of the enterprise.

The expectations which were based on the indifference of the Russian people were equally erroneous, and their attitude would have precluded submission, even if their rulers had been disposed to acquiesce in the demands of the intervening powers. In the course of my narrative I have shown how deeply public opinion was roused by the insurrection, and with what a proud and confident spirit the demands of diplomacy were met. There was no sacrifice which would not willingly have been submitted to for the sake of preserving the honour and integrity of Russia, and the nation rose as one man to vindicate her independence. It was this unanimous resolution which gave unwonted weight to the masterly despatches of Prince Gortschakoff, for it was felt that his policy was supported by the will of an united people.

From the time that these despatches were written the Polish question was virtually at an end; the alternative presented to Western Europe was acquiescence or war, and as war involved risks which neither England nor France cared to run, acquiescence became a necessity. Ceasing to be an European question, the Polish insurrection shrank back into its natural dimensions; it became merely the revolt of a disaffected class, a class which might have some claims on the generous sympathy, but had none on the armed support of foreign nations.

Unaided by the Western powers, it was certain that the insurrection must fail. A guerilla war might, indeed, be persevered in until winter drove the insurgents from their forests and other lurking-places; attacks might from time to time be made on posts which were defended only by a few soldiers, and detachments still be assailed as they crossed morasses or wound their way through woods. Sometimes also officials might be assassinated or peasants tortured and robbed. Such deeds were neither war nor insurrection, they were simple acts of brigandage, and would be so accounted by every impartial man; translated, however, into the language of telegrams and special correspondents, they wore a very different complexion, and for months after the revolt was virtually ended, the people of England and France regarded it as an existing struggle. At length winter set in, the bands were completely dispersed, and the Polish insurrection of 1863 was definitively suppressed.

The time had now arrived when dissimulation was of no

advantage to the Government. If its liberal professions were made with a fraudulent design, if it simply waited its opportunity to crush all improvement, and to revive the blighting rule of Nicholas, there was no one who had now the power to oppose it. Victorious over his rebel subjects, equally successful in his contest with diplomatic adversaries, the Emperor saw Poland prostrate before him, silently awaiting her doom.

APPENDIX A.*

TABLE I.—*Showing number of Poles as compared to other races in Western Provinces.*

	Name of Government.	Russian.	Letts.	Poles.	Jews.	Other Nations.	Percentage of Poles in every 100 Inhabitants.
White Russia.	Witebsk	428,651	139,295	63,432	62,628	10,189	9·2
	Mohilew	719,229	945	27,238	102,855	387	3·2
	Minsk ...	736,175	64,149	116,789	96,981	2,892	11·5
Lithuania.	Wilna ...	184,688	418,880	154,386	76,802	3,318	18·4
	Kowno...	6,852	730,933	25,189	101,337	40,727	2·7
	Grodno ..	293,489	201,897	193,228	94,219	6,814	24·0
Little Russia.	Kieff ...	1,370,250	38,026	83,351	225,074	1,655	4·6
	Volhynia	1,042,694	20,535	174,100	183,890	5,208	12·2
	Podolia	1,170,485	—	209,234	195,847	43,428	12·9
	Total ...	5,952,513	1,614,660	1,046,947	1,139,633	114,618	10·4

TABLE II.—*Showing the number of Free-born, Apanage, and Serf-born Individuals in Western Provinces.*

Government.	Free-born.	Apanage.	Serf.
Witebsk	142,831	13,336	446,233
Mohilew	75,378	9,412	572,269
Kovno	281,816	—	364,646
Wilna...	229,923	106	402,549
Grodno	243,529	—	361,302
Minsk	128,828	—	599,160
Volhynia	242,251	—	864,161
Podolia	324,906	—	1,041,051
Kieff ...	304,573	—	1,121,062
Total ...	1,974,035	22,854	5,772,433

[Jews and Colonists are not included in this table. Old soldiers are numbered in the Apanage column.]

* This and the two following tables are taken from A. von Buschen's work—"Bevölkerung des Russischen Kaiserreichs in den wichtigsten statistischen Verhältnissen dargestellt. Gotha, Verlag von Justus Perthes, 1862."

TABLE III.

Showing the number of the different religious communions in the Western Provinces.

Government.	Orthodox Greek Church.	Dissenters of Greek Church.	Roman and Armenian Catholics.	Protestants.	Total of Christian Population.	Jews.	Mahomedans.	Total of non-Christian Population.	Percentage of Greek Church to Christians.	Percentage of Christians to Population.
Witebsk	452,242	40,115	216,567	10,158	719,082	62,628	31	62,659	62·89	91·98
Mohilew	727,743	13,813	39,842	381	781,779	102,855	6	102,861	93·08	88·37
Kowno	29,596	14,269	802,358	40,309	886,532	101,337	418	101,755	3·33	89·71
Wilna	188,567	12,195	595,234	902	796,898	76,802	2,416	79,218	23·66	90·95
Grodno	487,009	—	293,839	5,564	786,412	94,219	1,250	95,469	61·92	89·17
Minsk	709,154	3,883	173,561	527	887,125	96,981	2,365	99,346	79·23	89·35
Volhynia	1,171,356	3,447	164,427	4,999	1,344,229	183,890	209	184,099	87·14	87·96
Podolia	1,319,975	9,913	220,906	1,780	1,552,574	195,847	45	195,892	85·01	88·79
Kieff	1,621,928	4,774	90,903	1,632	1,719,237	225,074	23	225,097	94·34	88·42

APPENDIX B.

PLAN OF THE EXISTING INSURRECTION.*

"HASTEN to Warsaw in order to obtain the fullest information as to the spirit and tendency of the demonstration of the 25th February on the subject of the resolution of the Agricultural Society relating to the grant of land to the peasants. Take this grant as the starting-point of all the measures destined to prepare for the national rising, and make use of the masses, who, by virtue of this wholesome resolution, have received lands in full and perpetual ownership, as the foundation-stone of the regeneration of the State.

"In traversing the eastern countries to the most distant limits of Poland, spread the news that the Agricultural Society, in evidence of its solicitude for the people, ordered, on the 24th February, the proprietors in all the provinces, without exception, to endow the peasants spontaneously with all the lands hitherto liable to statute labour (*corvée*). Admit no discussion on this matter; declare it in laconic terms and as an accomplished fact.

"In order to obtain permission from the Government that this order, emanating from the capital, be imposed on all the provinces, the Lithuanian and Ruthenian proprietors should send immediately to St. Petersburg a deputation intended to unite with that of Warsaw, and to submit itself implicitly to the injunctions of the latter.

"Our oppressors will not succeed in disuniting us if we are ourselves united.

"Write and print in the Russian language proclamations to inform the people of the benefits which come to them from Warsaw; combine the stipulations and the payments to be made to the proprietors in such a manner that this measure may surpass by far the advantages offered by the regulations of the St. Petersburg ukases.

"If the Czar, which it is difficult to suppose, should give his consent immediately to everything, spread at once the report that he has done it by intimidation, and that even he submits to the orders which are imposed on him from Warsaw.

"Organize in this case national solemnities, numerous and clamorous popular meetings directed by the lesser nobility (*Schliachta*). It is they also who should guide the people, without the smallest interference of priests or officials.

"Immediately after, openly, without the least hesitation, even though it

---

* This document may be regarded as the programme of the Red Republican Party.

involve a great loss, it is necessary to give effect to the resolution taken at Warsaw, without waiting, from which God preserve us, for the initiative of this application to come from St. Petersburg.

"The position of the Schliachta will be still more favourable if the Czar refuse to sign the ukase confirming the resolution of Warsaw, or if he delay the matter until the preparations for the insurrection are complete.

"Charge the Central Committee of Action (*Kapitoul*) at Warsaw to occupy the attention of Europe by newspaper correspondence and by deputations sent to the Governments of France and England.

"1. On the one hand, the opinion of the Western masses must be kept in a state of the most feverish excitement by means of ever-growing manifestations of the vitality of Poland and the impotence of Russia. To this end information must be sent to all the German, French, English, and Italian journals, *invented, if necessary,* on the civil commotions in Russia which shake the power of the Czars, and on the serious and irreconcilable dissensions which have broken out between the peasants, the boyards, and the *employés*; insisting particularly on the distress of Russia, financial and administrative, on the avenging and disintegrating influence exercised by the Polish idea on that structure created by Peter the Great, and which is now falling into ruins.

"It is necessary to persuade the world that Czarism can only be vanquished by the Poles.

"2. On the other hand, the Governments of France and England must be wearied with complaints and grievances emanating from Warsaw, fabricated for the purpose, and professedly remaining unnoticed at St. Petersburg. It is to be observed that these deputations will obtain nothing at first; but that must not cool our zeal, for our principal end should be to compromise these Governments with that of Russia, and, moreover, to furnish us with an occasion to complain of their indifference.

"We confidentially inform our fellow-citizens that these counsels have been given to us by persons in a position to know well the policy of the Tuileries, and who have cited to us the example of the Italians, who have succeeded in obtaining in a few years, by the force of patriotic perseverance, the overthrow of all diplomatic obstacles, in persuading the Emperor of the French to accomplish what he had never wished, or even thought of doing, and in forcing his Government, whether they would or no, to aid them in their attempt for emancipation.

"But God preserve us from employing emigrants in these missions, for this would be the best way of giving to the Western Governments—little sympathizing in general with the Polish movement—an excellent pretext for holding themselves apart from all relations with this movement.

"It is important, above all, to avoid those intriguers of the Hotel Lambert, who have abandoned the country, who have completely accustomed themselves to scrub (*frotter*) the ministerial antechambers in foreign countries, and who have covered themselves with ridicule in the eyes of all those who are little disposed in favour of our cause.

"The national emissaries should avoid too frequent resort to the Tuileries, where they may be easily detected ; but, as a set-off, they should visit the Palais Royal (residence of Prince Napoleon), where they are sure to receive every kind of assistance and information. The Deputy G. L. M. is in a position to furnish all the instructions and explanations required for this purpose.

"We repeat, these deputations must not expect from their proceedings and the parade of their grievances any other result than smoothing the way destined in the future to bring insurgent Poland nearer to the West, and to intimidate the Russians and the Germans by the belief that the Governments of France, of England, and of Italy are in secret relations with the Polish movement.

"We ought, in reality, to content ourselves with the knowledge that each Warsaw demonstration brings us nearer to the Italians, the Hungarians, and all the nationalities which aspire to break the Austrian chains. In regard to this, there is complete accord between Mieroslawski, Garibaldi, and Klapka.

"3. Restrain as long as possible, in the interior of the country, the propaganda of agitation within the limits of purely economic reforms; anticipate in every way an armed insurrection until the tribunes of the Schliachta have brought the whole population of the Western provinces to a degree of patriotic exaltation equal to that of the people of the Mazurie. In this way await the offensive operations on the part of the Muscovite troops; and, from the very commencement of these operations, whatever may then be the degree of maturity of the insurrection, join, without the least hesitation, for life or for death, the masses of the people; do not abandon them until the definitive and glorious deliverance of the *Kzecz pospolita;* take possession of them, and lead them wherever the desperate struggle against the oppressors may require.

"All should foresee—no long-sighted policy being able to mislead them—the fatal elements, *erostatiques*, and even *Khaïdaniachiques*, which will arise in this period of agitation, engendered by the leaven of a society corrupted by long servitude; but, at the same time, the duty of every one will be the quieting of these elements by practical sacrifices on a grand scale, and the alleviation of the fate of the people as much as may be possible and as means may permit. What, above all things, is necessary is to heal society by the discipline indispensable for military preparations, because none of the pseudo tribunes will sustain this trial.

"Besides, for the incurable demagogues it will be necessary to open the cage, that they may enrol themselves on the other side of the Dnieper; that they may there propagate the Cossack *haidamatchina* against the priests, the boyards, and the officials, by insinuating to the peasants that it is they who strive to maintain them in servitude. It will be necessary to hold in readiness an entire store of troubles, and to cast them into fire already kindled in the interior of Muscovy. Let all the agitation of little Russianism remove itself to the further side of the Dnieper; it is there that will be found the vast field of Pougatschew for our retarded *chmelnitchewstchina.**

---

* This word is derived from Chmelnicki, a Polish gentleman, and chief of the insurrection of the Cossacks against Poland in the first half of the seventeenth century. The name is stated by Russian writers to be associated with scenes of the most horrible cruelty and brutally atrocious acts.

"It is from there that our Panslavic and Communist school is composed. There is all the Polish *herzénisme*. Let it prepare silently and for a long time the enfranchisment of Poland by rending the entrails of Czarism. Here is a work as worthy as it is easy for the demi-Poles and the demi-Russians, who at present occupy all the degrees of the civil and military Government in Russia. Let anarchy replace everywhere the Russian Czarism, from which in the end the Russian nationality, our neighbour, will deliver and purify itself.

"Let us leave others to be seduced by the delusion that this Radicalism will promote *your liberty as well as ours:* but to transport it within the limits of Poland would be to betray the country; and this crime should be punished by death, as treason to the State. Within our country Radicalism must limit its impatience to preparations for the insurrection; on all points of the frontier must be introduced into the country powder, good arms, single-barrelled fowling-pieces—but not double-barrelled—and, if it be possible, carbines and all kinds of iron household utensils; all the manufactures of articles in iron in the hands of the Poles should be appropriated to the preparation for war; everywhere it will be necessary to prepare the materials necessary for cavalry and convoys, in order that all may be ready the instant when the necessity for them is felt.

"In the mean time it will be necessary to prepare and to organize the population beforehand, in the continual expectation of a sudden outbreak of war. In doing all this, it is necessary not to lose sight of the fact that the Schliachta furnish more volunteers for the cavalry, the citizens and the population of the woody countries for the sharpshooters, and the mass of peasants for the scythemen. All should be objects of solicitude and of particular care. Further, the pupils of the technical establishments may join the engineers or the artillery.

"The Poles of the Mosaic persuasion will work in factories with the needle, &c. &c. Everywhere let impatient patriotism understand that a period of suspense, which is to be one of activity and preparation, is indispensable to us in all respects, as much for the purpose of bringing back the people, especially in Lithuania, in Russia, and Galicia, to their ancient reliance upon, and submission to, the Schliachta, of which they have lost the habit under the influence of a long Muscovite and Austrian servitude, as for their material armament; and, finally, to await, in an approaching future, one of two consoling eventualities—a foreign war or an insurrection in Russia. May it please God that both may take place.

"4. It is only the fortunate concurrence of favourable circumstances in the interior and the exterior of the country which should be considered as the signal for a general insurrection in the whole country of Poland. Considering, however, that many provinces are in an exceptional position, and might, consequently, form an exception to the general rule, the insurrection should be organized in the following order:—

"(*a*) The masses of the agricultural population, prepared by the preceding economic agitation, armed with anything which may come to their hands, but absolutely under the command of the Schliachta, will hasten from all parts to the town of the district, annihilating by their unexpected attack the garrison of the oppressors, immediately barricading the streets and transforming the buildings into blockhouses, so that the town may take the appearance of a fortified castle.

"(b) The chiefs will choose, as quickly as possible, the best men from among this crowd, under the denomination of the first levy, distributing to them the best arms, especially arms which are not fire-arms, provisions for three days, and conducting them to a camp agreed on by the Woïwodie, or the Government, avoiding as much as possible any encounter with the enemy until all the levies are united in the same detachment, under the command of a single leader.

"As at least half of the fire-arms will remain in the towns of fortified districts, for the reserves, the chiefs of the camps of Woïwodies must rely principally on the cavalry and the scythemen; if, at each halt, they exercise the foot-soldiers, without intermission and with indefatigable zeal, to the easy management of arms, and teach the lancers to despise the enemy's fire, by inspiring them with the ardent desire to rush upon them, then the army will be sufficiently formed. The scythemen must be taught to lie on the ground before the fire of artillery, and to charge at a rapid pace under the fire of musketry. All the arms, whatever they may be, must be kept near some companies of sharpshooters, which must not be separated from the battalions of scythemen in any evolution, not even for an instant, with the sole exception of cases where the sharpshooters disperse themselves; and then they must disperse in sight of the scythemen.

"Menaced with an attack by the enemy, the sharpshooters must shelter themselves in the squares of the scythemen as well as in intrenchments formed of palisades; and it is from the third rank, above the heads of the kneeling scythemen, that they will deliberately fire (*avec sang froid*), allowing the enemy to approach as near as possible.

"The convoys, indispensable in every insurrection, must be placed in *tabors*, similar to those which were formerly in use among the Cossacks, the Poles, and the Tchèques. During the combat these *tabors* must be formed with the reserves, in the manner of movable fortifications, and in case of defeat, their retrograde movement must not be commenced until the enemy's attention is distracted, if only for a time, by some well-calculated offensive movement on our part.

"(c) The detachment, already exercised during the marches which will have preceded its general union, and trained during the few days which it will have passed in camp, must now march, according to the exigency of the case, either against the nearest detachment of the enemy, or for the chief place of the Government.

"It is at this phase of the insurrectionary action that our preliminary instructions must cease, because this phase of the local insurrection must absolutely correspond with that in which the foreign legion will be found ready to fly to the aid of the insurrection.

"5. The agitation in the interior of the country must not only not distract the people and prevent supplies being furnished, by material as well as moral means, to that army which is forming outside the country; but, on the contrary, this anchor of safety so near to them must be considered as the surest basis of the whole affair. Consequently, let none of the capital specially designed for this sacred object be retained under any pretext of more pressing need for interior operations; but let it be forwarded in time to the central fund of the legion, because foreign affairs are the most powerful lever of our whole enterprise; and God grant that we may not be taken unawares in the midst of a fatal irresolution.

"N.B.—In the present situation of affairs, the people must not allow to the enemy either recruitment or forced disarmament. The negotiations with the Muscovite Government will furnish a crowd of eloquent arguments on this subject; but if these negotiations do not lead to the desired end, force must be repelled by force.

(Signed) "LOUIS MIEROSLAWSKI.

"1st *March*, 1861."

APPENDIX C.

AMNESTY.

"SINCE the first news of the disturbances which have taken place in the kingdom of Poland we have followed the impulse of our heart in declaring that we did not consider the Polish nation responsible for an agitation which is, above all, fatal to herself. We have attributed it alone to external influences that have long been brought to bear upon the country by certain parties who have contracted, during the long years of an adventurous life, habits of disorder, of violence, and of obscure plots, which have perverted in them the noble sentiments of love for humanity, and even inspired the idea of sullying by crime the honour of the nation.

"These manifestations of another age, long since condemned by the judgment of history, are no longer in accordance with the spirit of our epoch. The object of our present generation should be to establish the welfare of the country, not by torrents of blood, but by the means of peaceful progress.

"This is the object we have had in view when, trusting in the Divine protection, we made before God and our conscience the vow to consecrate our life to the happiness of our subjects.

"But, in order to accomplish to the full extent this vow, which we shall always hold sacred, we need the assistance of all honest men who are sincerely devoted to their country, and who show their devotion not by interested calculations or criminal attempts, but by the maintenance of public tranquillity under the protection of the laws.

"In our solicitude for the future welfare of the country, we are ready to consign to oblivion all past acts of rebellion. Therefore, ardently desiring to put a stop to an effusion of blood as useless as it is regrettable, we grant a free pardon to all those of our subjects in the kingdom implicated in the late troubles who have not incurred responsibility for other crimes or for offences committed while serving in the ranks of our army, and who may before the 1st (13th) of May lay down their arms and return to their allegiance.

"It is upon us that the duty devolves of preserving the country from the recurrence of these turbulent agitations, and to inaugurate a new era of its political life. This can only commence by a rational organization of the local administrative autonomy as a basis for the whole edifice.

"We have already laid the foundations in the institutions granted by us to the kingdom; but, to our sincere regret, the result has not yet been tested by experience, owing to the intrigues which have substituted chimerical delusions for the conditions of public order, without which no reform is possible.

"While continuing for the present to maintain these institutions in their integrity, we reserve it to ourselves, when they shall have been tested by experience, to proceed to their further development in accordance with the requirements of the times and of the country. It is only by confidence in our intentions that the kingdom of Poland will be able to efface the traces of the present evils, and to advance surely towards the destiny which our solicitude assigns it. We invoke the Divine assistance that we may be permitted to accomplish that which we have ever considered to be our mission.

(Signed) "ALEXANDER.

"*St. Petersburg, March 31st,* 1863."

APPENDIX D.

Extract from the Address of the Municipality of St. Petersburg to the Emperor, April, 1863.

* * * * * *

"Enemies, envious of the progress of Russia, and only beholding in the revival of society the fermentation of subversive elements, have conceived the plan of striking a blow at the integrity of the Russian empire. They dream of the possibility of tearing from it provinces which are the cradle of the Russian orthodox faith, and which were restored to our common country at the cost of torrents of Russian blood.

"We, the citizens of St. Petersburg, feel convinced that any attempt against the integrity of the empire is an attack upon the existence of Russia, where the sentiment of national honour and attachment to its sovereign is more lively than ever.

"We do not reply to our enemies by hatred and a thirst for vengeance; but if it should please Providence to put Russia to the proof, we shall not recoil from any sacrifice; we will raise the standard for our Czar and for our country, and will march wherever your sovereign will may think fit to lead us."

APPENDIX E.

DIPLOMATIC CORRESPONDENCE.

EARL RUSSELL TO LORD NAPIER.

"*Foreign Office, April* 10*th,* 1863.

"My Lord,—Her Majesty's Government think it incumbent on them to state once more to the Government of his Majesty the Emperor of Russia the deep interest which, in common with the rest of Europe, they take in the welfare of the kingdom of Poland.

"The general sympathy which is felt for the Polish nation might of itself justify her Majesty's Government in making, in favour of the Polish race, an appeal to the generous and benevolent feelings of his Imperial Majesty, who has of late, by various and important measures of improvement and reform, manifested an enlightened desire to promote the welfare of all classes of his subjects. But with regard to the kingdom of Poland her Majesty's Government feel that the Government of Great Britain has a peculiar right to make its opinions known to that of his Imperial Majesty, because Great Britain, having, in common with Austria, France, Prussia, Portugal, Spain, and Sweden, become a party to the treaty of Vienna in 1815, her Majesty's Government are entitled to interfere with regard to any matter which may appear to them to constitute a departure from the provisions and stipulations of that treaty.

"By the first article of that treaty the grand duchy of Warsaw was erected into a kingdom of Poland, to be inseparably attached to the empire of Russia under certain conditions specified in that article; and her Majesty's Government are concerned to have to say, that, although the union of the kingdom to the Empire has been maintained, the conditions on which that union was distinctly made to depend have not been fulfilled by the Russian Government.

"The Emperor Alexander, in execution of the engagements contracted by the treaty of Vienna, established in the kingdom of Poland a national representation and national institutions corresponding with the stipulations of the treaty. It is not necessary for her Majesty's Government to observe upon the manner in which those arrangements were practically administered from that time down to the revolt in 1830. But upon the suppression of that revolt by the Imperial arms those arrangements were swept away, and a totally different order of things was by the Imperial authority established.

" Prince Gortschakoff argues, as his predecessors in office have on former occasions argued, that the suppression of that revolt cancelled all the engagements of Russia in the treaty of Vienna, with regard to the kingdom of Poland, and left the Emperor of Russia at full liberty to deal with the kingdom of Poland as with a conquered country, and to dispose of its people and institutions at his will. But her Majesty's Government cannot acquiesce in a doctrine which they deem so contrary to good faith, so destructive of the obligations of treaties, and so fatal to all the international ties which bind together the community of European states and powers.

" If, indeed, the Emperor of Russia had held Poland as part of the original dominions of his crown, or if he had acquired it by the unassisted success of his arms, and unsanctioned by the consent of any other power, he could have contended that might was equivalent to right, and without listening to the dictates of generosity and justice, he might have punished a temporary revolt of a portion of his Polish subjects by depriving the whole of them and their descendants for ever of those privileges and institutions which his predecessor had deemed essential to the welfare and prosperity of the Polish kingdom.

" But the position of the Russian sovereign with regard to the kingdom of Poland was entirely different. He held that kingdom by the solemn stipulations of a treaty made by him with Great Britain, Austria, France, Prussia, Portugal, Spain, and Sweden ; and the revolt of the Poles could not release him from the engagements so contracted, nor obliterate the signatures by which his plenipotentiaries had concluded, and he himself had ratified, those engagements.

" The question, then, having arisen whether the engagements taken by Russia by the treaty of Vienna have been and are now faithfully carried into execution, her Majesty's Government, with deep regret, feel bound to say that this question must be answered in the negative.

" With regard to the present revolt, her Majesty's Government forbear to dwell upon that long course of action, civil, political, and military, carried on by the Russian Government within the kingdom of Poland, of which the Poles so loudly complain, and to which they refer as the causes which occasioned, and in their opinion justified, their insurrection. Her Majesty's Government would rather advert to the much-wished-for termination of these lamentable troubles.

" What may be the final issue of this contest, it is not, indeed, for her Majesty's Government to foretell ; but whether the result shall be the more extended spread of the insurrection, and its assumption of dimensions not at present contemplated, or whether, as is more likely, that result shall be the ultimate success of the imperial arms, it is clear and certain that neither result can be arrived at without a calamitous effusion of blood, a great sacrifice of human life, and an extensive devastation of property ; and it is evident that even if Poland shall be reduced to subjection, the remembrance of the events of the struggle will long continue to make it the bitter enemy of Russia, and a source of weakness and of danger instead of being an element of security and strength.

" Her Majesty's Government, therefore, most earnestly entreat the Government of Russia to give their most serious attention to all the foregoing considerations ; and her Majesty's Government would beg, moreover, to submit to the Imperial Government that, besides the obligations of treaties, Russia, as a member of the community of European states, has duties of comity towards other nations to fulfil. The condition of things which has now for a long course of time existed in Poland is a source of danger, not to Russia alone, but also to the general peace of Europe.

"The disturbances which are perpetually breaking out among the Polish subjects of his Imperial Majesty necessarily produce a serious agitation of opinion in other countries of Europe, tending to excite much anxiety in the minds of their Governments, and which might, under possible circumstances, produce complications of the most serious character.

"Her Majesty's Government, therefore, fervently hope that the Russian Government will so arrange these matters that peace may be restored to the Polish people, and may be established upon lasting foundations.

"Your lordship will read this despatch to Prince Gortschakoff, and you will give him a copy of it. "I am, &c.,

(Signed) "RUSSELL."

EARL RUSSELL TO LORD NAPIER.

"*Foreign Office, April 24th*, 1863.

"MY LORD,—I have received and laid before the Queen your Excellency's despatch of the 12th instant, inclosing a copy of a manifesto on Polish affairs issued by the Emperor of Russia on 31st March (12th April).

"Her Majesty's Government have carefully and anxiously considered the contents of this document, in the hope to find in it the germ of a restoration of peace, and the hope of good government to Poland.

"I have to make to you the following remarks as the result of their deliberations.

"An amnesty may lay the foundation of peace in two cases :—

"1st. If the insurgents have been thoroughly defeated, and are only waiting for a promise of pardon to enable them to return to their homes.

"2nd. If the amnesty is accompanied with such ample promises of the redress of the grievances which gave occasion to the insurrection, as to induce the insurgents to think that their object is attained.

"It is clear that the first of these cases is not that of the present insurrection.

"It is not put down; it is, on the contrary, rather more extensive than it was a few weeks ago.

"Let us, then, examine the amnesty with reference to the second of the supposed cases.

"The Emperor, referring to the institutions which he has conferred (*octroyées*) on the kingdom of Poland, says :—

"'En maintenant encore aujourd'hui ces institutions dans leur intégrité, nous nous réservons, lorsqu'elles auront été éprouvées dans la pratique, de procéder à leur développement ultérieur selon les besoins du temps et ceux du pays.'

"This promise can hardly be satisfactory to the Poles. For it must be observed, with regard to the institutions already given, that it was during their existence that 2,000 young men were seized arbitrarily in one night, and condemned to serve as soldiers in the Russian army, in defiance of justice, and even in violation of the law of 1859, so recently enacted; so that it is evident no security would be obtained by submitting again to the same laws. With those institutions in full force and vigour, innocent men might be imprisoned as criminals, or condemned to serve as soldiers, or banished to distant countries, without a trial, without publicity, without any guarantee whatever.

"As to the promise held out for the future, it must be observed that it is made to depend on the practical working of these institutions, and on the wants of the time and of the country.

"The first of these conditions alone destroys all reasonable hope of the fulfilment of this promise; for the practical working of the institutions hitherto given depends on the co-operation of native Poles of property and character, as members of the Council of State, and of provincial and municipal assemblies. But the recent conduct of the Russian Government in Poland has deprived them of the confidence of all Poles of this description and forced all such Poles to withdraw from the bodies in which their functions were to be exercised.

"There are wanting, therefore, in this Imperial manifesto, the first elements of success; namely, a guarantee of security on the one side, and the feeling of trust and confidence on the other.

"In a despatch of Lord Durham, then ambassador at St. Petersburg, dated in August 1832, Lord Durham says—'There has long been a jealousy, nay hatred, existing between the Russians and the Poles.' Her Majesty's Government had hoped that the present Emperor, by raising the social condition of his Russian and securing the political freedom of his Polish subjects, might have united both by the link of loyal attachment to the throne.

"This hope has been unfortunately disappointed, and it is with great pain that her Majesty's Government observe that the feelings of hatred between Russians and Poles have not in the lapse of thirty years been softened or modified.

"The present amnesty does not appear likely to diminish the intensity of the insurrection, or give any solid security to the most moderate of Polish patriots. "I am, &c.,

(Signed) "RUSSELL."

PRINCE GORTSCHAKOFF TO BARON BRUNNOW.

"*St. Petersburg, April* 14*th*, 1863.

"M. LE BARON,—On the morning of the 5th (17th) of April Lord Napier delivered to me a copy, herewith enclosed, of a despatch from Her Britannic Majesty's Principal Secretary of State relative to the present situation of the kingdom of Poland.

"The first part of this document is devoted to a retrospective examination of the question of right; the second expresses the wish that peace may be restored to the kingdom of Poland, and established on a lasting basis. I will reply to these two points of Lord Russell's despatch.

"As regards the question of right, her Britannic Majesty's Principal Secretary of State reproduces the arguments already recorded in his despatch of the 2nd of March; I can, therefore, refer to the observations which I then made to the ambassador of England.

"The Government of her Britannic Majesty takes a position on ground where the Imperial Cabinet will never hesitate to meet it—that of treaties.

"Nevertheless, it is here a question less of the text than of the interpretation of treaties. We have the right not to admit without reservation every interpretation which it might be wished to give them.

"Lord Russell says in his despatch that, by article 1 of the General Act signed at Vienna, the 28th of May (9th of June), 1815, 'the duchy of Warsaw was erected into a kingdom of Poland to be inseparably attached to the empire of Russia under certain conditions.'

"Now, this is what the Act of Congress of Vienna stipulates in respect to those conditions:—

"'Poles, subjects of Russia, Austria, and Prussia respectively, shall enjoy representation, and shall obtain national institutions to be determined in conformity with the political existence which each of the Governments to which they belong shall consider it useful and expedient to grant to them.'

"The Emperor Alexander I. developed these principles in accordance with his personal views. He granted to Poland the constitution of the 12th (24th) of December, 1815. It was a spontaneous act of his sovereign will, and it did not constitute an irrevocable engagement towards foreign powers, inasmuch as the act of the constitution, posterior to the treaty of Vienna, was not even communicated to them.

"Lord Russell contests the principle according to which the revolt of Poland in 1830, having resulted in the declaration of the forfeiture of the sovereign dynasty, should be held to annul the bases of political existence granted in virtue of the Act of Vienna.

"Although history has more than once confirmed this conclusion of natural right, theory may afford matter for controversy. We think it may be laid down that if the revolt does not invalidate the national engagements, it at any rate annuls the spontaneous development of them which had been generously added, and which have led to fatal results to Poland and to Russia.

"But the Principal Secretary of State of her Britannic Majesty gives to this argument a prominent place in his despatch, while I had only incidentally put it forward in the course of my conversation with Lord Napier.

"The English ambassador alludes to it in the following terms in the despatch which he had the goodness to communicate to me:—

"'Prince Gortschakoff also said to me that, desiring to treat this question in a spirit of conciliation and humanity, he had abstained from employing an argument which lay at his disposal—that of the right of conquest.'

"Moreover, everything has been said on both sides in this discussion, and to prolong it on that ground would be a useless task.

"I proceed to the second part of Lord Russell's despatch.

"The design of our august master is to arrive at a practical solution. We assume that such is also the desire of the Government of her Britannic Majesty. Since its aim is to see assured to the kingdom of Poland the repose and welfare which are the objects of the solicitude of his Majesty the Emperor, it appears to us difficult not to arrive at an understanding.

"The difference in our points of view lies in the fact that the English Government appears to believe that the constitution of 1815 is the sole panacea calculated to calm the present agitation of Poland.

"But the English Government and nation, whose practical good sense has founded the greatness of England, can hardly assert that there is only one form of government possible for all peoples, whatever may be their history and development. Before arriving at the political maturity of which England offers the example, there are many degrees to pass through, and each nation must proceed in this path according to its own instincts. It is just and natural that a sovereign, animated by the most benevolent intentions, should calculate the bearing and extension of institutions destined to place his subjects in the most favourable conditions of existence.

"The idea of our august master has been shown ever since his accession to the throne, and cannot be ignored by any one in Europe.

"His Majesty has resolutely entered upon the path of reform. Relying upon the trust and devotion of his people, he has undertaken and accomplished in a few years a social transformation which other states have only been able to realize after a long lapse of time and many efforts. His solicitude has not ceased there. A system of gradual development has been applied to all the branches of the public service, and to existing institutions. It opens to Russia the prospect of a regular progress. The Emperor perseveres in it without precipitation or impulse (*entraînement*), taking into account the elements which it is the work of time to prepare and mature, but without ever deviating from the line he has traced for himself.

"This measure has conciliated to him the gratitude and affection of his subjects. We think it gives him a title to the sympathies of Europe.

"The same designs have not ceased to influence his Majesty since his solicitude has been brought to bear upon the kingdom of Poland.

"We shall not enter here into an enumeration of the national institutions, for the most part elective, with which this country has been endowed.

"They do not appear to have been sufficiently understood in Europe, either on account of remoteness, or rather, because chimercial passions and the interested labours of a hostile party have stood in the way of an equitable and impartial judgment.

"The system inaugurated by our august master contains a germ which time and experience must develop. It is destined to lead to an administrative autonomy on the basis of the provincial and municipal institutions which in England have been the starting-point and the foundation of the greatness and prosperity of the country. But in the execution of this idea the Emperor has encountered obstacles, which are found principally in the agitations of the party of disorder.

"This party has understood that if it allowed the peaceable majority of the kingdom to enter upon this path of regular progress, there would be an end to their aspirations. Their intrigues have not allowed the new institutions to be carried into effect. It has been impossible to show how they work, or how far they respond to the real necessities and to the degree of maturity of the country.

"It is only when this experiment shall have been made that it will be possible to pass a judgment upon this work and to complete it.

"The manifesto of the 31st of March indicates the wishes of our august master in this matter.

"By the side of an act of clemency, to which it has been possible to give a large extension since the dispersion of the most important armed bands, the Emperor has maintained in force the institutions already granted, and has declared that he reserved to himself the power of giving to them the developments indicated by time and the requirements of the country.

"His Majesty can, then, refer to the past in the rectitude of his conscience; as to the future, it necessarily depends on the confidence with which these institutions will be met in the kingdom.

"In taking a stand upon this ground, our august master considers that he acts as the best friend of Poland, as the only one whose aim it is to secure her welfare by practical means.

"Lord Russell calls upon Russia to discharge those duties which, as a member of European society, she owes to foreign states.

"Russia is too directly interested in the tranquillity of Poland not to understand the duties of her position towards other nations.

"It would be difficult to assert that she has met, in this respect, with scrupulous reciprocity. The continual conspiracy which is being organized and armed abroad to keep up disorder in the kingdom is a fact of public notoriety, the inconvenience of which principally consists in the moral effects which the favourers of the insurrection deduce from it, in order to lead astray the peaceable population by gaining credit for the belief in direct assistance from abroad.

"In this manner we have seen produced two influences, both equally grievous—that exercised by foreign agitation on the insurrection, and that which the continuation of the insurrection itself exercises in its turn upon public opinion in Europe.

"These two influences react one upon the other, and have ended by bringing affairs to the situation which the Powers at present point out to the vigilance of the Imperial Cabinet.

"It is asked of it to restore the kingdom to the conditions of a lasting peace.

"The Powers are inspired with this desire by the conviction that the periodical troubles of Poland cause to the states placed in the immediate vicinity of its frontiers a shock, the reaction of which is felt by the whole of Europe, that they excite the minds of the people in a disquieting manner, and that they might, if prolonged, bring about, under certain circumstances, complications of the most serious nature.

"The Government of her Britannic Majesty, in expressing this desire, further relies upon the engagements of 1815, which affect the condition of the different parts of Poland. We do not hesitate to declare that these wishes are entirely in accordance with those of our august master.

"His Majesty admits that in the peculiar position of the kingdom the troubles which agitate it may affect the tranquillity of the adjoining states, between which were concluded on the 21st of April (3rd of May), 1815, separate treaties intended to determine the condition of the duchy of

Warsaw, and that they may interest the powers who signed the general transaction of the 28th of May (9th of June), 1815, in which were inserted the principal stipulations of these separate treaties.

"The Emperor believes that explanations on the basis and in the spirit of the communications which have just been addressed to us may conduce to a result conformable to the general interests.

"Our august master notices with satisfaction the sentiments of confidence which the Government of her Britannic Majesty testify towards him in relying upon him to bring back the kingdom of Poland to conditions which would render possible the realization of his benevolent views.

"But the more the Emperor is disposed to take into account the just prepossessions of the neighbouring states, and the interest which the powers who signed the treaty of 1815 show in a state of things which is the cause of deep solicitude to his Majesty himself, the more our august master considers it a duty to request the serious attention, to the true causes of this situation, and to the means of remedying it, of the courts who have addressed themselves with confidence to him.

"If the Government of her Britannic Majesty lays stress upon (*relève*) the reaction which the troubles of Poland exercise on the peace of Europe, we must be still more struck with the influence which the agitations of Europe have in all times had the power to exercise upon the tranquillity of Poland.

"Since 1815 this country has witnessed the development of a material welfare unknown until then in her annals, while other states have in the same interval undergone many interior crises.

"This repose was only troubled in 1830 by the consequences of commotions coming from abroad; eighteen years later, in 1848, while almost the whole of Europe was convulsed by the revolution, the kingdom of Poland was able to preserve its tranquillity.

"We are persuaded that it would be the same at present, were it not for the continual instigations of the party of cosmopolitan revolution. If this party, everywhere devoted to the overthrow of order, at present concentrates all its activity upon Poland, a grave error would be committed in supposing that its aspirations will stop short at that limit. What it seeks there is a lever to overturn the rest of Europe.

"Those cabinets which attach importance to seeing the kingdom of Poland return a moment earlier to the conditions of a durable peace, cannot therefore more certainly insure the realization of this desire than by labouring, on their side, to appease the moral and material disorder which it is sought to propagate in Europe, and thus to exhaust the main source of the agitations at which their foresight is alarmed.

"We entertain the firm hope that in strengthening in this respect the ties which bind them together, they will effectually serve the cause of peace and of the general interests.

"I have the honour to request that you will communicate a copy of this despatch to the principal Secretary of State of her Britannic Majesty.

"Receive, &c.,

"GORTSCHAKOFF."

EARL RUSSELL TO LORD NAPIER.

"*Foreign-office*, May 2nd.

"MY LORD,—Baron Brunnow came to me this morning, and, before giving me a copy of the despatch of his Government in answer to mine to your Excellency of the 10th of April, said to me in substance what follows:—
'You have declared to me that the step which Lord Napier was instructed to take was taken with a pacific intention. The Imperial Cabinet has received your despatch in a similar spirit of peace and of conciliation.

"'You have told me that the representation you have made is founded upon the basis of the stipulations of the treaty of Vienna of 1815.

"'The Imperial Cabinet on its part accepts this basis.

"'The Imperial Cabinet is ready to enter upon an exchange of ideas upon the ground and within the limits of the treaties of 1815.'

"I enclose a copy of the communication of Prince Gortschakoff.

"I shall, in another and a later despatch, furnish you with the views of her Majesty's Government upon the contents of that communication.

"I am, &c.,
"RUSSELL."

EARL RUSSELL TO LORD NAPIER.

"*Foreign-office*, June 17th, 1863.

"MY LORD,—Her Majesty's Government have considered with the deepest attention the despatch of Prince Gortschakoff of the 26th of April, which was placed in my hands by Baron Brunnow on the 2nd of May.

"Her Majesty's Government are not desirous, any more than Prince Gortschakoff, of continuing a barren discussion. I will therefore pass over all the controversy regarding my previous despatch; I will not endeavour in the present communication to fix the precise meaning of the article regarding Poland in the treaty of Vienna, nor will I argue, as Prince Gortschakoff seems to expect I should do, that there is only one form under which good government can be established. Still less will I call in question the benevolent intentions of the enlightened Emperor who has already in a short time effected such marvellous changes in the legal condition of his Russian subjects.

"Her Majesty's Government are willing with the Emperor of Russia to seek a practical solution of a difficult and most important problem.

"Baron Brunnow, in presenting to me Prince Gortschakoff's despatch, said, 'The Imperial Cabinet is ready to enter upon an exchange of ideas upon the ground and within the limits of the treaties of 1815.'

"Her Majesty's Government are thus invited by the Government of

Russia to an exchange of ideas upon the basis of the treaty of 1815, with a view to the pacification and permanent tranquillity of Poland.

"Before making any definite proposals, it is essential to point out that there are two leading principles upon which, as it appears to her Majesty's Government, any future government of Poland ought to rest. The first of these is the establishment of confidence in the government on the part of the governed.

"The original views of the Emperor Alexander I. are stated by Lord Castlereagh, who had heard from the Emperor's own lips, in a long conversation, the plan he contemplated.

"The plan of the Emperor is thus described by Lord Castlereagh :—' To retain the whole of the duchy of Warsaw, with the exception of the small portion to the westward of Kalisch, which he meant to assign to Prussia, erecting the remainder, together with the Polish provinces formerly dismembered, into a kingdom under the dominion of Russia, with a national administration congenial to the sentiments of the people.'

"The whole force of this plan consists in the latter words.

"Whether power is retained in the hands of one, as in the old monarchy of France, or divided among a select body of the aristocracy, as in the republic of Venice, or distributed among a sovereign, a house of peers, and a representative assembly, as in England — its virtue and strength must consist in its being a 'national administration congenial to the sentiments of the people.'

"The Emperor Alexander II., speaking of the institutions he has given, says, ' As to the future, it necessarily depends on the confidence with which these institutions will be received on the part of the kingdom.'

"Such an administration as Alexander I. intended, such confidence as Alexander II. looked for, unhappily do not exist in Poland.

"The next principle of order and stability must be found in the supremacy of law over arbitrary will. Where such supremacy exists, the subject or citizen may enjoy his property or exercise his industry in peace, and the security he feels as an individual will be felt in its turn by the Government under which he lives.

"Partial tumults, secret conspiracies, and the interference of cosmopolite strangers, will not shake the firm edifice of such a government.

"This element of stability is likewise wanting in Poland. The religious liberty guaranteed by the solemn declarations of the Empress Catherine, the political freedom granted by the deliberate charter of the Emperor Alexander I., have alike been abrogated by succeeding governments, and have been only partially revived by the present Emperor.

"It is no easy task to restore the confidence which has been lost, and to regain the peace which is now everywhere broken.

"Her Majesty's Government would deem themselves guilty of great presumption if they were to express an assurance that vague declarations of good intentions, or even the enactment of some wise laws, would make such an impression on the minds of the Polish people as to obtain peace and restore obedience.

"In present circumstances it appears to her Majesty's Government that nothing less than the following outline of measures should be adopted as the bases of pacification :—

" 1. Complete and general amnesty.

" 2. National representation, with powers similar to those which are fixed by the charter of the 15th (27th) November, 1815.

" 3. Poles to be named to public offices in such a manner as to form a distinct national administration, having the confidence of the country.

" 4. Full and entire liberty of conscience ; repeal of the restrictions imposed on Catholic worship.

" 5. The Polish language recognized in the kingdom as the official language, and used as such in the administration of the law and in education.

" 6. The establishment of a regular and legal system of recruiting.

" These six points might serve as the indications of measures to be adopted after calm and full deliberation.

" But it is difficult, nay, almost impossible, to create the requisite confidence and calm while the passions of men are becoming daily more excited, their hatreds more deadly, their determination to succeed or perish more fixed and immovable.

" Your lordship has sent me an extract from the *St. Petersburg Gazette* of the 7th (19th) of May. I could send your lordship, in return, extracts from London newspapers, giving accounts of atrocities, equally horrible, committed by men acting on behalf of Russian authority.

" It is not for her Majesty's Government to discriminate between the real facts and the exaggerations of hostile parties.

" Many of the allegations of each are probably unfounded, but some must in all probability be true. How, then, are we to hope to conduct to any good end a negotiation carried on between parties thus exasperated ?

" In an ordinary war, the successes of fleets and armies, who fight with courage, but without hatred, may be balanced in a negotiation carried on in the midst of hostilities. An island more or less to be transferred, a boundary more or less to be extended, might express the value of the last victory or conquest. But where the object is to attain civil peace, and to induce men to live under those against whom they have fought with rancour and desperation, the case is different. The first thing to be done, therefore, in the opinion of her Majesty's Government, is to establish a suspension of hostilities. This might be done in the name of humanity by a proclamation of the Emperor of Russia, without any derogation of his dignity. The Poles, of course, would not be entitled to the benefit of such an act, unless they themselves refrained from hostilities of every kind during the suspension.

" Tranquillity thus for the moment restored, the next thing is to consult the powers who signed the treaty of Vienna. Prussia, Spain, Sweden, and Portugal must be asked to give their opinion as to the best mode of giving effect to a treaty to which they were contracting parties.

" What her Majesty's Government propose, therefore, consists in these three propositions :—

" 1st. The adoption of the six points enumerated as bases of negotiation.

" 2nd. A provisional suspension of arms, to be proclaimed by the Emperor of Russia.

" 3rd. A conference of the eight powers who signed the treaty of Vienna
" Your Excellency will read and give a copy of this despatch to Prince Gortschakoff.
" I am, &c.,
" RUSSELL."

PRINCE GORTSCHAKOFF TO BARON BRUNNOW.

" *St. Petersburg, July 1st.*

" M. LE BARON,—Lord Napier has been instructed to give me the annexed despatch from her Britannic Majesty's principal Secretary of State to read, and a copy of it. We have pleasure in learning that Lord Russell admits with us the barren nature of a prolonged controversy relative to the signification of the 1st article of the treaty of Vienna ; and that with us, likewise, he desires to place the question upon ground which should offer more opportunities for arriving at a practical solution. Before taking our stand upon this ground, we deem it useful to put in a clear light our positions respectively. The Imperial Cabinet admits the principle that every power signing a treaty has the right to interpret the sense thereof from its own point of view, provided always that that interpretation remains within the limits of the meaning that is possible to be put upon it according to the text itself. In virtue of this principle the Imperial Cabinet does not dispute this right in any one of the eight powers which have concurred in the general proceedings of Vienna of 1815. Experience has, it is true, demonstrated that the exercise of such right issues in no practical result. The experiments made already in 1831 have had no issue but to place on record the divergence of opinions. Nevertheless, this right exists. It extends as far as the limits which I have indicated above, and is incapable of obtaining a wider range but with the express consent of the contracting party most directly interested. Accordingly, it depended upon the Imperial Cabinet to maintain the strict application of this principle, observing the line of action taken towards them in the course of the month of April last, with respect to events which occurred in the kingdom of Poland. If, in reply to that appeal, they went further into the subject, it was entirely owing to their perfect readiness to seek to conciliate, and in order to reply with courtesy to an appeal which bore a similar character. I will add that another cause was, that in the intentions which his Majesty the Emperor cherishes towards his Polish subjects there was no purpose which could dispose us to remove them from the light. This consideration was perfectly brought out by your Excellency when you informed the principal Secretary of her Britannic Majesty that the Imperial Cabinet was ready to enter upon an exchange of views upon the basis and within the limits of the treaties of 1815. That declaration we adhere to, and my despatch of this day will furnish the best proof of our perseverance in the same disposition. Having thus confirmed the genuine and sole character of the invitation which we have addressed to the English Cabinet, we will permit ourselves, after Lord Russell's example, to precede the observations which we have to communicate to his Excellency by some reflections in reply to the questions which he has entered upon and proposed at the outset.

"The principal Secretary of State of her Britannic Majesty says that the basis of government is in every case the confidence which it inspires in the governed, and that the ascendancy of the law over the arbitrary element must be the foundation for order and stability. *A priori*, we subscribe to these principles. We will only recall to mind that their indispensable corollary is respect for authority. The confidence with which a government inspires the governed depends not only on the goodness of its intentions, but also on the conviction imparted that it has the power of carrying them into effect. If Lord Russell affirms that partial tumults, secret conspiracies, and the influence of cosmopolite strangers, will not shake a government based upon confidence and respect for the laws, he will also admit that neither confidence nor legal conduct would be possible were that government to allow that a fraction of the people was vested with the right of seeking elsewhere than under the legitimately constituted authority, by armed rebellion supported by hostile or foreign parties, the well-being and the prosperity which they might declare that they could not realize without the aid of inspirations from abroad. Lord Russell places before us six articles, which he considers to be of a nature to provide for the pacification of the kingdom of Poland. In communicating them to us, her Britannic Majesty's Principal Secretary of State adopts in part the point of view put forward by my despatch of the 14th of April. This is an exchange of sentiments, and to that form of expression we have no objection to raise. I have clearly indicated in the despatch to which I refer the germs of practical conduct laid down by our august master, and the developments reserved in his Majesty's purpose to be given them when he should deem the proper time to be come. In comparing them with his own views, Lord Russell will convince himself that the greater part of the measures which he points to have already been decreed or prepared on the initiative of our august master. The Principal Secretary of State of her Britannic Majesty expresses the hope that the adoption of these measures would lead to the complete and permanent pacification of the kingdom of Poland. We are unable to share this hope without certain reserves. Viewing the subject as we do, re-organization of the kingdom must in all cases be preceded by the re-establishment of order in the country. That result is dependent upon a condition to which we had called the attention of the Government of her Britannic Majesty, and which is not only unfulfilled, but is not even alluded to in the despatch of Lord Russell. We refer to the material assistance and moral encouragement obtained from abroad by the insurgents. We are not aware from what sources of information the Government of her Britannic Majesty have formed their judgment of the state of affairs in Poland; we must presume that they are not of impartial origin. Indeed, we find Lord Russell himself establishing a kind of similarity between the news published by the St. Petersburg journal from statements furnished under the control and upon the responsibility of the recognized agent of the Government, and the information of every kind which the London journals borrow, without discernment or any guarantee, from the most suspected publications of the Polish revolutionary press. The confidence inspired by these publications has more than once given cause for declarations which, in spite of the formal denials given to them by daily events, have contributed to mislead opinion in England. In this manner have been propagated, in relation to the brave Russian soldiers who fulfil in Poland a painful duty with devotion and self-denial, calumnies and outrages which all Russia has felt with profound indignation. If Lord Russell were exactly informed of what passes in the kingdom of Poland, he would know, as we do, that wherever the armed rebellion has striven to acquire substance, to give itself a visible head, it has been crushed. The masses have kept aloof from it, the rural population evinces even hostility to it, because the disorders by which agitators live ruin the industrial classes. The insurrection sustains itself alone by a terrorism unprecedented in history. The bands are recruited principally from elements foreign to the country. They gather together in the woods, and disperse at the first attack to reunite in other places. When they are too closely pressed they cross the frontier, to re-enter the country at another point. Politically, it is a stage display intended to act upon Europe. The principle of action of the directing committees from without is to keep up agitation at all cost, in order to give food for the declarations of the press, to abuse public opinion, and to harass the Government by furnishing an occasion and a pretext for a diplomatic intervention which should lead to military action. All the hope of the armed insurrection is in this—it is the object at which it has laboured from its rise.

"Lord Russell will admit that in this situation the measures which he recommends to us would with difficulty find application practically. The greater part, I repeat it, have already been decreed; the state of the country has, up to the present time, paralyzed their execution. As long as that condition of things shall subsist, the same causes will produce the same effects. The presence of armed bands, the terrorism of the central committee, and the appearance of an immediate pressure from without, would, moreover, take from these measures the fitness of time, the dignity, and the effectiveness which we could promise ourselves in their spontaneous adoption. We will go further. Even when they could be put into execution with the full extension with which they are invested in the mind of the principal Secretary of State of her Britannic Majesty, they would have no prospect whatever of attaining the result which he has in view—that of pacifying the country. If Lord Russell follows attentively the productions of the press devoted to the Polish rebellion, he must be aware that the insurgents demand neither an amnesty, nor an autonomy, nor a representation either more or less complete. The absolute independence of the kingdom even would be for them only a means for arriving at the final object of their aspirations. This object is dominion over provinces where the immense majority are Russians by race or by religion; in a word, it is Poland extended to the two seas, which would inevitably bring about a claim to the Polish provinces belonging to other neighbouring powers. We desire to pronounce no judgment upon these aspirations. It suffices for us to prove that they exist, and that the Polish insurgents do not conceal them. The final result at which they would arrive cannot be doubtful. It would be a general conflagration, which the elements of disorder scattered through all countries would be brought to complicate, and which seek for an opportunity to subvert Europe. We have too much confidence in the principal Secretary of State of her Britannic Majesty to allow that he can approve an object as irreconcilable with the peace and with the equilibrium of Europe, with which are bound up the interests of Great

Britain, as they are with the maintenance of the treaties of 1815, the only basis and the only starting-point of the overtures which he has just made to us. Lord Russell quotes a passage related by Lord Castlereagh of a conversation which that statesman had with the Emperor Alexander I. in 1815, and which mentions the project formed by this sovereign to combine the duchy of Warsaw 'with the Polish provinces anciently dismembered, into a kingdom under the sovereignty of Russia, with an administration in accordance with the wishes of the people." This idea was a passing inclination of the Emperor Alexander I., and one which that sovereign did not accomplish when he was enabled to consider more maturely the interests of his kingdom. At all events, this question must be excluded even in an exchange of ideas made within the limits of the treaties of 1815. The only stipulation of these treaties which can have made it appear doubtful that the Emperor of Russia possessed the kingdom of Poland by the same title as that by which he holds his other possessions, the only one which might have made his rights dependent upon any condition whatever, and which explains the possibility of an exchange of ideas with foreign courts upon the subject of his relations with that portion of his dominions, is the vague phrase of article 1, which says 'that the Emperor of Russia reserves it to himself to give to this state, enjoying a distinct administration, such an internal extension as he shall deem advisable ;' and that article which says 'that the Poles, the respective subjects of the high contracting parties, shall obtain representation and national institutions, regulated in conformity with the mode of the political existence which each of the Governments to which they belong shall deem it expedient and proper to bestow upon them.' But the history of this period is not so remote that the remembrance can be lost of the position which Russia held at the termination of the European crisis which was brought to an end by the treaty of Vienna. From that time we should not be far from the truth if we affirmed that the 1st article of the treaty of Vienna was prepared by and directly emanated from his Majesty the Emperor Alexander I. The conversation with Lord Castlereagh cited by Lord Russell is an additional evidence of this fact.

"After saying this, the Principal Secretary of State of her Britannic Majesty will dispense us from giving an answer to the proposed arrangement for a suspension of hostilities. It would not resist a serious examination of the conditions necessary for carrying it into effect. If it were to be defined between whom it was to be negotiated, of what nature the *status quo* was to be which it would guarantee, and who was to watch over its execution, it would readily be perceived that the provisions of public law could not be applied to a situation which would be a flagrant violation of such law. His Majesty the Emperor owes to his faithful army, which struggles for the maintenance of order, to the peaceable majority of the Poles who suffer from these deplorable agitations, and to Russia, on whom they impose painful sacrifices, to take energetic measures to terminate them. Desirable as it may be speedily to place a term to the effusion of blood, this object can only be attained by the insurgents throwing down their arms and surrendering themselves to the clemency of the Emperor. Every other arrangement would be incompatible with the dignity of our august master, and with the sentiments of the Russian nation. It would, besides, have a result diametrically opposed to the one recommended by Lord Russell. As to the idea of a conference of the eight powers who signed the treaty of Vienna, which should discuss the six points adopted as bases, it presents to us serious inconveniences, without our being able to see in it any advantage. If the measures in question are sufficient for the pacification of the country, a conference would be without object. If the measures were to be submitted to ulterior deliberation, there would result a direct interference of foreign powers in the most intimate details of the administration—an interference that no great power could admit, and which certainly England would not accept in her own affairs. Such an interference would be neither in the spirit nor in the letter of the treaties of Vienna, on the base of which we have invited the powers to a friendly exchange of ideas. It would result in removing still further the end which they propose to themselves by depriving the Government of its prestige and its authority, and by further increasing the pretensions and illusions of the Polish agitators. The course which was followed in 1815 appears to us to indicate clearly enough the nature of the deliberations which may take place upon questions bearing, on the one side, on the general interest, and on the other upon administrative details of the exclusive dominion of the neighbouring sovereign states. At that epoch a distinction was practically established between these two classes of interests; the first have been the object of separate negotiations on the part of the courts of Russia, Austria, and Prussia, between which the traditions of history, a permanent contact, and an immediate neighbourhood created a strict solidarity. All the arrangements destined to regulate the interior administration and the mutual relations of the Polish territories placed, since the congress of Vienna, under their respective dominions, have been laid down in treaties concluded directly between these three courts on April 21st (May 3rd), 1815. They have been successively completed by a series of special conventions whenever circumstances have required it. The general principles mentioned in these treaties, and which could interest Europe, have alone been inserted in the Act of the Congress of Vienna, signed on May 27th (June 8th), by all the powers invited to concur in it. At present it is not a question of these general principles, but the administrative details and ulterior arrangements would furnish useful matter for discussion by the three courts, in order to place the respective position of their Polish possessions, to which the stipulations of the treaties of 1815 extend, in harmony with present necessities and the progress of time. The Imperial Cabinet declares itself from the present time ready to enter into a similar understanding with the Cabinets of Vienna and Berlin. In any case the re-establishment of order is an indispensable condition, which must precede any serious application of the measures destined for the pacification of the kingdom. This condition depends greatly upon the resolution of the great powers not to lend themselves to calculations which the instigators of the Polish insurrection found on or expect from an active intervention in aid of their exaggerated aspirations. Clear and categorical language on the part of those powers would contribute to dissipate these illusions, and to thwart these calculations which tend to prolong the disorder and excitement of public opinion. They would thus bring nearer the moment which we invoke—that in which the tranquillization of passions and the return of material order will permit our august master to labour for the moral pacification of the country by putting into execution the measures which his Majesty maintains both in the germs already laid down, and in the development of them which he has allowed to be foreseen. Your Excellency will have the goodness to read and give a copy of this despatch to the principal Secretary of State of her Britannic Majesty. "Receive, &c., "GORTSCHAKOFF."

EARL RUSSELL TO LORD NAPIER.

"*Foreign Office, August* 11*th*, 1863.

"MY LORD,—On the 18th of last month Baron Brunnow communicated to me a despatch which he had received the evening before from Prince Gortschakoff.

"This despatch, of which I enclose a copy, is far from being a satisfactory answer to the representation which, in concert with France and Austria, her Majesty's Government addressed to the Cabinet of St. Petersburg.

"The despatch begins, indeed, by stating that 'the Imperial Cabinet admits the principle that every power signing a treaty has a right to interpret its sense from its own point of view, provided that the interpretation remains within the limits of the meaning that it is possible to put upon it according to the text itself.' Prince Gortschakoff adds, 'In virtue of this principle, the Imperial Cabinet does not dispute this right on the part of any one of the eight powers which have concurred in the general act of Vienna of 1815.'

"Prince Gortschakoff, however, departing widely from the question of the interpretation of the treaty of Vienna, proceeds to ascribe the continuance of the insurrection in Poland to the moral and material assistance which it receives from without; admits vaguely the six points; rejects the proposed suspension of hostilities; refuses to accept a conference of the eight powers who signed the treaty; and, finally, declares that the re-establishment of order must precede the serious application of any measures destined for the pacification of Poland.

"Her Majesty's Government will now proceed to examine calmly the principal topics of Prince Gortschakoff's reply to the considerations brought before him in my despatch.

"1. Prince Gortschakoff, while he admits that confidence on the part of the governed, and the ascendancy of law over arbitrary power, must be the foundation of order and stability, adds that the indispensable corollary to these principles is respect for authority. But the Russian Cabinet cannot be ignorant that clemency and conciliation are often more effective in establishing respect for authority than material force. It would be a lamentable error to seek to restore that respect by force of arms alone, without the addition of some adequate security for the political and religious rights of the subjects of the king of Poland. Such security the proposals of the three powers held out to Russia and to Poland alike.

"It has pleased the Cabinet of St. Petersburg not to avail itself of this mode of restoring respect for authority.

"2. Prince Gortschakoff affirms—and this view is the theme of the beginning and end of his despatch—that the re-establishment of order in Poland is dependent upon a condition to which he had called the attention of the Government of her Britannic Majesty, 'and which is not only unfulfilled, but is not even alluded to in the despatch of Lord Russell; we refer to the material assistance and moral encouragements obtained from abroad by the insurgents.'

"Her Majesty's Government would have been glad to have avoided this topic, and, instead of commenting on the past, to refer only to healing measures for the future.

"But, thus compelled by Prince Gortschakoff's reference to allude to the subject, her Majesty's Government have no hesitation in declaring their conviction that the principal obstacle to the re-establishment of order in Poland is not the assistance obtained by the insurgents from abroad, but the conduct of the Russian Government itself.

"The Empress Catherine in 1772 promised to the Poles the maintenance of their religion. The Emperor Alexander I. in 1815 promised to the Poles national representation and national administration.

"These promises have not been fulfilled. During many years the religion of the Poles was attacked, and to the present hour they are not in possession of the political rights assured to them by the treaty of 1815, and the constitution of the same year.

"The violation of these solemn engagements on the part of the Russian Government produced disaffection, and the sudden invasion of the homes of Warsaw, in a night of January last, was the immediate cause of the present insurrection.

"Unless the general feeling in Poland had been estranged from Russia, the moral and material assistance afforded from abroad would have availed the insurgents little. It is true, however, that lively sympathy has been excited in Europe in favour of the Poles. In every considerable state where there exists a national representation—in England, in France, in Austria, in Prussia, in Italy, in Spain, in Portugal, in Sweden, in Denmark—that sympathy has been manifested. Wherever there is a national administration, the administration has shared, though with prudence and reserve in expression, the feelings of the legislature and the nation.

"Russia ought to take into account these sympathies, and profit by the lesson which they teach.

"3. Prince Gortschakoff lays much stress on the fact, which cannot be denied, that 'the insurgents demand neither an amnesty, nor an autonomy, nor a representation more or less complete.'

"But it would be a mistake to suppose that in cases of this kind there are only two parties, viz., the Government occupied in suppressing the insurrection, and the leaders of the insurgents, busy in fomenting and extending it. Besides these parties there is always in such cases a large floating mass who would be quite contented to see persons and property secure under a just and beneficent administration. The confidence of this great mass has not been obtained, and their continued inaction can hardly be depended upon.

"Her Majesty's Government must again represent the extreme urgency of attempting at once the work of conciliation which is so necessary for the general interest.

"In profiting by the loyal and disinterested assistance which is offered her by Austria, France, and Great Britain, the Court of Russia secures to herself the most powerful means towards making ideas of moderation prevail in Poland, and thus laying the foundations of permanent peace.

"4. In referring to the treaty of Vienna, Prince Gortschakoff says that 'we should not be far from the truth if we affirmed that the first article of the treaty of Vienna was prepared by and directly emanated from his Majesty the Emperor Alexander I.'

"Her Majesty's Government readily admit the probability of this supposition. In 1815, Great Britain, Austria, France, and Prussia would have preferred to the arrangement finally made a restoration of the ancient kingdom of Poland as it existed prior to the first partition of 1772, or even the establishment of a new independent kingdom of Poland, with the same limits as the present kingdom.

"The great army which the Emperor Alexander then had in Poland, the important services which Russia had rendered to the alliance, and, above all, a fear of the renewal of war in Europe, combined to make Great Britain, Austria, and Prussia accept the arrangement proposed by the Emperor Alexander, although it was, in their eyes, of the three arrangements in contemplation, the one least likely to produce permanent peace and security in Europe.

"But the more her Majesty's Government see in the decision adopted the prevailing influence of Russia, the more they are impressed with the conviction that the Emperor of Russia ought to be, of all sovereigns, the most desirous to observe the conditions of that arrangement.

"It would not be open to Russia to enjoy all the benefits of a large addition to her dominions, and to repudiate the terms of the instrument upon which her tenure depends.

"In stating these terms Prince Gortschakoff says that the only stipulation which can have made it appear doubtful that the Emperor of Russia possessed the kingdom of Poland by the same title as that by which he holds his other possessions, the only one which could make his rights dependent upon any condition whatever, is contained in two passages which he proceeds to quote.

"But there is another passage which he does not quote. It is found in the beginning of the first article, and says :—

"'The duchy of Warsaw, with the exception of the provinces and districts which are otherwise disposed of by the following articles, is united to the Russian empire, to which it shall be irrevocably attached by its constitution, and be possessed by his Majesty the Emperor of all the Russias, his heirs and successors, in perpetuity.'

"Were not a national representation intended by this article, it would have been sufficient to say, 'to which it shall be irrevocably attached,' without any mention of a constitution.

"It is therefore evident that the constitution is the link by which Poland was connected with Russia. It is important to know what this constitution was which united Poland and Russia. It was not prescribed by the treaty; it was not promulgated by the European powers; its construction was left entirely to the Emperor Alexander; but nevertheless, when once promulgated, it must be taken to be the constitution meant by the framers of the treaty of Vienna.

"It was for this reason that her Majesty's Government proposed as the second of the six points laid before the Government of Russia, 'national representation with powers similar to those which are fixed by the charter of the 15th (27th) November, 1815.'

"5. Passing to the specific propositions of her Majesty's Government, Prince Gortschakoff says, in regard to the six points, that the greater part of the measures which were pointed out by the three powers ' have already been either decreed or prepared on the initiative of our august master.'

"Towards the end of the despatch an allusion is made to ' the measures which his Majesty adheres to, both in the germs already laid down, and in the development of them which he has allowed to be foreseen.'

"This passage, though far from being a definite assurance either of a national representation with efficacious means of control, or of a national administration, gives some hope that the Emperor Alexander will ultimately listen to the inspirations of his own benevolent disposition and to the counsels of Europe.

"The proposal of a suspension of hostilities is rejected, 'in justice to the Emperor's faithful army, to the peaceable majority of Poles, and to Russia, on whom these agitations impose painful sacrifices.'

"The proposal of a conference of the powers who signed the treaty of Vienna is rejected, and with it the prospect of an immediate and friendly concert.

"In the place of this fair and equitable proposal, the Russian Cabinet suggests that the three powers who proposed the separate treaties between Austria and Russia, and Prussia and Russia, previously to the general treaty of Vienna, should meet together, and that France and Great Britain should be afterwards informed of the result of their deliberations.

"There are two reasons, either of which would be sufficient to condemn this suggestion :—

"1. The treaties in question, taken apart from the provisions inserted in the general treaty of Vienna, have reference only to material objects—the use of the banks of rivers, the regulations for towing-paths, the free passage of merchandise from one province to another, and such other matters of convenience and of commerce. No political developments or details are contained in them.

"2. It is obvious that such a conference would place Austria in a false position, and be inconsistent with her relations to France and Great Britain.

"His Majesty the Emperor of Austria, therefore, with a proper sense of his own dignity, has at once rejected the Russian proposal.

"In communicating their views to Prince Gortschakoff, it remains to her Majesty's Government to discharge an imperative duty.

"It is to call his Excellency's most serious attention to the gravity of the situation, and the responsibility which it imposes upon Russia.

"Great Britain, Austria, and France have pointed out the urgent necessity of putting an end to a deplorable state of things which is full of danger to Europe. They have at the same time indicated the means which, in their opinion, ought to be employed to arrive at this termination, and they have offered their co-operation in order to attain it with more certainty.

"If Russia does not perform all that depends upon her to further the moderate and conciliatory views of the three powers, if she does not enter upon the path which is opened to her by friendly counsels, she makes herself responsible for the serious consequences which the prolongation of the troubles of Poland may produce. "I am, &c., -

(Signed) "RUSSELL."

PRINCE GORTSCHAKOFF TO BARON BRUNNOW.

(Translation.)

"*Tsarkoe-Selo, August 26th (Sept. 7th)*, 1863."

"LORD NAPIER has, by order of his Government, communicated to me a despatch from Lord Russell, of which your Excellency will find a copy hereunto annexed.

"It is in answer to my despatch of the 1st (13th) July last, which you were invited to communicate to the Principal Secretary of State of her Britannic Majesty.

"The overtures which we had set forth in that document were dictated to us by the desire to arrive at an understanding.

"In receiving the observations which they have suggested to Lord Russell with the attention which we always pay to the opinions of her Britannic Majesty's Government, we cannot but regret that we must come to the conclusion that we have not attained the end which we had proposed to ourselves.

"From the moment that this discussion could only end in establishing and in confirming the divergence of our views, it would be too contrary to our conciliatory disposition for us to seek to prolong it; and we believe that in this we are not acting at variance with the sentiments of the Principal Secretary of State of her Britannic Majesty.

"We prefer to fix our attention only upon the essential points of his despatches, upon which we find ourselves agreed, at least in intention.

"Her Britannic Majesty's Government desire to see promptly re-established in the kingdom of Poland a state of things which shall restore tranquillity to that country, repose to Europe, and security to the relations of the cabinets.

"We entirely share in this desire, and all that can depend upon us shall be done to realize it.

"Our august master continues to be animated by the most benevolent intentions towards Poland, and by the most conciliatory towards all foreign powers. To provide for the welfare of his subjects of all races and of every religious conviction is an obligation which his Imperial Majesty has accepted before God, his conscience, and his people. The Emperor devotes all his solicitude to the fulfilment of that obligation.

As regards the responsibility which may be assumed by his Majesty in his international relations, those relations are regulated by public right. The violation of those fundamental principles can alone involve responsibility. Our august master has constantly respected and observed those principles with regard to other states. His Majesty has the right to expect and to claim the same respect on the part of the other powers.

"You will be pleased to read and give a copy of this despatch to the Principal Secretary of State of her Britannic Majesty.

"Receive, &c.,

"Gortschakoff."

Accompanying this despatch, a copy of the following memorandum was presented to Lord Russell :—

MEMORANDUM.

The powers which have expressed to the Cabinet of St. Petersburg their wishes and opinions relative to the troubles in the kingdom of Poland have taken for their starting-point the treaty of 1815.

According to all the known rules of international right, and even in virtue of the more modern principle of non-intervention, their diplomatic proceedings could have no other basis.

It is, then, only within the limits of this treaty that the discussion should be confined relative to the questions of right belonging to the kingdom of Poland.

Treaties should be interpreted in their letter and in their spirit.

The treaty of 1815, notwithstanding the caution observed in its formation, in order to spare and to conciliate different opinions and interests, is, however, sufficiently precise in its terms to leave but a very small space for differences of opinion.

If we desire to deduce the precise meaning of this document from the spirit by which it was dictated, it must be judged by the ideas and circumstances prevailing at the period in which it was concluded, and not by those to which it is now attempted to give the ascendancy.

Let us see what was the position of the duchy of Warsaw at the time of the congress ; it was as follows :—

In 1812, Russia had conquered and occupied the duchy of Warsaw by its unassisted power, by the incontestable right of war. She had retaken it from Saxony, an ally of the power with which she was in declared hostility.

She had the greater right to consider it as a legitimate and irrevocable conquest, as the duchy of Warsaw had not only been the theatre of war : it had also taken an active part in the foremost rank of the enemies of Russia ; it had furnished numerous contingents to the power which had invaded the territory of the Empire ; it had served as the basis of its operations.

Russia was fully justified in a moral and political, as well as in a legal point of view, in wishing to rid itself, once for all, of a permanent menace to its security.

The Emperor Alexander I. had, nevertheless, been restrained by two considerations :

First, he had seen in the hostility of the Poles a moral evil requiring other than material remedies for its extirpation.

It is a law of human nature that each generation acts under the dominion of sentiments and impulses which are often forgotten by the following generation. Placing itself in antagonism to it, the latter frequently undoes the work of its predecessors.

The Empress Catherine II., living nearer to the period of the struggles between Poland and Russia, influenced by their traditions and the duties they imposed on her, a witness of their calamities, had adopted the policy of separation as an inexorable necessity. The Emperor Alexander I., beholding the consequences of this policy, the animosity and the agitation of the Poles, attributed them exclusively to the fact of the separation, and was led to think of remedying this state of things. This idea, conceived in his youth, had grown with him; towards the end of the year 1812 he had asked himself whether the time had not arrived for Russia to extinguish this hotbed of hatred and disorder in his vicinity, by raising Poland and rendering it a reconciled and allied nation. But he would not proceed in this until the great work he had begun was completed. This was the meaning of the words he addressed to the Poles. "My intentions have not changed," said he, "but I shall await the conclusion of the struggle." "It is as conqueror that I will regenerate Poland." This work—and this was the second motive which influenced his resolutions in respect to the duchy of Warsaw—this work was the deliverance of Europe, and the great design of consolidation which the calamities of twenty-five years' war had implanted in his soul; the design whose inspiration gave the energetic impulses of the years 1813, 1814, 1815.

Under this impression, the Emperor Alexander I. desired to set an example of self-denial and disinterestedness, and to remove every element that might disturb the union he wished to establish with the great powers.

It had been already arranged at Kalisch, on the 16th (28th) of February, 1813, in the course of the negotiations with the Cabinet of Berlin, "to unite ancient Prussia to Silesia, by a territory which should answer this end perfectly in every respect, military as well as geographical."

During the negotiations of Görlitz with Austria, the 1st (13th) May, 1813, this power had stipulated for "the annihilation of the duchy of Warsaw."

By the treaty of Töplitz, the 28th of August (9th of September), 1813, it was agreed "that an amicable arrangement between the three courts should determine the fate of the duchy of Warsaw."

Finally, in all the treaties subsequently completed and settled by the alliance, the Emperor Alexander I., generously forgetting that the duchy of Warsaw had been conquered by the arms of Russia alone, from an enemy in whose ranks Prussia and Austria then figured, had admitted the principle that "the fate of conquered territories should be ultimately settled in a congress which should be assembled at Vienna."

Such was the attitude in which the Emperor Alexander I. presented himself to the congress, after the accomplishment of the great work to which he had devoted himself.

It is incorrect to allege that the Polish question occupied the first place in these memorable deliberations It had a marked place, thanks to the disinterestedness of the Emperor Alexander I., but did not hold the only place, nor the first. The fate of all Europe, and almost that of the whole world, was then to be settled. If the chief discussion was on the questions of Saxony and Poland, it was because Russia and Prussia had neglected to stipulate for themselves at Paris in 1814, immediately after the victory, and had neglected their own interests in the general interest : it is also because they did not think of opposing either the views of England or those of Austria, while questions which interested them excited ill-feeling.

In the general settlement of affairs, England obtained considerable aggrandisement : Malta, the Cape, the Isle of France, the island of Heligoland, and several important colonies, were adjudged to her. She had also caused her views and her interests to predominate in Europe, particularly by the creation of the kingdom of the Netherlands, which included the important question of Antwerp.

Austria was aggrandised in the Tyrol, in Lombardy, in Venice, in Dalmatia—she ruled Italy. Prussia itself, although not seeking an element for compensation, succeeded in establishing the principle of the restoration of her possessions of 1805, with a more compact and more homogeneous geographical configuration.

It would have been strange that at the time when all the great powers of Europe obtained such increase of territory, Russia alone—Russia which had been the first to shake the conquering power against which all Europe was contending Russia, which had given the signal for the struggle for general independence, which had devoted herself to it at the price of the greatest sacrifices, and which had been the connecting link between the great European alliance—should have been deprived of every species of advantage and compensation.

She did not even demand aggrandisement ; but the power of carrying out an intention of pacification and reparation, of closing a long-standing wound by restoring to reconciled Poland a national existence under the sceptre of the sovereigns of Russia.

The resistance the Emperor Alexander encountered in this path from his allies was certainly one of his most painful disappointments. This resistance was of a very complex nature.

On a careful examination of the documents of the period, there is only one conclusion to be arrived at ; it is, that the powers who opposed themselves to the realization of the wishes of the Emperor Alexander I. were in no degree actuated by solicitude for Poland. She then weighed but little in the balance of interests, and the clamour that had been made around her was lost in the momentous crisis that was taking place in Europe.

That which the allies feared was the aggrandisement of the power which had now revealed itself with so much splendour.

It was feared that the addition of Poland, uniting under the same sceptre the greater part of the population of the Sclavonian race, would double the material and moral power of Russia, and carry its advanced posts to the heart of Germany and of Europe. The event has not justified these anticipations, but they are evident at every step in the documents of the epoch.

The powers would then have preferred, in deference to views which were purely theoretic, the re-establishing a Poland which should have been completely independent. But this independent Poland could only be re-established at the expense of the three partitioning powers, and it would have been inadmissible that, immediately after the glorious struggle to the success of which Russia had materially contributed with so much energy, while the other victorious powers derived from it ample advantages, the proposal could have been seriously made to her that she should subscribe to her own dismemberment.

Lord Castlereagh declared "that such a combination would impose sacrifices so great that the British Cabinet would never have thought of making the proposal; that the only means of avoiding new troubles would be to persevere in the system of partition, and that it appeared to him that no power could desire the maintenance of this system more than Russia."

Prussia and Austria opposed themselves to the re-establishment even of the name of Poland. Prince Metternich said, in a conference of the 15th (27th) September, 1814 : "The consequence of a war would unfortunately be still easier to foresee if, as is supposed, the Emperor Alexander should intend to lend himself to the accomplishment of the ideas of some Poles, by giving to these new acquisitions the name of Poland. Under this supposition we must consider Galicia as lost to us, and this question is therefore more important than that of territory. It comprehends all the elements of future troubles, and is entirely contrary to existing treaties, the tripartite powers having at the time of the partition pledged their word no longer to make use of that name."

On his side Chancellor Hardenberg, in the same conference, enlarged especially " on the danger that equally menaced Prussia should the name of Poland be given to the acquisitions of Russia."

It was only at a later period, when the Emperor Alexander I. had testified a resolution not to draw back even in case of war, and that to avoid such an extremity by carrying conciliation to the utmost possible limits, he had consented to agree on the questions of Posen, Cracow, and the saltmines of Wieliczka, as well as on the question of Saxony; it was not till then that the powers, unwilling to be behindhand in demonstrations of sympathy towards Poland, finally agreed to the propositions of the Emperor, propositions reduced very considerably from those of his original design.

It would be committing a grave error to allege that those conditions which governed the arrangements then made were in their liberal character dictated to Russia at the conclusion of preliminary conferences having a European character.

First one may repeat that it was not at the time when Russia had taken so considerable and so decisive a part in the affairs of Europe, and when all her strength weighed down the balance, that the Emperor Alexander I., who possessed in the highest degree the conviction of his sovereign dignity, would have permitted such interference in the internal administration of a portion of his dominions.

On the contrary, he peremptorily opposed all discussion on the constitution he intended giving to the Poles reunited under his sceptre.

But more than this. It may be affirmed that the initiative of liberal intentions emanated from the Emperor Alexander I., and that the resistance to his intentions proceeded from the other powers.

With the exception of England, which had long lived under a constitutional government, the generality of the powers were unfavourable to these ideas.

The trials attempted in some of the German states were very incomplete. Prussia had adjourned all reforms of this kind. As to Austria, no government was further removed from constitutional principles.

In this state of things it cannot be supposed that these principles could have been imposed on, or even recommended to, the Emperor in respect of Poland.

Far from this being the case, the powers were seriously engaged in considering the bearing of the Emperor's views, and the rebound which might result from it in their own Polish possessions.

Chancellor Hardenberg said, in a memoir transmitted to Prince Metternich on 2nd December:—

"The affair of Poland is reduced to the widening of the aggressive boundary and the preventing of the political existence of the new kingdom from becoming hurtful to the tranquillity of its neighbours and of Europe, and making it rather turn to their profit. It is necessary then, in the first place, to demand of the Emperor Alexander of what nature the existence and the constitution of the new kingdom are to be, what guarantees he will give to the neighbouring powers, and also what he will require on their part."

Now, the guarantees which the Emperor Alexander first demanded of his neighbours were to secure to the Poles under their dominion institutions conformable to the popular wishes.

This demand was formally made by Count Razoumowski, the 10th of December, in a proposal in which it was said:—

"When this deduction is made . . . . . the rest of the duchy of Warsaw has devolved to the Russian crown as a united territory to which his Majesty reserves to himself the right of giving a national constitution, and what extension of boundaries he may judge fit.

"The Emperor of Russia, desiring to make all the Poles participate in the benefits of a national administration, *intercedes* with his allies in favour of their subjects of this nation, with the design of obtaining for them provincial institutions which may preserve proper respect for their nationality, and give them a share in the administration of their country."

The counter-project, presented January 3rd, 1815, by Austria, indicated the views by which that power was animated. It bore:—

"The duchy of Warsaw shall be re-united to the dominions of his Majesty the Emperor of all the Russias, to be possessed by him in full property and sovereignty."

Thus this project carefully excluded every allusion to the kingdom of Poland as *a state united to Russia,* to a *national constitution,* and to the *provincial institutions* which the Russian scheme proposed to bestow on the Polish subjects of the three Courts.

These explanations preceded by some days the notes of Lord Castlereagh and Prince Metternich, from which the inference has been deduced that the powers represented by these two plenipotentiaries testified their sympathy with the Poles, and recommended the Emperor of Russia to respect their nationality. This fact proves that the initiative of sympathy for Poland emanated from the Emperor Alexander I., and that if the other powers rallied round it, it was because the principles of the policy of the times cautioned them against leaving to Russia the merit of this initiative, and counselled them to divide it with her, in order to lessen the overwhelming strength which they feared to see this power acquire, and which they would otherwise be unable to prevent.

They did not foresee, doubtless, at that time, the embarrassments which would be occasioned to Russia by the tendencies the Poles would find in Europe.

It is argued that *it was of little consequence that these engagements should have emanated from the initiative of the Emperor of Russia, from the moment they were contracted by him.* On the contrary, these considerations are of essential consequence, because they mark precisely both the nature of the engagements taken by the Emperor of Russia and the aim of the rights which are alleged to flow from the powers of the mind which presided in the transactions of 1815.

The assertion, amongst others, must fail that the liberal intentions manifested by the Emperor Alexander I. were a motive for adhering to the reunion of Poland to Russia. It clearly results from what has preceded, that it is the contrary which is true; that the Emperor Alexander I. would have encountered fewer obstacles had he renounced the revival of the Polish name and the Polish nationality; and had he confined himself to insisting on the territorial question, which nominally the court of Vienna put down as a secondary one, and had he incorporated purely and simply the duchy of Warsaw with his other dominions.

It is both possible and probable that *the fear of rekindling the war had* (as has been affirmed) *great effect in this adhesion of the powers.*

But this desire of preserving peace was entirely for their own interest. They were emerging from twenty-five years of war; they were principally indebted to Russia for their deliverance; they knew the enormous power she had possessed in this war, and the power she might yet throw into the scale, should the work of pacification to which she had so energetically contributed be once more shaken.

As to the arguments which are endeavoured to be drawn of the intentions of the Emperor Alexander I., they do not appear to us to bear profound examination. These illusions of a generous mind, and the disappointments in which they resulted, teach a useful lesson, but could constitute no engagement. The Emperor Alexander I. made an attempt at conciliation. He did not succeed. He stopped before the obstacles revealed to him by experience, which showed that the institutions with which he had endowed the kingdom were so many weapons placed in the hands of the Poles, and that they would use them only to attain the aim of their chimerical aspirations, that is to say, the reconstitution of a Poland in the most extended sense, independent, at the price of the dismemberment of three mighty neighbouring powers.

Morally, the promise he had made to the Poles was annulled by the use they had made of his gifts. Materially, the international engagement he had contracted was limited by the treaty of 1815. These limits were ascertained by a stipulation which one passes over willingly in silence: it is that which reserves to the three Courts the right of settling the representative and national institutions of their Polish subjects after the manner they shall judge it fit and suitable to grant.

Animated as he then was by liberal intentions, which were not bounded by the frontiers of the kingdom of Poland, the Emperor Alexander I. appears not to have thought of putting this reservation in form. He was led to do so by the scruples of the Cabinet of Vienna. The Austrian plenipotentiaries, on presenting their counter-project in the conference, accompanied it by verbal observations, which, on the demand of the Emperor, were embodied in the form of the article, in which it was said that "the Poles are the qualified subjects of the high contracting powers, and considered as such under their distinct denominations, and in this quality, and according to the forms of political existence which each Government shall judge fit to grant them, they shall obtain the institutions which secure the preservation of their nationality."

This was the root of the reservation stipulated afterwards in article 1 of the definitive treaty. The idea which inspired the Emperor Alexander is easily deduced.

That sovereign never intended to cause revolution, but conservation. He was convinced that to satisfy the just wishes of the people by an enlightened and beneficent administration was to disarm the revolution. He wished authority to be loved, in order that it might be more respected. Every act of the Emperor Alexander I. bears the impress of this conviction. Even in 1820, when his faith in the realization of this principle began to be shaken, whilst he concurred energetically in the suppression of the revolutionary movement of Naples, he suggested, by his advice to the king of the Two Sicilies, a wisely liberal constitution, and invited the Italian princes to unite in adopting analogous principles in the government of their dominions. With such views it could not enter into the intentions of the Emperor to weaken in any degree the sovereign authority, either in his own territory or in that of others, which would have been the case had the powers which possessed parts of Poland been compelled to govern their Polish subjects according to the principles they would have judged compatible with the condition of their other possessions. The kingdom of Poland being indissolubly united to Russia, as Posen and Galicia are irrevocably attached to Prussia and Austria, these possessions were subjected to conditions which were indispensable to the unity of the three powers of which they made part. Prussia and Austria had exacted these guarantees which the Emperor Alexander I. could not think of refusing to them. He had then confined himself to stipulating that the Polish subjects of the three Courts should have national representation and institutions; he intended to apply them himself, and hoped to see them applied by the others in the widest sense; but he had expressly reserved to the three Governments the power of regulating them according to that form of existence they should judge it useful and suitable to grant.

The same considerations apply equally to the internal development which the Emperor Alexander I. had reserved himself the power to give to the kingdom of Poland. To infer from this an obligation would be to change the nature of the character of the stipulations, which, while evincing generous intentions, attest, on the other hand, to what a great extent the sentiment of dignity and sovereign independence was carried at this epoch. Doubtless, the idea of extending the frontiers of the kingdom of Poland had at one time occupied the mind of the Emperor; but the realization of it depended on the manner in which the Poles would justify on their part the hopes he had founded on this combination, and the Emperor had expressly reserved to himself the application of it *according to* what he might judge useful and suitable. It could not be otherwise. The argument that some pretend to draw from the denomination *Polish subjects*, in order to apply equally to the Polish inhabitants of the Western provinces of Russia the clause Art. 1, which stipulates in their favour representative and national institutions, is inadmissible. In these provinces the Poles hardly form a seventh part of the population. It is then evident that there the only *national institutions* are those of the majority. Besides, article 1 of the treaty of Vienna has so clearly established that these stipulations apply exclusively to the ancient duchy of Warsaw, *with the interior extension which the Emperor of Russia may judge suitable to give to it*, that the Imperial Government must peremptorily repel every allusion to provinces which do not constitute a part of it, and which are consequently shut out from the international engagements which might spring from the treaty of Vienna.

From these premises it results, that, whether we inquire into *the spirit* or *the letter* of the treaty of 1815, it is impossible to arrive at any other conclusions than the following:—

The kingdom of Poland is indissolubly united to Russia, with any internal extension that the Emperor of Russia may think fit to give it.

The Polish subjects of the three Courts are to have national institutions and representation, according to the species of political existence which each of the Governments to which they belong may judge useful and convenient to grant them.

The rights and the duties of all parties engaged in the question are perfectly limited by the terms of these stipulations.

The Poles of the Empire should respect the ties which bind them to Russia.

It is the duty of foreign powers to do nothing to weaken these ties.

The three Courts are under obligation to grant to their Polish subjects national representation and institutions, administered according to their own judgment.

This is the position which springs from the treaties of Vienna.

The Emperor Alexander I. saw fit to give to the Polish subjects of his kingdom the institutions specified by the constitution of 1815. He might have clothed them in another form, and given them more or less extension, provided they preserved a national and representative character. The terms of this constitution were not, could not be, obligatory.

The Congress of Vienna had wisely recognized this in leaving the institutions to be granted to the free choice of the sovereigns.

The argument drawn from the fact that, according to the text of the 1st article, the kingdom of Poland is bound to Russia *by its constitution*, is not admissible. It is erroneously concluded from this that if the powers had not had in view a certain *constitution* they would have confined themselves to saying that the kingdom of Poland is bound to Russia, without adding the words *by its constitution.*

But, besides that the word constitution had not then the meaning now assigned to it, it would be more exact to conclude that if the powers had in view a *certain constitution*, they would have defined it with precision, since they must have guaranteed it.

The preparatory conferences which were summoned were confined to general principles—they did not, they could not, bear on details of internal administration, or on any particular form of constitution, necessarily variable according to time and place : it would have been entirely contrary to the ideas of the epoch. Neither of the three sovereigns would have admitted it. No foreign power would have proposed it.

The proof of this is, that the constitution of 1815 was promulgated nearly six months after the Congress, without having been communicated to either of the Cabinets ; it may be added that, when it was promulgated, many considered it too liberal.

There can, then, be no doubt on this question ; and even if there were any, the authority of Vattel, who decides that *in case of doubt the interpretation should be given against him " who dictated the law,"* could with difficulty be applied to it.

The Emperor Alexander I. no more intended to dictate the law than he intended to submit to it. That which occurred during the following years is sufficiently known. The Poles had not been in any way satisfied by the constitution accorded them by the Emperor Alexander I. They dreamed of the reconstitution and the independence of Poland in its ancient limits. Their Diets presented so factious a character that it was necessary to adjourn them, and secret societies multiplied. The Government of the Emperor Alexander I. is reproached with having restricted by decrees the exercise of the political rights which it had granted to the Poles.

It is certain that the agitations of Europe after the year 1820 had dispelled the illusions of this sovereign. It is possible that the novelty of constitutional principles and the struggles of the tribune which are the ordinary consequences of them, may have produced a strong impression on his mind, especially by the contrast they formed with the order subsisting in the rest of the empire. But while we admit these impressions, which were also produced in all European states, and everywhere complicated the relations between the government and the people, it is impossible to deny two facts.

The first is, that, in spite of these internal collisions, the kingdom of Poland, from 1815 to 1825, enjoyed a tranquillity and a prosperity which it had never before known.

The second is, that the Poles made a use of the liberties which had been granted them, showing the same factious spirit which had led to the loss of their political independence.

The French revolution of 1830 occurred.

The rebound which it had on Poland attests one truth ; namely, that it is not Poland which troubles the security of Europe, but the situation of Europe which invariably reacts on the tranquillity of Poland.

When the insurrection broke out in the kingdom, nearly the same facts were produced which we now witness. The insurgents called to their aid the sympathies of liberal Europe. Cabinets offered their diplomatic intervention. It was rejected. The Emperor Nicholas was firmly resolved to quell the rebellion. It was repressed. The Western powers protested against this repression in the name of the treaty of 1815, and insisted that the Polish constitution should be re-established as an international engagement. This demand was declined. The Imperial Government affirmed that the rebellion of the Poles had destroyed all engagements; that Russia, compelled to have recourse to war, had henceforth all the rights which conquest confers.

This theory was not agreed to by other cabinets. The Russian Government maintained it.

The international discussion had no other result. It would be fruitless now to recur to these controversies. The question is not how to recriminate as to the past, but how to resolve the difficulties of the present and to prepare a better future.

To effect this, it is important to define the present situation.

His Majesty the Emperor Alexander II., from the time of his accession to the throne, has given undeniable pledges of his liberal and reforming intentions.

The kingdom of Poland obtained institutions bearing the impress of this spirit.

Whatever judgment may be formed of these institutions, it must be acknowledged, first, that they endow the kingdom with an administrative autonomy, with a national government, and with a representation based on the principle of election.

The Emperor of Russia made use of his rights in tracing for these institutions the limits he judged suitable for the good of a country where it was desirable to avoid the melancholy experiences of the past, and for that of the empire, whose development, prepared by the care of the sovereign, was to be accomplished gradually.

Secondly. That these institutions constituted a marked amelioration for the present, and opened a path for progress in the future.

Now this was the moment chosen by the Polish agitators to raise the standard of revolt. This is a sufficient starting-point to enable us to define clearly the cause and the aim of this insurrection.

However, the three Courts of England, France, and Austria roused themselves at the troubles of Poland, in the name of the treaty of Vienna and the security of Europe. They concerted together to address representations to the Russian Government, and to express their desire for the prompt and durable pacification of the country.

The Imperial Cabinet deferred to this desire of an understanding, and consented to an exchange of amicable ideas on the basis and within the limits of the treaty of 1815.

The conciliatory overtures which it made in reply to the propositions of the three Courts met, *nevertheless*, with objections forwarded in their last despatches, which suggest the following observations :—

Firstly. It has been remarked, that, *if respect for authority is the indispensable condition of confidence and legality, it would be an error to believe that it is possible to restore respect for authority by the force of arms alone, without adding to it a corresponding security for the political and religious rights of the subjects.*

The Imperial Cabinet has always shared in these convictions. His Majesty the Emperor has so little sought in force alone the conditions of respect for his authority, that he has spontaneously endowed the kingdom of Poland with institutions granting to it an administrative autonomy based on representative and elective principles. His Majesty has loudly proclaimed his intention of maintaining and developing them.

But the grant of these institutions was precisely the signal for the insurrection, which even drew from it the arms for its organization and propagation. It follows evidently from this that the evil does not reside in the intentions attributed to the Government of employing force alone, nor in the absence of legitimate security for the subjects, but in the moral agitation and the insensate aspirations kept up by the permanent conspiracy abroad. These motives have prevented the application of the reforms granted by his Majesty the Emperor.

The Polish rebels, who wish for complete independence and the limits of 1772, are not contented with these institutions, any more than with the six points indicated by the three Courts. They declare this loudly.

It is then indispensable that before everything else the rebellion shall be subdued, and respect for authority re-established. There is not a government in Europe that has proceeded differently; not one which has admitted the possibility of concession before armed revolt. The history of all nations (even of those who now address themselves to Russia) offers numerous and recent proofs of this.

Secondly. The assertion of the Russian Government that, the insurrection of the kingdom of Poland is kept up by material and moral encouragement from abroad, has been the object of a refutation tending to prove—*That the principal obstacle to the re-establishment of order in Poland arises from the Russian Government not having fulfilled the promises which the Empress Catherine II. in 1772, and the Emperor Alexander I. in 1815, made to the Poles, as to the maintenance of their religion and their political rights, national representation and administration.* We cannot understand on what basis the assertion rests *that during a great number of years the Polish religion was attacked.* There is evidently here an appreciation of facts which is incorrect. In the kingdom of Poland, the predominant religion, which is Catholicism, enjoys a liberty to which few states in Europe offer the equivalent. This liberty is only bounded at the limits where it could degenerate into propagandism. Beyond this legitimate prohibition, the only restrictions on the full liberty of exercising the Catholic worship are those usual in almost every state in Europe, even in those where the Catholic religion is that of the State. These restrictions, which figure in almost all concordats, have for their object the limitation of the spiritual jurisdiction and direct relations of the Church of Rome. They are occasioned by the character of temporal sovereignty inherent in the papacy, which does not permit any sovereign to admit that his subjects can be placed under the authority of a foreign sovereign.

As to political institutions, those which the Emperor Alexander I. had granted to the kingdom of Poland produced results on which experience has pronounced. His Majesty Alexander II. granted to his subjects belonging to the kingdom of Poland representative and national institutions, such as he has judged useful and suitable, after the experience that had been acquired, having in view the well-being of the country, the generous principles of his Government towards the rest of his empire, and within the limits of his international engagements.

These liberal institutions did not prevent the insurrection: they gave the signal for it.

The fact of recruiting, which is assigned as the cause of the rising, was but the consequence of it.

The three powers, who address themselves to the Government, have sufficient means of information to know that the Polish movement had been fomented for a considerable period by the emigration; that it only awaited a favourable occasion, and especially that, two years before the measure of the recruitment, all was preparing for the outbreak. The recruitment, which was not a violation of the law, but the application of the ancient custom which the new law had not yet definitively replaced, aimed only at baffling and defeating these machinations. It may have served as the pretext for the insurrection, but it would be incorrect to assert that it was the cause of it.

Thirdly. The cause is deeper and more inveterate—it partly resides in the "*sympathy which in England, in France, in Prussia, in Italy, in Spain, in Portugal, in Sweden, in Denmark, wherever a national administration exists, is pointed out as having been manifested towards the Poles, although with prudence and reserve.*"

Without denying that these evidences have been the result of very pressing diplomatic action, and that the prudence and reserve which characterize them have been carried by several Governments to the point of not transgressing the limits of a humane wish, accompanied by assurances of confidence in his Majesty the Emperor, yet it cannot be contested that they have exercised an influence on Poland, which is much to be regretted.

Fourthly. It has been attempted to explain this by different motives. It has been endeavoured to establish a difference *between the efforts of a people defending its nationality, making an appeal to all that is most lofty in the heart of man, to ideas of justice, of country, and of religion, and the disordered aspirations of unhealthy minds attacking the very basis of social order.* It has been observed on another side, "*that in cases of this kind there are not two parties only, viz., the Government occupied in suppressing the insurrection, and the leaders of the insurgents engaged in fomenting and extending it. But that, besides these parties, there is always in such cases a large floating mass who would be quite contented to see persons and property secured under a just and beneficent administration.*"

From the moment when the insurgent Poles, who pillage, hang, assassinate, torture, ravage, and terrorize their country, shall be considered as defending all that is most sacred in the heart of man—the ideas of country, nationality, and religion,—it would be perfectly useless to discuss the question of rights founded on treaties. It would remain only a question of strength between Governments possessing subjects of different races and different religion, and people aspiring to free themselves from all the ties created by history and by treaties. The map of the world must be re-drawn on principles entirely new, and escaping all criticism, because they have not undergone the trial of experience.

The distinction attempted to be established between the disturbers of public repose and the masses who live by repose and by work, and are essentially conservative, is perfectly just.

The Russian Government has relied on, and still continues to rely on, *that great floating mass* to bring back the kingdom of Poland to the condition of order and tranquillity indispensable to its prosperity and to the application of useful reforms. But it is precisely there also that its efforts have been paralyzed by external influences.

It is impossible not to be amazed by seeing that Governments, which could not be suspected of favouring revolution, could be brought to support the same cause as its most accredited organs and its most ardent leaders ; that Governments attached to the maintenance of the European equilibrium founded on the treaties of 1815, and who took the text of these treaties for the starting-point of their diplomatic intervention, should have been brought to defend the same cause as the Polish insurgents, and the party of the cosmopolitan revolution, who dream aloud of the re-establishment of Polish independence with the boundaries of 1772, and a general derangement of Europe, that is to say, the negation and the destruction of the state of things founded on treaties.

These anomalies must necessarily have unsettled minds already over-excited by the appeal to traditions of national independence, always so easy to be aroused. They contributed to confirm the illusions of a crusade composed of almost all the powers of Europe to attain an aim diametrically opposed to the interests and to the views of the majority of these very powers.

This illusion has precisely acted on *this great floating mass* which is everywhere hostile to disorder, and which is the healthy and solid medium on which a just and enlightened government may place the prosperity of a country by the application of measures destined to guarantee the security of persons and property.

This mass is not ignorant of the fact that it can only expect these guarantees from the authority of Government, and not from the powers of an anarchy contending for the right to pillage and oppress the country. With very few exceptions, it has never favoured disorder, unless when constrained to do so by violence, executions, and terror. It has remained, and will remain, the firm stay of the Russian Government, despite the weight of revolutionary pressure.

But in this mass there are credulous and timid minds easily led astray, and on whom the excitements from without, the goading of the press, and above all, the comments circulated on the subject of the diplomatic action and the intentions of foreign powers, must necessarily exercise influence. The agitators of the kingdom of Poland have been careful not to neglect this means of drawing away the weak and the undecided, by making them anticipate as immediate the active intervention of foreign powers in favour of their most extreme aspirations. These seductions on the one side, and on the other the terrorism of a secret committee, shrinking from no crime, have contributed to swell the ranks of insurrection, and to multiply the number of victims.

The Powers were thus unintentionally induced to work directly against the aim they had in view. Whilst they demanded of the Russian Government the speedy pacification of the kingdom of Poland, their diplomatic action, designed (*exploitée*) and perverted by the chiefs of the rebellion, became the principal obstacle to the restoration of tranquillity, by favouring the attempts made to deprive the Russian Government of the concurrence of the masses.

Consequently, instead of affirming that *the moral and material assistance from abroad would have influenced the insurrection but little if the general feeling had not been alienated from* Russia, it would be more correct to acknowledge that public feeling would not have been led to err without the moral support which the insurgents derived from the attitude and the diplomatic intervention of foreign powers.

This influence is incontestable ; it is clearly revealed by the fluctuations manifested in the disposition of the minds of the kingdom, according to the manner in which foreign diplomacy appeared to favour or to discourage the hopes of the revolution. It manifests itself now still more clearly, when the masses, disabused, wearied with the disorders, the crimes, and the terrorism of the Central Committee, manifest more and more their aversion to these enemies of public repose.

It cannot, then, be doubted that the problem which agitates the kingdom of Poland, preoccupies Russia, and interests Europe, will be near its solution when the attitude and the language of those powers who desire only the good of the country, the peace and security of Europe, shall be calculated to prove in the eyes of the Poles that they do not intend to favour the dream of the reconstruction of one great and independent Poland, the realization of which could only be accomplished by the dismemberment of three mighty powers and a general conflagration ; that they intend to maintain the order of things founded on treaties ; and that the Poles must expect national prosperity alone from an indissoluble union with Russia under a just and beneficent monarch, from the application and the regular working of the institutions which have been granted to them, from the progressive development which the sovereign has given them reason to foresee, and for which every act of his reign, and the actual tendencies of his government, offer a secure pledge.

5thly. It is useless to return to the amnesty and suspension of hostilities proposed by the three powers. *It is affirmed that the suspension of hostilities was not impracticable ; that a great country cannot derive dignity from prolonging unequal strife ; that the most bitter enemies of Russia would not have dared to violate the armistice ; that the trial deserved to have been made, and would have honoured those who had attempted it ; in short, that an amnesty subordinate to the political usages of the Russian Government, could not influence the disposition of the Poles, as is attested by the trifling effect of the last amnesty.*

It is sufficient to state that there may be different opinions on questions of dignity, but that each government must be the sole judge of its own. Even had the insurgent Poles not violated the armistice, they would certainly have profited by it to complete their armament and their organization. A government has too much responsibility to stake its honour on experiments which could end only in prolonging deplorable struggles in which blood too precious to be lavished must flow. As to an amnesty, if that spontaneously granted by the Emperor has not influenced the dispositions of the Poles, why should the proposed amnesty have produced more effect? If, on account of being offered and guaranteed by foreign powers, it must be acknowledged that the Russian Government was right in preferring making it subordinate to its own political convenience rather than to that of foreigners.

6thly. As to the conference, it is affirmed that *from the moment when the Russian Government admits the right of interpretation by the powers who sign a treaty, it must admit that these powers have the right to unite together to exercise it. All that can be granted to it in such matters is the material fact that its refusal to take part in such reunion would render it impossible.*

Had it been a question of modifying the fundamental principles of the treaty of Vienna, there is no doubt that the Congress ought to have seized it. But it was a question only of the application of these principles, and it is impossible to deny that any discussion relating to this would have touched upon the most intimate details of the administration. It would have been necessary to state precisely the character which constitutes *national* institutions, the mode and degree of representation, the competency of representative assemblies, the electoral census, &c. Questions more delicate or interference more direct cannot be imagined. A government which could have accepted it would have virtually given up its authority into the hands of the conference.

The proposition substituted by the Russian Government, that of an agreement of the three neighbouring powers, the result of which should be made known to those who signed the treaty of 1815, does not appear to have been well understood. It was alleged that *it departed from the precedents of 1815, that the powers were then without the basis of the treaties which are now the starting-point of their diplomatic action. It was remembered that the particular treaties concluded at this epoch between the three Courts, had been confined to questions of details of commerce, of navigation, towing-paths, &c. &c.; that besides the stipulations of these separate treaties had been finally comprised in the general act as constituting a part of it and having the same force and same value. It was observed also that the Court of Vienna had always repulsed every preliminary understanding on subjects of this sort, as contrary to its dignity.*

The despatch of the Austrian minister for foreign affairs containing no allusion to this last point, it is useless to raise it. It belongs to him only to appreciate that which may affect the dignity of his country. It is certain that the Imperial Cabinet in proposing an agreement between the three neighbouring Courts, according to historical precedent, cannot be suspected of wishing to lessen the dignity of any one. It suffices, besides, that the Austrian Government should have found such an agreement incompatible with the new ties it has contracted.

As to the foundation of the question, the Russian Government has had no other aim than that of calling attention to the important distinction established by the precedents of the Congress of Vienna, between the general principles in which all Europe was interested, and the internal question exclusively appertaining to the adjoining powers. These countries, possessing each parts of ancient Poland, may have derogated from their own rights of sovereignty by concerting together in order to establish a certain harmony in their Polish possessions, according to the general principles laid down by the Congress ; they could never have consented to alienate these rights, and place them in the hands of all Europe.

This distinction springs clearly from the stipulations of 1815. If, at that epoch, the separate treaties concluded between the three Courts touched only on questions of commerce, of navigation, of tonnage, &c. &c., it is because these questions alone were discussed. Nevertheless, it must be allowed that these questions of detail were not without importance. The questions of frontier, for example, were of very grave import. The treaties concluded between the three Courts in 1818 and 1825, as to custom-houses, extradition of deserters, &c. &c., had a certain political value. Lastly, the treaties concluded between them in 1833, and still later in 1846, on the subject of the free state of Cracow, were yet more serious. And yet all these treaties were concluded without the participation of those who signed the general act of Vienna.

This fundamental distinction applies itself perfectly to the present situation.

The principles laid down by the general treaties (*acte*) of Vienna are not now in question, since, on one side, the three powers which have made representations on the subject of Poland have taken as their basis the stipulations of 1815, and on the other side the Russian Cabinet has declared its willingness to respect these stipulations.

It is then only necessary to apply them ; but in doing so, internal questions are touched upon which have been always considered by the three powers as belonging to their sovereign dominion, and to which they are exclusively competent.

To sum up all, if from the region of dissertation one passes to the field of practice, the only place where so grave a problem can be resolved, the result is that the three Courts desire the return of the kingdom of Poland to the conditions of a durable peace. This is also the most constant and the dearest wish of the Emperor of Russia.

The three Courts have declared their wish to seek the means for this within the limits of the engagements of 1815 ; the Russian Emperor declares his determination to maintain these engagements in their full extent.

To satisfy this, his Majesty has granted to Poland institutions formed on the principle of an administrative autonomy and elective representation.

He maintains these institutions, reserving to himself the right of developing them.

The three Courts have on their side recommended six points, as likely to contribute to the pacification of the kingdom of Poland : the greater part of these are already in existence ; some are in the course of preparation, or lie in the same direction as the views of the Emperor of Russia, and the developments which his Majesty has given cause to expect. But at the same time, the three Courts think that the application of these measures should be immediate, and would secure the re-establishment of order and tranquillity in the kingdom.

The Russian Government, on the contrary, is of opinion that, after the experience it has acquired, these measures cannot be adopted in face of armed insurrection ; that they should be preceded by the re-establishment of order; and that to be efficacious they must emanate directly from the sovereign power, in the plenitude of its strength and liberty, without any foreign diplomatic pressure. These are the shades which separate opinions.

But these shades do not appear of a nature to occasion serious discussion between the Cabinets, still less to trouble the peace of Europe.

It could not take this character if the evident plans of the agents in the Polish revolution were allowed to develop themselves; these agents on one side weigh on the public opinion of Europe, by the spectacle of a struggle of which they endeavour to multiply and to aggravate the calamities, whilst, on the other hand, by prolonging and propagating disorder, they deprive the Russian Government of the possibility of adopting and applying the measures of moral pacification which would correspond with its own intentions not less than with the desires of the Cabinets and the sentiments of public opinion.

There would be no reason to fear such a toleration on the part of those powers, unless they were determined to pursue, under the appearance of diplomatic action, within the limits of international engagements, the realization of the most extreme desires of the Polish revolution, leading to the overthrow of treaties, and of the equilibrium of Europe.

One cannot evidently expect this from those Cabinets which are interested in the maintenance of this equilibrium, and who have taken as the basis of their intervention the scrupulous execution of the treaties of 1815.

Tsarskóe Selo, 26th August, 1863.

EARL RUSSELL TO LORD NAPIER.

Foreign Office, Oct. 20th, 1863.

MY LORD,—Baron Brunnow has communicated to me a despatch from Prince Gortschakoff, dated August 26th (September 7th), in reply to my despatch to your Excellency, No. 178, of the 11th ultimo, of which you were instructed to give a copy to his Excellency.

Her Majesty's Government have no wish to prolong the correspondence on the subject of Poland for the mere purpose of controversy.

Her Majesty's Government receive with satisfaction the assurance that the Emperor of Russia continues to be animated with intentions of benevolence towards Poland, and of conciliation in respect of all foreign powers.

Her Majesty's Government acknowledge that the relations of Russia towards European powers are regulated by public law; but the Emperor of Russia has special obligations in regard to Poland.

Her Majesty's Government have, in the despatch of the 11th of August and preceding despatches, shown that, in regard to this particular question, the rights of Poland are contained in the same instrument which constitutes the Emperor of Russia King of Poland.

I am, &c.,

(Signed)   RUSSELL.

P.S.—Your Excellency is instructed to give a copy of this despatch to Prince Gortschakoff.

INDEX.

ABICHT, Assassination of	Page 113
Administration, Laxity of in Western provinces	107
Agitation, unarmed	50, 57, 67
„ Secret progress of	64, 78
Agricultural Society	56
„ Intended uses	65
„ Political purposes	65, 66
„ Dissolution of	68
„ resented by demonstration	72
„ Various narratives of demonstration	73, 74, 75
„ at Kieff, dissolved	106
Alecot, People of, assist those of Kovno in procession	101
Alexander the Emperor, his views	16
„ Visit to Warsaw	19
„ Address to the nobles	20
„ Reforms introduced by	21
„ Oukase of	68
„ Polish view of his reforms	104
Amnesty, Proclamation of	185
Arrest of students	98
Assassination attempted, of Count Luders	85
„ Grand Duke Constantine	87
„ Wielopolski	88
„ Count Berg	267
Assembly of Nobles, Address from St. Petersburg	184
Austria, Policy of	140
BANDS, Composition of insurgent	129
Berg, Count, appointed Viceroy of Poland	253
„ his character and antecedents	253
„ his vigorous policy	254
„ Search of convents	255
„ Attempt to assassinate	257
„ Measures for suppression of revolt	258
„ imposes property tax on proprietors in Warsaw	259
„ prohibits mourning	260
Bismarck, Herr von, Explanation of convention to Prussian chambers	137
„ Explanation to Sir A. Buchanan	140

Buchanan, Sir A.—Statement of convention between Russia and
               Prussia . . . . *Page* 136
     "   Explanation of 138

CATECHISM, Polish 9
Central Committee defy Government to effect conscription . . . 113
    "   Proclamation of, after conscription 119
    "   authorize the murder of Wielopolski . . . 125
    "   their letter to General Langiewicz 158
    "   resume power on the defeat of Langiewicz . . 167
Church, Roman Catholic, Influence of 28–31
        "   how exercised towards Russia . . . 30
        "   "   towards Austria . . . 30
Churches, Warsaw, blockaded 81
Clanricarde, Lord, his speech in the House of Lords . . . 201
Clergy, Roman Catholic, favour the revolt 130
Committee, Polish, in Paris, Address of 215
Comparative position of peasantry 24
Congress kingdom, Condition of peasants 16–26
    "   Population analyzed and classified . . 23–26
    "   historically defined 89, 90
    "   Advantanges of Poles in 124
Conscription, effected 113
    "   Evil consequences of 115
    "   Exaggerations respecting 116
Conscripts, Number of 113
Constantine, Grand Duke, appointed Viceroy of Poland . . 85
    "   Character 69–85
    "   Resignation of 247
Convents, search of 255
Council of State, Withdrawal of Polish nobles from . . . 180

DEMOCRATIC Prejudices, how exhibited 51
Demonstrations, Political, prohibited 79
   "   "   98
Domeiko, M., Attempt to assassinate 214

EDUCATIONAL Projects 70
Education of Poles after suppression of their universities . . 4
Ellenborough, Lord—Observations in the House of Lords . . 149
    "   his speech in the House of Lords . . 201
Engineer absconds with railway engine 118
England—Feeling in favour of insurrection 149
Executions by General Mouravieff 205

GENDARMES hanging, Murders committed by 247
German Press, feeling of 141

INDEX.

Gortschakoff (General)—Policy as lieutenant . . . . *Page* 57–72
      „   Death of 76
      „   Retrospect of policy 76
Gortschakoff (Vice-Chancellor)—Statements in reply to Lord Russell's despatch 151
      „   Effect of his despatches . . . 154
Government, National. See *National Government*.
Grockovo, Commemoration of battle of 52

History, Study of Polish, forbidden 7
Horodicki, Defeat of 225
Hostile Demonstrations 98

Insurgents, Excesses of 126
      „   Exaggerated statements of 142
Insurgent, Composition of bands 129
Insurrection, Outbreak of 114
            Collapse of 261

Jaroszynski, Louis, attempted assassination of Grand Duke Constantine by 87
Jews and Poles, mutual feelings of 63
Jitomir, Demonstration in 106

Kieff, Rising in 221
Kovno, Demonstration at 100

Lambert, Count, appointed Viceroy 78
Langievicz, commands the insurgents in Radom, establishes provisional government there 131
      „   Defeat of, at Winchock 133
      „   his partisan system of warfare 155
      „   his assumption of dictatorship . . . 157
      „   Letter received by him from the Central Committee . 158
      „   surrounded by Russians 161
      „   his last skirmishes 162
      „   resolves to resort to guerilla war . . . 164
      „   Consternation and flight of his army . . . 164
      „   his capture by the Austrians 165
      „   denounced by his enemies 166
Lelewel, Death of 249
Lepel, Scene of patriotic demonstration 102
Liberal party in Russia; their views of the policy of Emperor Nicholas 14
Lithuania, Commemoration of union with Poland . . . 90
Losses of the Russians in engagements with insurgents . . 129

Massacre of Russian soldiers 117
Mieroslawski 28–53
Miracles alleged on behalf of Poland 216

Moral force, mistaken theory regarding . . . . *Page* 190
Mouravieff, General, appointed Governor of North-western provinces . 194
    „   Character of 194
    „   Proclamations against wearing mourning . . 197
    „   Success of proclamation 200
    „   imposes property tax on landlords . . 202
    „   Sequestrations of property by . . . 202
    „   Executions by order of 205
Mourning adopted by Poles 84
    „ Proclamations against, by General Mouravieff . . 197
    „ misrepresented in England 200
    „ Statements in House of Lords concerning . . 201

NAPIER, Lord—Explanation of convention between Russia and Prussia 139
    „   On patriotic agitation in Russia 183
Napoleon—Policy of Emperor 144
    „   his designs on Prussia 145
    „   Character of 146
    „   Difficulties of his position 147
    „   Close of his diplomatic correspondence . . . 239
National Government, Popular impressions regarding . . . 168
    „   Explanations of its apparent power . . . 169
    „   Proceedings of 171
    „   its secret police 171
    „   Murders committed at the instance of . . 173
    „   its diplomatic circular 173
    „   its interference in land question . . . 175
    „   denounces the amnesty 185
    „   denounces the constitution of 1815 . . 194
    „   Terrorism exercised by 248
    „   desires employeés of official journal to abandon
                  their employment 259
    „   prohibits payment of property-tax . . 260
    „   prohibits mourning 260
Nazimoff, Governor-General of Wilna 90
    „ his wavering policy 105
    „ replaced by General Mouravieff 194
Nicholas the Emperor, Policy of, after revolt of 1830 . . . 3
    „ Suppression of Polish universities 4
    „   „   Results upon education of Poles . . 5
    „ his death and its effects 14
    „ his advice to Emperor Alexander 15
    „ his restraints relaxed—consequences 104
Nullo, death of Francisco 217

OPINION (public) in Russia 246
Order of the day of the revolutionary chief of Warsaw . . 125

PAULUCCI, Marquis of, President of Delegation . . . 61

INDEX.   331

Paskievitch, Viceroy of Poland . . . . . *Page* 19
Peasants Guard, formation of 178
  „   Conduct of 181
  „   Disposition of, in the South-western provinces . . 218
  „   Arrest fugitive insurgents 220
Petersburg (Saint)—assembly of nobles—address . . . 184
Peto, Sir Morton—his contract declared void by National Government 177
Podolia, address of nobles of 108
Points, the six—motive of Western Powers in proposing . . 229
  „   Indignation of Russians at six 232
Poland, State of during the Crimean war 18
  „   Division of into military districts 128
Pole, Letter of a patriot 226
Poles, Education of—subsequent to 1830 4
  „   Hostility of to Russia 5
  „   holding office—conduct of 7
Polish literature restricted 7
  „   nobility 23
  „   proletarians 25
  „   peasantry 24
  „   soldiers, conduct of in Crimean war 19
  „   exiles, effect of their return 23
  „   aristocrats 27
  „   women, patriotism of 31
  „   Position of peasantry, reviewed 33–49
  „   „   compared with that of Austria and Prussia 46
  „   delegation, influence of 59
  „   National Hymn 29
  „   mayors' duties and responsibilities, and how fulfilled . 40
  „   insurrectionary leaders 58
  „   „   policy of 95
  „   Council of State 68
  „   commissioners of public instruction and public works . 69
  „   costumes 75
  „   address to the Grand Duke Constantine . . . 90
  „   nobles, dissatisfaction of 179
  „   „   withdrawal of from State Council . . . 180
  „   Character of some of the leaders 252
Posen, Policy of Prussia in 134
  „   Proclamation of Governor of 137
Powers, Western, effect of interference of 193
Property-tax imposed by General Mouravieff . . . 202
Proprietors, Hostility to Government 9
  „   Commercial activity of 22
  „   Position of in the Western Provinces . . . 26
  „   Prejudices of 67
  „   Resentment of on behalf of Agricultural Society . 72
  „   Embarrassed position of 120
  „   Views of patriotic party amongst . . . 122

Provinces, Western, effect of reforms of Emperor on . . . *Page* 124
Prussia, her policy in Posen 134
   „   her alarm at the Polish insurrection 135
   „   her convention with Russia as to refugees . . . 136
   „   Report of Sir A. Buchanan upon 136

RACES, Analysis of 25
Radziwilow, Attack upon 224
Railway, Destruction of 118
Red and White parties, Disputes between 241
 „ party, Views of 242
Religion, Influence of 29–63
Religious veneration of Russians 83
Revolt, Plan of 95
   „   Polish, of 1830 3
Revolutionary hymns prohibited 79
   „   press, suggestions and instigations of . . . 94
   „   education and preparations 108
Roman Catholic clergy, influence in Kovno 100
Rossiny, Demonstration at 100
Russell, Lord—Despatch to Sir A. Buchanan 138
   „   Further Despatch to Sir A. Buchanan . . . 139
   „   withdraws his demands 140
   „   Speech in the House of Lords 149
   „   Despatch of to Lord Napier 150
   „   Apparent ignorance of Polish question . . 153
   „   Incompetency to cope with Prince Gortschakoff . 153
   „   View of Amnesty 187
   „   proposes the six points 229
   „   his ignorance of the Treaty of Vienna . . 234
   „   he closes diplomatic correspondence . . 238
Russia — her convention with Poland as to refugees . . 136
   „   Report of Sir A. Buchanan upon 136
   „   Anxiety of people of 183
   „   Public opinion of 246
Russian tombs violated 51

SEQUESTRATIONS by General Mouravieff 202
Seriakoffski appointed commander of insurgents in Lithuania . 207
   „   Defeat of 208
   „   Capture of 209
   „   Execution of 213
Six points, Objections to 235
Skarga, Opinion of on the state of the peasantry . . . 35
South-western provinces disarmed 106
Stanton, Colonel, Despatch of, announcing conscription and revolutionary
    outbreak 114
Synkiewicz, Major, Escape of 225

TREASURY, Robbery of in Warsaw 248

INDEX.

VOLHYNIA, Invasion of . . . . *Page* 221

WALDECK, Herr Von, speech of in Prussian chambers . . . 137
Warsaw, Suppression of University of 4
  ,,   Massacres of February 27th, 1860 54
  ,,   Public funeral of killed in 60
  ,,   Re-establishment of university 70
  ,,   Disturbance in 74
  ,,   Proclamation of state of siege 79
  ,,   Resignation of municipal council . . . 182
  ,,   Treasury, robbery of 248
Wengrow, Capture of by Russians 132
Western provinces, Revolutionary sympathies of 95
White and Red parties, Disputes between 241
Wielopolski, Marquis of, insists on conscription 113
  ,,   appointed Chief Minister 85
  ,,   Character and state craft 86-92
  ,,   sentenced to death by National Committee . . 125
  ,,   Change in policy of 127
  ,,   suspected both by Russians and Poles . . 182
  ,,   Resignation of 247
Wilna, Suppression of university of 4
  ,,   Demonstration in 98
  ,,   Arrest of students at 99
  ,,   Martyrs of, funeral services for 103
  ,,   Proprietors, Roman Catholic, taxed . . . 106
Wysocki, General, appointed to command in Volhynia . . 221
  ,,   Description of his army 222
  ,,   Defeat of 225

ZAMOYSKI, Count Andrew 23, 54, 56, 59, 61, 90
  ,,   Exile of 92
  ,,   Popularity of 97
  ,,   Palace, confiscation of 258

www.ingramcontent.com/pod-product-compliance
Lightning Source LLC
Chambersburg PA
CBHW031853220426
43663CB00006B/612